Ohio States

To Liz,
  I hope this book
gives you as much pleasure
as it gave me.
Happy summer reading!

    Yours,
    Jim

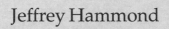

Jeffrey Hammond

Ohio States

A Twentieth-Century Midwestern

The Kent State University Press ⬧ Kent & London

© 2002 by The Kent State University Press, Kent, Ohio 44242
All rights reserved.
Library of Congress Catalog Card Number 2001007202
ISBN 0-87338-733-3
Manufactured in the United States of America

06 05 04 03 02   5 4 3 2 1

Library of Congress Cataloging-in-Publication Data

Hammond, Jeffrey.
Ohio states : a twentieth-century midwestern / Jeffrey Hammond.
p. cm.
ISBN 0-87338-733-3 (pbk: alk. paper)
1. Hammond, Jeffrey—Childhood and youth.
2. Findlay (Ohio)—Social life and customs—20th century.
3. Findlay (Ohio)—Biography.
4. Middle West—Social life and customs—20th century.
I. Title.
F499.F4 H36 2002
974.1'45—dc21
2001007202

British Library Cataloging-in-Publication data are available.

for Norma

Contents

Acknowledgments

This book grew out of a scheme of self-preservation through writing, initially hatched in a desperate effort to stay sane while chairing an English department. Although the scheme worked, sort of, it would have failed utterly without the support of sympathetic friends and editors: Beth Bergmann-Loizeaux, Jeff Carr, Laura Carr, Jennifer Cognard-Black, Jeff Coleman, Maureen Corrigan, Ray Craig, Tom Davis, Virginia Davis, Todd Feil, Robert Fogarty, Michael Glaser, Rosemary Guruswamy, Andrea Hammer, Lawrence Hetrick, Janie Hinds, Harold Jaffe, Altie Karper, David Kuebrich, Rick LaFleur, Dan Latimer, Daniel Liberthson, Lisa Logan, Bill Loizeaux, Joe Mackall, Bill Meiners, Alan Paskow, Jackie Paskow, Richard Peterson, Bill Scheick, Norma Tilden, Hadley Tremaine, Elizabeth Velez, Larry Velez, Hilary Woodward, and Rich Yeselson.

Earlier versions of several chapters appeared in *The Missouri Review, The Southern Review, The Virginia Quarterly Review, ISLE: Interdisciplinary Studies in Literature and the Environment, Salmagundi, Shenandoah, Fourth Genre,* and *The American Scholar.* I wish to thank the editors—Evelyn Somers, Michael Griffith, Staige Blackford, Scott Slovik, Peg Boyers and Robert Boyers, Rod Smith and Lynn Leech, Mike Steinberg, and Anne Fadiman—for encouraging these forays into what was, for me, a new kind of writing. I am especially grateful to Joanna Hildebrand Craig and John T. Hubbell of The Kent State University Press for their enthusiastic response to a collection of these pieces.

My greatest debt is to Evan Hammond, Jeanne Hammond, David Hammond, and Susan Hammond Long. Despite occasional discomfort at confronting versions of themselves in story form, they supported these attempts to recover how things seemed—and may even have been—a long time ago in Findlay, Ohio. My family sometimes remembered things a little differently, and their input helped keep me within the bounds of probability. To respect the privacy of those who had no input, I've given everyone else in these stories different names. Although some Findlayites—past and present—might object to my depiction of the town, I hope they will remember that a hometown is much like a family: as time goes by, exasperation and affection become nearly impossible to tell apart.

The High Places Club

The view from atop a horse barn in our neighborhood on the east edge of Findlay, Ohio, was spectacular: miles of cornfields stretching to the horizon, broken only by the occasional silo and several far-off stands of trees. If you've ever driven through northwest Ohio—on the turnpike, say, between Cleveland and Toledo—you know how flat it is and how far you can see. If you are ten years old and growing up in such a place, finding a spot high above the ground is a very big deal. Being on the roof of that barn felt like riding in an airplane, or at least what my friends and I imagined riding in an airplane would feel like. "Neat!" and "Gaw!"—the latter a euphemism for "God," which none of us were allowed to say—are the words I said and heard while gazing at those cornfields. What other words are possible when you can see the curvature of the earth, or think you can, outlined in green and gold against a bright blue sky?

The barn roof was one of our high places. There were five others: the taller of two pines in my front yard, a huge maple down the street, and the rooftops of my house, Lenny's grandparents' house, and Robbie's garage. These were our secret places for congregating unseen. In a flat landscape, getting ten or fifteen feet above the ground will make you wonderfully invisible. People who live in flat places don't have cause to look up very often except to read the weather.

The High Places Club was my idea, though I don't remember how I got it. I suppose it had something to do with finding a special place of our own, one that offered relief from the relentlessly horizontal grid that

Bedroom view, 1956.

made up our world: the right-angled streets of town, the rectangular yards, the surrounding fields that were either big squares or little squares, the county roads that preserved the geometric regularity of the range-township system with which our part of Ohio had been surveyed. A special place is by definition an exotic place, different from the places you normally inhabit. Since we knew every inch of our neighborhood turf, the only way to escape the everyday was to go up.

The High Places Club didn't have much of an agenda. Lenny, Robbie, and I would simply gather on one of these secret perches to talk, or sometimes to keep quiet and, aided by Lenny's binoculars, observe neighborhood comings and goings. Sometimes we would each climb to a different high place and communicate what we saw by whistling in Morse Code. We made tiny cheat sheets to help us do that, but our efforts never quite concealed the fact that there was precious little to report. Endless sporadic whistles: "What . . . do . . . you . . . see?" More endless sporadic whistles: "Mister . . . Brown . . . is . . . taking . . . out . . . his . . . trash."

The club fostered an air of danger as well as secrecy. The pine tree swayed in strong winds, which made for dizzying meetings that consisted of little more than just hanging on. The roof of my house, with its heavy slant, was our riskiest spot, and not just because my parents forbade us to go out there. "You're going to break your necks," my mother said whenever she ordered us down. I knew that this was no empty warning. One time I lost my footing and slid down on my belly until my tennis shoes caught in the gutters. Shaken, I inched my way back up to the window like an alligator and crawled inside, my fingernails black with shingle grit.

Our spot on the horse barn, nestled between two gently sloping gables, had the best view and was also the least scary high place. The barn's roof was flatter than the others, and the gables provided a wedge of shade that made the tin bearable even on sunny days. It was there that we spent most of our time and did most of our idle talking. I remember being on that roof as we watched a summer thunderstorm blow in, a wall of purplish blue that slowly darkened the fields as it approached.

We instinctively knew that a high place was a place to be still. Our usual roughhousing was out of the question because, after all, a kid could break his neck. There was power in knowing that whenever a parent called, all we had to do was be still and we would never be discovered— a scenario that was fun to imagine, though hardly necessary. It's not that the High Places Club offered escape from overburdened and abused childhoods. We were all, in fact, dimly aware that we were enjoying pretty good childhoods. The High Places Club simply offered another plane on which to exist, a handful of places that were mysterious because they were *different*.

I don't remember how or why the High Places Club disbanded. Maybe it was the fact that the neighborhood grownups got wise to us and started breaking up our meetings so often that the club got to be more trouble than it was worth. One time Lenny's grandmother heard us on her roof and rushed out with a broom, thinking that we were giant raccoons. "You kids get down from there! You're going to break your necks!" As we shinnied down the spout with hooded eyes and sullen expressions, I was sure that Lenny's grandmother had been talking to my mother. How else to explain this exact duplication in their words? Then, too, around this time we were starting to make other friends at school and go our separate ways, as neighborhood pals usually do. Or maybe the club faded away simply because we outgrew it, embarrassed because the secrets we had shared in those high places now struck us as childish.

While it lasted, though, the High Places Club was great fun. I've always suspected that its appeal had something to do with why those pyramids and ziggurats got built in the ancient Near East. Egypt and Mesopotamia are flatlands, too, and maybe a flatlander is hardwired to look upward when searching for something different, whether it's that "Gaw" feeling or just a place in which to be still. Years later I read in the Bible that God met Moses on a mountain, which made perfect sense to me, and that the Temple in Jerusalem had been built on a high place—a "threshing place" where the winds were strong. The prophets railed against people who kept setting up other altars atop other high places. What impulse lay behind all those pesky altars, those unauthorized attempts to get above it all? What to make of the fact that the word "altar" comes from the Latin word for "high"?

Sometimes I almost think I know. I was twenty-one, driving back to Ohio from Phoenix in a 1963 Volkswagen, when I saw real mountains for the first time. Leaning forward in a futile attempt to ease the car's burden as it chugged up the inclines of southwestern Colorado, I found it all a bit unsettling. When I finally made it to Durango and camped for the night, I wondered what I was doing in such a place and whether my VW would ever make it back to the plains, to liveable territory. Yes, the mountains were beautiful—though oddly unreal, like huge stage sets—and yes, this place was *different*. But an hour or so earlier, as I inched along and caught a glimpse of Hesperus Peak to the north, a kind of terror had swept over me. This was not a human place, a place where people were meant to be. This felt more like the top of Khufu's pyramid, the crown of Sinai, or maybe even the upper branches of that tall pine on windy days when I had to look straight out because if I looked down I'd get dizzy and my legs would start aching.

Even as a kid I understood that sacred spaces make their own demands. I knew that if I ever went crazy on the ground and started running around like a wildman, the worst that could happen was that I'd twist an ankle in a drainage ditch. But when you're in a high place, being a wildman is not an option. You have to watch your step and avoid sudden movements—and be sure to keep your foot on the gas or you'll break your neck and maybe even disappear. In all high places, whether on U.S. 160 in Colorado or near the top of a swaying pine in Ohio, you need to keep your wits about you. You need to keep still.

The Pagan of East Sandusky Street

I am four. As it grows dark outside, my older sister and I are sitting on either side of our mother on the massive, fuzzy couch in the front room. She is reading to us, as she often does just before my bedtime. Our father, settled in the recliner that is exclusively his in the evenings, is reading the paper and sipping a beer. I am aware, dimly, of my older brother working on a model at the dinner table in the next room.

Our mother's voice rises and falls in comforting rhythms as she makes her way through a poem that we have heard many times before. I know from watching her finger skip over whole blocks of words that she is leaving out large portions of it. Still, it is very long, and I've only recently been able to stay awake to the end. As she draws out the closing words in a dramatic flourish, my sister and I, cuing each other with exaggerated nods and widened eyes, join in with an excited shout: "Turn down an empty glass!"

• • •

By the time I knew how *The Rubáiyát of Omar Khayyám* turned out, I could already see that our mother was different. There would come a time, some ten years later, when that difference would be obvious even to outsiders, but when I was little it was still a family secret. We kids weren't particularly alarmed by it, though we often discussed it among ourselves with the curiosity that children usually have about their parents. We could not say *how* Mom was different, exactly, and we had no name for her strangeness. It simply *was*, like Dave's acne or Sue's freckles or my poor hearing,

7

which improved once my tonsils were taken out. Only forty years later did I find a word to describe how she was: our mother was a pagan.

In an era when everybody seems to be the adult child of *something*, this characterization could easily be misconstrued as the lament of yet another middle-aged ingrate, mad as hell and ransacking memory for ready targets. A pagan's child might be expected to tell lurid stories of ritual abuse, blood-smearing rites involving the Thanksgiving turkey, perhaps, or an all-American family chanting softly to the moon after doing the dinner dishes. But I have no such stories—no confessions of slow letter carriers or pushy salesmen stiffly rendered into tiny Play-Doh figures stuck with hatpins, no freshly killed goats lying gutted on the kitchen table, their entrails laid open for guidance on whether to buy a new radio or fix the old one. To my knowledge, Mom never consulted our dead ancestors on whether Sears or JC Penney's was the better source for school clothes.

At their best, the pagans of the ancient Mediterranean world felt an insatiable hunger for truth and beauty. Later, anyone bold enough to pursue these qualities with no special regard for the Judeo-Christian God became suspect. To be an outsider—and just this *sort* of outsider—pretty much sums up our mother's situation. A pagan in ancient Athens or Rome would have had lots of company, but if you were a pagan disguised as a twentieth-century midwestern housewife, you'd have to go it alone. There would be nobody around to tell you in how to wear a toga or when to pour libations to Dionysus.

"Like a woman from Mars" is how our mother later described her feelings during those years. As she remembers it, she could be strolling the aisles of FoodTown or watching the gas station attendant check the oil— when suddenly she wouldn't know what to do with her face. Feeling that her features were transforming into objects requiring deliberate manipulation, like hands or feet, she would be forced to consider how to arrange them so as to appear normal. Such unease might well be expected for a pagan—or a Martian, for that matter—living in the 1950s in Findlay, Ohio. Mom recalls a constant restlessness, a sense that a cosmic joke with no punchline was being played at her expense. Mostly she remembers that time as a constant search for "kindred spirits," always few and far between.

Now in her early eighties, our mother does not object to the "pagan" designation with which I tease her. She even wishes she had hit upon the word four decades ago. Unlike Martians, pagans were human beings, and having a label for self-consciousness that felt, at the time, like arbitrary weirdness might have saved her considerable anguish. She might have felt less need to wonder, as she placed packages of Mrs. Paul's fish sticks into her shopping cart, if *this* was how an Ohio housewife placed fish sticks into a shopping cart. Was this how an Ohio housewife should look—should *be*—as she absently watched the numbers spin and heard the pings of the gas pump? As she waited in line at the butcher shop? As she deposited part of her husband's paycheck into the Christmas Club at the First National Bank?

Our mother swears that entire lives can be lived in the wrong place and time. When I remember her as she was in the 1950s, it is easy to imagine her lounging at a table on the Champs Elysées, sipping espresso and talking animatedly to a man with a beret and an eye patch. It is no stretch to picture her sitting on a bench in front of the British Library, rubbing her eyes after a long morning of research, or bobbing her head to Monk or Mingus in a Village jazz club, her cat's-eye glasses reflecting a spotlight cutting down through the curling smoke and glancing off a saxophone. She *should* have lived in Paris or London or New York, and in fact she felt unaccountably at home in these cities when she finally visited them years later. She does not recall this mismatch of self and situation with regret. A pagan understands the futility of struggling against fate, especially after the fact: there was simply no way to get to these places from where she started.

. . .

If places can have their opposites, our mother grew up in the antithesis of the Left Bank. Her father left southeastern Kentucky as a young man in 1896, planning to live with relatives in downstate Illinois while he found a job and established himself. After jumping a troop train heading for the Spanish-American War, when he had second thoughts about becoming a Rough Rider, Henry Weldon married Susan Foster, a daughter of German immigrants, and started a family that eventually included four children. After several years the family moved to Rugby, North Dakota, where my mother—their third child—was born. Then they moved to Slayton, Minnesota, where Grandpa opened a dress and fabric store called Weldon's Style Shop. After the shop closed due to competition from Silverberg's department store, he went into partnership in a dry-goods store with a big, gregarious Swede named Risberg, who later swindled him—so the story went—out of his investment. Working as a traveling salesman and, during the Depression, as a records clerk for the WPA, Grandpa eventually took the family back to Martinsville, Illinois, a town of a thousand souls twenty-five miles west of Terre Haute, Indiana, and sold dry goods and fabrics in Martinsville's general store.

My mother, who was about to start her senior year of high school, resented the move—and soon after coming to Illinois she committed her first act of rebellion. Christened Henrietta after her father, she officially changed her name to Jeanne. She had never really felt like a Henrietta: Jeanne suited her much better, especially with the French spelling.

Gawky and precocious, Jeanne had trouble adjusting to the flat rhythms of life in Martinsville. Suspecting that her Minnesota accent sounded overprecise and little-girlish to Illinois ears, she missed her best friend back home and their endless talks about Whitman, Tennyson, and Sir Walter Scott. But she soon found some Martinsville girls who also loved books, threw herself into her English class, and played baritone horn in the twelve-member high school band. Her family also joined the local Methodist church, which her parents deemed infinitely more civilized than the Baptist church or the nonaffiliated Bible Church, where people gave tearful witness to what Jesus had done for them that week.

Except for the name change, Jeanne tried to be a dutiful daughter, and in the Weldon household "dutiful" meant being a good Christian. Increasingly, though, she couldn't believe that a loving God could create hell, let alone send anyone there. Her mother patiently explained free will, sin, and salvation through Jesus, but something in Jeanne's nature recoiled at the whole system. Real rebellion might have been possible had Grandma not been such a sweet and gentle woman; once Jeanne realized that it broke her mother's heart to hear such doubts, she kept them mostly to herself. A pagan daughter can still be a good daughter, anxious to please her parents and keep the peace. Still, Grandma's Jesus had posed a test that Jeanne could not pass, and a painful self-consciousness that came from having been put on the spot would never really leave her. "Are You Washed in the Blood of the Lamb?" Well, *are* you?

My mother met my father toward the end of her senior year. Evan Hammond, a shy farm boy who looked like Glenn Ford, was three years out of school and working in the post office. The story was—and we kids had ample reason to believe it—that Mom took the initiative, "forgetting" pieces of her family's outgoing mail so she could return to the handsome young man behind the barred window. It took Dad, who figured she was too "classy" for him, months to work up sufficient nerve to ask her out. One day, when he spotted her talking with some girlfriends on the street, he summoned his courage and asked if he could buy her a bowl of chili at the Hi-Way Café.

A member of the infamous Bible Church, my father had grown uneasy with the weeping and wailing, and spent his Saturday nights worrying that the preacher might call on him to give a "testimonial" the next morning. Although his parents, reclusive farmers who lived out in the country, had not attended church for years, Dad continued to go because he sang tenor in the gospel quartet. Hearing about hellfire still seemed an acceptable trade-off, though a steep one, for the fun of singing those Stamps-Baxter gospel tunes. Once he and Mom started dating, they were a decidedly "mixed" couple by Martinsville standards. In small towns where there are no Catholics and no Jews, distinctions among Protestants loom large. Willing—eager, he later confessed—to escape the theatrical enthusiasms of the Bible Church, Dad agreed to become a Methodist.

Soon after they married, Dad took a better-paying job as a pipeline worker at the Marathon Oil tank farm west of town. A year later my brother was born, and my sister four years after that. When an opportunity to supervise a crew opened up at a tank farm in Ohio, the family moved to Lima, and a few years later, after my father completed a tour in the navy, I was born. Now responsible for three children, Dad took correspondence courses in accounting under the GI Bill. When he landed a job in the company's accounting department, the family moved thirty-five miles up the road to Findlay, where Marathon's home offices were located. Like most men of his generation, my father was pursuing the American Dream, and it was unfolding pretty much as it was supposed to, in orderly increments on a flat and seemingly limitless landscape.

One of the first things our parents did in Findlay was to shop for a Methodist church. By this time they had settled on a better-safe-than-sorry policy regarding religion and the kids. Despite her doubts, Mom wanted us to learn about God and Jesus so that when the time came, we could decide for ourselves what we believed. After the First Methodist Church, a huge Gothic edifice with two pastors, proved too large and impersonal, they settled on a smaller church on the north side of town. The Howard Methodist Church had a motto that was printed on every pledge envelope: "Large enough to serve you, small enough to know you." That sounded appropriately cozy, but I don't guess that the other church ladies got to know my mother all that well, at least as far as her beliefs were concerned. Mostly she kept them to herself.

· · ·

More visible escapes from Grandma's rigid faith were pursued by the other Weldon children, who spent twenty-five years concealing whole chunks of their lives from Grandma and Grandpa. Mom's older sister, Elizabeth married a quick-tempered musician who had briefly played organ for Lawrence Welk in North Dakota. Dreaming of snowless winters, cheap Mexican beer, and a fortune to be made in the oil business, Uncle Frank took Aunt "Biba" to San Antonio, where they ran a gas station. Mom's older brother, Foster, who had left Slayton to become an engineering student at the University of Minnesota, began to earn pocket money playing jazz trumpet in Minneapolis bars. Grandma, had she ever found out, would have declared with sadness that Uncle Foster "fell hard." Having acquired a lifelong taste for liquor, he always made a point, in drunken Christmas Day calls to Mom, of announcing that there was no God. After working for Matson Lines in San Francisco and helping to design the BART system, Uncle Foster moved to Detroit and worked for Ford as a shaper of aerodynamic fins and consumer demand. Mom's younger brother, Jim, who studied physics at Miami University in Ohio, joined the space age and tracked sunspots for NASA in Washington, D.C. During holiday visits he regaled our family with exciting stories of Georgetown nightlife—censored, I'm sure, for the sake of us kids. One Christmas Uncle Jim showed up in a Porsche, which could have been a spaceship as far as we were concerned. That visit he played some bossa nova records he had brought along; I remember Mom swaying to the catchy beat as she cut up a chicken.

Our mother envied her brothers deeply. Except for a bus trip to visit Aunt Biba and Uncle Frank in Texas the summer after her high school graduation, Findlay was as far from Martinsville, Illinois, as she had ever been. There was no possibility that she would go to college—an option, she later recalled, that never occurred to her. While the Weldon boys chose their majors, the Weldon girls chose their husbands and resigned themselves to fate. This was what was expected, and certainly not just of Mom and Aunt Biba: thousands of other midwestern girls could just as easily have wound up keeping house in San Antonio or Findlay.

Indeed, living on East Sandusky Street felt like an inevitability. Even when it came to religion, the habit of making do with narrow choices proved hard to break. Dad, who had come to detest everything about religion but the music, would not have raised us Methodist or even Christian had it been up to him. But Mom had been given a tighter script to follow and was determined to do right by it. Being Methodist was like having two eyes, a nose, and a bungalow on the east edge of Findlay: realistic alternatives were not yet imaginable. This, too, would be a sacrifice, a mandated suppressing of pagan identity.

While paganism may have claimed Mom as a matter of semiconscious recognition, it was hardly a source of pride. Something, she thought, must be wrong with *her*. It's difficult to pinpoint how far our mother had gone in rejecting Grandma's faith, but I suspect that she began to work things out somewhere on old U.S. Route 40 in Indiana, driving Dave and Sue in the car behind Dad's rented truck as the family left Illinois for their new home in Ohio. I faintly remember some family Bible reading when I was very small, but that had ended long before Sue and I were chanting along with Omar Khayyám. In those very early days, we still took turns saying grace before dinner, but whenever I peeked, Mom's and Dad's eyes were open. Still, Grandma's gentle reach was exceedingly long. Even two states away, our mother could not bring herself to let Susan Weldon's grandchildren grow up unchurched and unsaved. Besides, being a pagan entailed grave risks. Although Mom could not embrace Grandma's religion, that didn't mean it might not be true. She may have resigned herself to a pagan sensibility and a future in hell, if hell existed, but she wasn't about to gamble on the chance of taking her children down with her.

If you had observed the Hammond family sitting in a pew at Howard Methodist on a Sunday morning or heard Mom chatting with the other ladies as they set out their dishes for a tureen supper in the church basement, you would have sensed nothing amiss. We kids recognized, however, that this was a different mother from the one we knew at home. Mom's doubleness created in us an unstated respect for her privacy, and we instinctively sought to protect her. Without ever being told, we learned early that there was a clean line between what went on inside the house and what went on outside.

This was no hypocrisy on our mother's part, no attempt to fool people. At first she said what she thought, sometimes with a directness that her church friends found off-putting. In time, though, these encounters fostered a habit of passive concealment, of holding back. The only place in Findlay where Mom could be herself, at least in the early days, was in our little house. The effects of that are still with her children. If you are raised Methodist *and* pagan in a small midwestern town, you will acquire a habit

Jeanne Weldon Hammond, 1959.

14

of reticence, not because you're ashamed of who you are but because there would be no point in revealing it to other people except to shock them—and why do that? Although my sister stood this reticence on its head and began a relentless pursuit of popularity, she went against the family grain. To this day, my brother and I are compulsively private, comfortable only on our own turfs and painfully ill at ease everywhere else. We have managed to become reasonably adept at feigning a measure of comfort in social situations, but our words and faces never tell the whole story. Like our mother, we are not easy to know.

All three children share an affinity for strange juxtapositions and surprising turns. From our mother we learned to be militant ironists, sharing her profound belief that an essential arbitrariness lies at the heart of things. Add this to that and get *this*. Add something else and get *that*. How could we believe otherwise, hearing Victorian translations of Persian carpe diem poems while knowing that Dad's old pipeline hardhat, perfect for neighborhood games of war, hung on a peg on the back porch? The double self that we sensed in Mom was matched by a doubleness in our house, situated near cornfields tended by the Hancock Hybrids company. We knew that our house was a kind of hybrid, too, an ongoing experiment in the crossing of opposite strains. Such a house might be expected to contain a copy of the *Sporting News*, which our father sometimes picked up on his way home from work, or the issues of the *Reader's Digest* neatly stacked in the bathroom, complete with pencil marks recording Dad's answers to "It Pays to Increase Your Word Power." But what could account for *The Fireside Book of the Opera*, open to *Carmen* on the kitchen table because Mom had been reading the story before listening to the record as she started dinner?

Our father was constantly ambushed by the beautiful things—these bits of art and culture—that his bespectacled Illinois bride kept bringing into the house. Mom's music, for instance, wasn't remotely like the Protestant hymns of their youth, or even the Glenn Miller tunes that other young people—the ones who were allowed to dance—had heard at the armory in Terre Haute or the Legion Hall in Lima. Dad never yelled "Honey, I'm home" when he came in from work: Mom's music was too loud for that. He would silently slip in, give her a kiss over the kitchen counter, where she would be stripping carrots or peeling potatoes, and head for the bathroom to decompress from the day and increase his word power. We kids got used to making our after-school snacks wordlessly, spreading peanut butter in rhythm to the rushing afterbeats of the "Hungarian Rhapsody," which was high fun but resulted in messy sandwiches.

Our friends' houses were usually quiet, except for what was then called "country & western" music—Red Foley, Bob Wills, Hank Williams. If there were teenagers in the family, you might hear Elvis or Chuck Berry, who also boomed through our house whenever Dave controlled the radio. But Mom's music was different. She liked her music big, with loud brass and sweeping strings to prove it. We would come home to hear "Dance of the Valkyries" or "Rhapsody in Blue" blasting a lush greeting. If Mom was in a light mood, it might be "Cherry Pink and Apple Blossom White" or "Hernando's Hideaway," and she would be dancing some sort of tango as she stirred away in a mixing bowl clasped to her hip.

It might also be "Lisbon Antigua" or "The Poor People of Paris," reflections of Mom's growing love for all things European. "Those people know how to live," she would often proclaim. None of us kids could figure out exactly what that meant, though it was mildly disturbing to hear. All we knew about Europeans was that they smoked a lot and made dirty movies, and that we sometimes took up collections at school for their children. Such concerns were forgotten, however, in our Saturday night ritual, when Sue and I, fresh from our baths, danced wildly in our pajamas to one of these records while Mom conducted us with a baton that Grandpa Weldon had made for her when she was fifteen. One of her prized possessions, that baton got hard use. Whenever she wasn't cooking or ironing or otherwise using her hands, she conducted her music alone in the afternoons. The neighborhood housewives grew accustomed to pounding on the door to get her attention whenever they stopped by to chat or to borrow some flour.

We had an old upright piano that the former occupants of the house hadn't bothered to move. Mom occasionally picked out songs from sheet music, but was too impatient to work at it. She wanted to hear beautiful music *now*, not these halting clinks and clunks of a learner. Dave and Sue took piano lessons and actually learned to play a little, but you could tell from Mom's face that she hated hearing them practice. For her, music wasn't something to suffer through or to hear badly played, as other mothers willingly did at school concerts. Although Mom dutifully attended these events, she sometimes embarrassed us by wincing or rolling her eyes whenever some kid hit a clunker. It didn't matter whose kid it was. One time when Sue was playing cornet in the junior high band, she caught Mom flinching during one of her solos.

Dad was the kind of man who spends considerable energy trying not to be noticed. The worst thing you could do, in his view, was to "put on airs," and I can only guess what went through his mind as Mom's paganism, so aggressive in its pursuit of finer things, began to assert itself. But Mom's saving humility—the fact that her love for these things was utterly devoid of pretense—prompted him to accept them as well. She didn't play her music so that other people would consider her a "cultured" person. How could she, when she allowed herself to get lost in it only within the confines of the house? Only the neighbors knew—and then only in warm weather, when it blared out through the screening. When Mom ran into an acquaintance at the supermarket, she never brought up Wagner or Puccini. What would be the point, except to advertise her weirdness? Her motives were as pure and uncomplicated as a pagan's: she played her music because she loved it.

We came to love Mom's music, too, though it forced Dad into a dizzying expansion of his tastes. He liked nothing better than good singing, but opera proved a far cry from his beloved barbershop quartet albums, which featured winners of the annual contests of the SPEBSQSA, The Society for the Preservation and Encouragement of Barbershop Quartet Singing in America. Dad, a card-carrying member of the society's "Johnny Appleseed" district, sang in a quartet, too. Although he loved unadorned vocal tones, free of showy vibrato, he tried to meet Mom halfway and sat uneasily through *La Bohème, Aïda,* and the rest of them. At the crescendo of a soprano aria, however, he could never resist cracking "Someone get that woman a doctor," at which Mom would reply, in mock exasperation, that he should give himself a chance with it. Dad wound up getting plenty of chances.

When I first heard the expression "opposites attract," it made perfect sense. Dad was a singer but not a talker, so quiet that he seemed embarrassed by the sound of his own voice. Mom's music, I figured, allowed him to remain silent without anyone thinking him strange. While Mom liked her music loud, Dad liked his pure. A peas-over-here, potatoes-over-there aesthetic accounted for his dislike of opera and musicals, which mixed things up too much. In his own quartet, The Four Mugs (they used a different name when they hired out to sing at funerals), he hated coordinated gestures and other forms of showmanship. When the Mugs' young baritone once tried to get them to use some "choreography," Dad's response was, "Are we gonna sing or are we gonna dance?" Whenever my father came home early from work, he was likely to find his wife doing both. As he heard *I Pagliacci,* he must have thought that this shrieking Italian clown was directing unintelligible words straight into his bewildered heart.

Later Dad softened a bit and actually got to like *The Music Man,* which featured the Buffalo Bills, an honest-to-God barbershop quartet even though they committed barbershopper's treason by using instrumental accompaniment. He also learned to tolerate the music from *Breakfast at Tiffany's.* Mom bought the album after making Dad take her two or three times to see the movie. She said she identified with it, though I never understood why until many years later. "You've got a Holly Golightly mother," she'd brightly say—at which point Dad would immediately add ". . . and a Haile Selassie father." Who knew what *that* meant? Sue and I would look at each other as if our parents were both insane. A topic of endless speculation was how Mom and Dad had ever gotten together.

. . .

Trapped in a realm hostile to pagan reveries—a practical world of milk bottles, clothespins, and mousetraps—our mother was determined to give that world some color and light. The most thumb-worn books in the house were Uncle Foster's college literature textbook and Mom's girlhood copy of *The Best Loved Poems of the American People,* which was later superseded by individual volumes of Dickinson, Whitman, and Frost. Anne Morrow Lindbergh's *Gift from the Sea* and Somerset Maugham's *The Razor's Edge* headed her list for prose. There was also an endless succession of books from the public library, where she did volunteer reshelving on Saturday mornings. Mom's favorite library books, renewed for months at a time, included Richard Halliburton's adventure and travel books, assorted poetry anthologies, and volumes from Will and Ariel

Durant's *The Story of Civilization*. She began to write poetry, too, which she hadn't done since she was a girl. She entered her final versions, along with other thoughts and observations, into a three-ring notebook with "Jeanne's Meditations" written on the cover. Sometimes she would show me one of her poems; it was usually about walking through the woods or watching a bird through the kitchen window.

Reading and writing became the avenues by which our mother connected with the few kindred spirits she managed to find in our town. She bought a pillbox hat and a camel's-hair coat and started attending poetry readings and lectures at Findlay College, where she made friends with some faculty members. Before long she and Dad became part of a regular crowd in which they were the only couple who had never been to college. Sometimes faculty couples came to our house for dinner, and after clearing the table, Mom would put on a record and get everyone talking about music or literature. As I played quietly on the floor and listened until bedtime, I noticed that our "happy" mother, the inside-the-house mother, seemed to glow on these nights, asking questions of the professors and their wives and leaning in for their responses with an almost scary gleam in her eyes. These conversations went on long after I went to bed, and I would fall asleep to the comforting drone of talk and laughter downstairs. The next morning, Mom's notebook was often still on the kitchen table, where she had jotted down her thoughts after the guests had left.

Mom soon joined her Findlay College friends in a "great books" reading group, which sometimes met at our house. Sitting in a rack in the front room, next to a used set of *Encyclopedia Americana* that she and Dad had bought soon after they were married, were the boxed sets—pink, green, blue, and purple—of little paperbacks that the Great Books Society sent out with the annual reading plans. Mom was never more excited than when one of these boxed sets arrived in the mail and a new program was about to start. I loved those sets, too; compact and neatly squared, they seemed to bear brave witness that all knowledge was readily available, that anyone could learn anything. Dad was a kind of honorary member of the group. He read the books too, and he and Mom would talk about them before the guests arrived. Often, though, he was too tired from work to finish that night's assignment, and even when he did finish it, he rarely said anything once the discussion started. Whenever there was a spirited debate—about what sort of Plato's Cave illusions were afoot in Findlay, or how Saint Thomas Aquinas differed from the local Baptists—Mom was always right in the thick of it. Dad, never comfortable with loud talk even when it was friendly, would retreat to the kitchen under the guise of loading more snacks onto a tray.

. . .

Other friends helped Mom feel more at ease with who and where she was. One, an offbeat housewife and painter named Miriam Clowers, lived around the corner on Fishlock Avenue. Mrs. Clowers specialized in portraits, with cool blue backgrounds, greenish flesh tones, and faces that looked sad and dreamy. She had done a painting of Dave when he was nine; it made him look depressed and pensive. Her portrait of Mom, gazing out into the middle distance through some apple blossoms, had the same melancholy spookiness about it. I thought that Mrs. Clowers's paintings were scary and wouldn't let her paint me when she offered. Something about her pictures reminded me of dead people.

If Miriam Clowers fed Mom's hunger for beauty, Mary Shawcross offered bracing doses of truth—and precisely the sort of truth that my mother was seeking. Mrs. Shawcross, the toothy, wild-haired wife of the local pharmacist, was a cheerful atheist who kept an elaborate garden and made vicious fun of Christians. A stout vessel of common sense, she annually protested the Nativity display on the courthouse lawn, which was maintained, outrageously enough, by her tax dollars. Whenever she threatened to write to the Findlay *Republican Courier* to defend non-churchgoers' rights, her husband warned her that it might hurt business at the drugstore. Of Mom's friends, I liked Mrs. Shawcross the best: she talked to us kids as if we were regular people, without the fake smile and singsong tones that grownups usually affected. Sometimes, though, she could be a little unsettling. I remember hearing her describing Holy Communion as a cannibal feast while she and Mom shared a plate of Oreos. Mom told me to run outside and play, but later, when I peeked though the window, she was listening intently and nodding her head.

Mrs. Shawcross was not just a pagan but a "psychic." She had premonitions, which she recounted in the same matter-of-fact tone with which she mocked Christian dogma. The story went that years before, while on a shopping trip to Cleveland, she had refused to get on an elevator that then crashed and killed everyone on board. Mrs. Shawcross said that she had seen death on the passengers' faces, but the doors closed before she could warn them. Mom sometimes lamented the fact that she had no such powers, so fully did they attest to a pagan's attunement to cosmic forces. More often, though, she admitted that she didn't want them. Wouldn't the joy go out of life if you always knew what was going to happen? And since everybody died, wasn't *that* the thing which was always going to happen anyway? Turn down an empty glass. Pick up Sue's Pep Club sweater from the cleaners, take Jeff to the eye doctor, and help Dave fill out his application to Ohio State. But turn down an empty glass.

. . .

Our mother's beliefs could not remain private, especially in a church that was small enough to know her, and she eventually got into a series of doctrinal arguments with Reverend Detweiler and his successor, Reverend Karlson. Once Mom realized that my sister and I hated going to church, she agreed, in a family vote, that we should leave the Howard Methodist Church. She still believed that Jesus was all right—but look at what the Christians had done to him, especially this business about hell. When would these Methodists ever outgrow it? If *The Rubáiyát* summed up our mother's attitude toward this world, another favorite poem, Leigh Hunt's "Abou Ben Adhem," summed up her attitude toward the next one, if it existed. Waking from a "deep dream of peace," Abou Ben Adhem sees an angel writing the names of those who love God into a golden book. After learning that his name is not there, Ben Adhem asks the angel, "Write me as one that loves his fellow-men."

> The Angel wrote, and vanished. The next night
> It came again with a great wakening light,
> And showed the names whom love of God had blessed,
> And, lo! Ben Adhem's name led all the rest!

Mom figured that Abou had gotten it just about right. If pagan sensibilities render you incapable of loving a God who created hell, you might indeed resign yourself to loving your "fellow-men"—and if you do, your paganism will take a political turn. After trying a number of different churches, Mom discovered Findlay's Episcopal church and Father Ashcroft, who preached the Social Gospel and admitted privately that the Resurrection was probably a folktale. Mom had found a new kindred spirit and a church fit for Abou Ben Adhem—and her children—to attend.

Father Ashcroft's politics matched perfectly with Mom's developing activism. During the Eisenhower/Stevenson election of 1956, she had joined the League of Women Voters even though the organization's neutrality frustrated her. Four years later she worked for the Kennedy campaign, a lost cause in Hancock County. Some kids at school told me what their parents had said: if JFK won, the pope would be running the country. When I told this to Mom, she said it was a stupid lie—but even if it were true, it would be better than having the Southern Baptists in charge. On election night Sue and I got to stay up until the California returns came in and Nixon was sent back into oblivion, where Mom and Dad figured he belonged. I remember keeping track of the electoral vote by arranging my armymen into "good guys" and "bad guys," Democrats and Republicans, on the living room rug.

In three years JFK was dead, and Mom cried bitterly, but around that time she read Betty Friedan's *The Feminine Mystique,* which helped her recover. She later recalled that the book seemed like her own feelings put into words. By the time we joined the Episcopal church, she was a feminist and a civil rights activist, showing up at realtors' offices and asking them to sign petitions promising not to discriminate against minorities. She got kicked out of a few offices, and we started getting crank phone calls, some of them threatening. Dad volunteered to give the callers "one of these," as he said while making a fist, but the calls eventually petered out—largely, I think, because Sue was on the phone so often. Mom's political awakening proved to be catching, though a thirteen-year-old might be expected to take it too far. One time I talked the neighborhood kids into choosing sides for football on the basis of Democrats versus Republicans. When it ended up being two kids against seven, we dropped the idea. What kind of a game would *that* make?

In these years Dad stayed home in the evenings and checked our homework while Mom went off to civil rights discussion panels at the Episcopal church and Chamber of Commerce meetings, where she demanded low-income housing for the migrant workers who harvested the county's sugar beets. Cooking might as well have been quantum physics to Dad, so Mom served dinner early in order to make her meetings. Sue once announced that she wished we kids were colored or Mexican, because maybe *then* we could eat at a normal time and have something good for a change. Truth to tell, our mother had never been a great cook: it's hard to be a great cook when your thoughts are elsewhere. She usually made meatloaf or chicken, with mashed potatoes and a vegetable that nobody ate. Her most exotic dish was Spanish rice. Years later Sue and I would gain twenty-five pounds apiece in our freshman years at college. We were among the few kids who actually liked dormitory food.

. . .

Mom never felt at home in our town, but by the late sixties she began to feel more at home with the times. When the Vietnam War heated up, she became a draft counselor. I was the only boy I knew whose mother was urging him to prepare a conscientious objector's file. While I agreed with her politics and was grateful for her advice, something in me rebelled against it. If she couldn't be a regular mother, how was I supposed to be a regular son? What was I supposed to rebel against?

The war brought a long-standing family issue to a crisis. It had never been easy for us kids to accept the fact that our mother was hipper than we were. She had always been a force to reckon with, and each of us had managed to carve out a space apart from her, some breathing room. My brother, like Uncle Foster, turned to science, virtually a foreign language to our mother. My sister cultivated an obsession with social acceptance that disappointed Mom in its ordinariness. Why worry whether Jim Beech is going ask you out when you could be listening to Verdi? I had always been the child who responded most deeply to the strange, artsy things with which our mother filled our lives—but don't we always rebel most strongly against what we are? Repelled by her maddening currency, I withdrew from her orbit even more than my brother and sister did. I began to identify more with Dad and started acting more like the down-home kid that I thought I was supposed to be. My mother and I had some terrible arguments during the sixties. "Why don't you act your age?" was one of the hurtful things I'm ashamed to have said to her.

23

Caught up in my own rebellion, I could not tell her how proud I was that she had never taken her cues from people her own age, who watered their lawns, watched Lawrence Welk (Uncle Frank's old boss), and voted Republican. But when the hippie counterculture hit full force and the country got more on Mom's wavelength, we kids found it taxing to keep up with her. During visits home we would find her in Cesar Chavez blue jeans or flowered dashikis, often sporting a headband. A peace cross became a constant accessory, along with the same wire-rimmed glasses that my college friends were wearing. Sue and I called her new look—which she wore mainly to Democratic Party fund-raisers so sparsely attended that they barely filled someone's living room—the "Full Woodstock." Mom even got Dad into flared pants and paisley shirts with wide, lounge-singer collars. Clothes, however, don't always make the man: when our father walked in those flared pants, he still covered a little too much ground with each stride, like the farm boy he had once been.

Around that time, soon after Grandma and Grandpa Weldon died, our house began to see a daily ritual that would have made Grandma, who belonged to the Women's Christian Temperance Union, spin in her grave. Mom started a "happy hour," complete with bowls of beer nuts, manhattans and martinis for her, and bourbon on the rocks for Dad. Whenever I hitchhiked home from college for the weekend, I usually arrived just as happy hour was gearing up. The house would be filled with the sounds of Dylan or Joni Mitchell, and a framed portrait of "The Laughing Jesus" could be seen hanging on the wall next to the bathroom. Mom had clipped it, if I remember right, from *Hustler* magazine.

• • •

In 1970 Dad had a heart attack and took early retirement. Thinner now, he joked that he owed his new look to Lucky Strikes, workplace stress, and Jeanne. After he recovered, he and Mom realized that with the kids grown and his working days over, there was no reason to stay in Findlay. Seeking a haven for a pagan and a pagan's husband, they decided on Phoenix, where Dad joined a barbershop chorus and Mom started taking sociology courses at Maricopa Community College. Arizona seemed a good a place to start over—to be who they wanted to be—and Mom left Ohio vowing never to darken a church door again. One Sunday, however, when they went with some friends to a Unitarian church, she changed her mind. The Unitarians seemed to offer the next best thing to a community of pagans, a church so tolerant that Mary Shawcross, Miriam Clowers, Father Ashcroft, Omar Khayyám, and Abou Ben Adhem—all sorts of kindred spirits—might find a home there.

Fellowship with such freethinkers was dizzying. One night Mom and Dad tried marijuana with some other Unitarian Universalists, who were probably never more universal than at that moment. Dad pronounced it "pleasant," but Mom could not force herself to inhale and came away disappointed. Progressive to a fault, these Arizona Unitarians proved the perfect crowd with whom to savor Watergate, which brought our parents months of elated fascination. They embraced the scandal as a personal vindication, an all-encompassing "I told you so" issued to the Republican citizenry of Findlay, Ohio. They had no trouble believing that Nixon was a crook; what they could *not* believe was that they had finally found people who agreed with them.

The move to Arizona felt like a spiritual homecoming, but it was also a homecoming in a more literal sense. Having severed their Methodist roots by breathing the intoxicating air of the secular city, all four of Henry and Susan Weldon's aging children had regrouped under the clean desert sun. Uncle Foster was retired and living with his second wife in Scottsdale; Uncle Jim and *his* second wife ran a jewelry shop in Lake Havasu City; Aunt Biba, now widowed, lived with her daughter and son-in-law in Albuquerque. Mom got to see her sister and brothers regularly, and even visited her artist friend Miriam, who had moved to Santa Fe years before. Despite these renewed ties, however, daily life in Phoenix began to assume a hard monotony. A pagan loves nature—but what could be less natural than a pipe-fed city slapped down in the middle of an uninhabitable desert? The few weeks when the desert was in bloom proved no substitute for the changing seasons and their all-encompassing cycles. Hadn't Bliss Carmen's "The Vagabond," with its celebration of autumnal colors, been another one of Mom's favorite poems?

After two years our parents moved to Atlanta, but the freeways were too frenetic to negotiate. Then they moved to Terre Haute, which proved too close to Martinsville and a past that they had left far behind. Finally they settled in Columbus to be near Sue, who had just given birth to twins and would surely need a helping hand. They became active in a Unitarian congregation there, and Mom joined an interpretive dance group that occasionally performed at the services, donning black tights and enacting slow-motion mimes of themes like "Love," "Peace," and "Rebirth." She also began to read spiritual self-help books that spoke to inner peace, unity with nature, and a cleansing of guilt—everything dear to a pagan soul, ancient or modern. After sixty years of asking questions for which everyone else seemed to have all the answers, she devoured these books as confirmations that she had not been entirely crazy. *Nosce teipsum*, "Know yourself," as her ancient predecessors put it. Wasn't that what she had been trying to do all along?

Mom also became a strict watcher of diets, hers as well as other people's, as I was reminded at every encounter with no-fat ice cream, skim milk, and the unsalted soy nuts that she now served at happy hour. This too reflected an old pagan truth: *Mens sana in corpore sano:* "A sound mind in a healthy body." She also found renewed expression of a pagan's desire for social tolerance by becoming an activist for gay causes. As that devout pagan Horace had written, *De gustibus non est disputandum,* "There's no arguing in matters of taste," including taste in love. It seemed inevitable that Mom would find kindred spirits among gay men and lesbians, many of whom had lived much of their own lives feeling like Martians or, if they came from Christian homes, like pagans. At odds with their own times and places until they discovered that they needed only to *be*, they shared with my mother a hard journey toward self-acceptance. People who have made that journey, for whatever reason, will naturally be drawn to one another.

Mom and Dad began hosting monthly potlucks for their gay friends. I was home for visits during several of these gatherings, and as I talked with the guests, most of whom were around my age, I heard once again how "remarkable"—that was always the word—my mother was. By this time, with the dizzying swirl of dashikis and Laughing Jesuses well behind us, I could nod in genuine agreement.

· · ·

It was characteristic that at the first signs of physical decline, our parents sold their house and moved into an assisted-living facility. When they informed us kids of this decision—a little too cheerfully, we thought—there was a curious reversal of roles. *They* were the ones calmly noting that it was time to prepare for the inevitable, while their children, middle-aged and thus only half-convinced of the fact of death, complained that they shouldn't rush things, that they would surely feel more mobile again, that it was all too soon.

It was a natural desire, I suppose, to stop time—to shield our parents from that inexorable slide toward the end. But midwestern pagans, like their ancient predecessors, don't waste much time worrying about death. Socrates, who once spoke for everyone who never knew—or who managed to escape—the Christian story of judgment and hell, speculated that either there will be nothing after death and thus nothing to fear, or there will be a regathering of spirits for stimulating conversation, a sort of Great Books group in which everyone understands all the readings perfectly. I recently asked my mother what she thinks about this, and while she wouldn't mind another session with the old Great Books crowd, she doubts that things will be that way. The pagan preference for the here and now, as opposed to heavenly pipe dreams, prevents her from being overly concerned about it. Besides, there's too much going on. Some of those kindred spirits at the Unitarian church still need a few lessons in political awareness; the French conversation group that she attends is bound to enjoy the Baudelaire poem she wants to discuss; and the local branch of the Columbus Public Library has not yet exhausted its supply of mind-food: spiritual revelations for her, large-scale popular histories for Dad.

Mom's latest discovery is Evelyn Underhill's *Practical Mysticism*, which is starting to convince her that "mystic" might be a more accurate characterization than "pagan" after all. When I remind her that she never had Mary Shawcross's gift for receiving visions, she declares that she's not so sure about that. Maybe she had them all along. She says she'll give the matter some more thought.

. . .

I remember the last potluck I attended while our parents were still in their house. I was nibbling on something healthy, probably a carrot, when I spotted my father in a corner of the room chatting with two young men, one of whom was draping his arm across the other's shoulders. Dad was listening intently and nodding, but his face wore a half-smile that was not, to my eyes, entirely relaxed. The old pipeliner whose first lessons in morality had come from the Bible Church in Martinsville, Illinois, was still a little uncomfortable with all this, but as always, he was in there kicking. In the back of his mind he may have been wondering how an Illinois farm boy wound up picking at broccoli covered with low-fat cheese while listening to two strapping men, a choral director and an elementary schoolteacher, describe how they met and fell in love. If pressed, however, my father would know that the answer is obvious: once upon a time in the Midwest, he married the Pagan of East Sandusky Street. As he listened to the men his gaze followed my mother, who was working the room and freshening some drinks. When their eyes met for an instant his smile became genuine, and I knew exactly what he was thinking: This has been one hell of a ride.

Science Boy

It was hard to grow up in the 1950s without absorbing an unshakeable faith in science. The American Way of Life seemed to depend on science, and the results were already pouring in. Polio was beaten, Detroit was making the most powerful cars in the world, interstate highways were on the drawing board, planned communities were popping up in the suburbs, and space-age "convenience" foods were filling the shelves of those new, aptly named "supermarkets." We kids were told that the Russians could take it all away, of course, but not if our science stayed ahead of their science. At the time the race seemed pretty close. Vice President Nixon scored points for our side when he showed Khrushchev the kitchen of the future, but shame and fear nagged at our hearts as we peered into the night sky for a glimpse of Sputnik.

The government began pushing science education as a matter of national survival. In school we watched movies, usually produced by power companies, in which avuncular scientists in lab coats (it didn't occur to us that they were actors) soothingly described the benefits of the coming nuclear age. As a hedge against bad times, we also practiced A-bomb drills. What I remember most from elementary school was hearing that we couldn't afford to fall behind "the rest of the world," meaning the Soviet Union. Being smart in school was a patriotic duty, and being smart meant being smart in science.

A particular kind of kid resulted from all this: the Science Boy. My older brother Dave was a pure specimen of the type. He entered the 1950s at the age of nine, primed to ingest the wonders of the new era just as they were leaping from blueprints. I was born eight days after the decade began, and when I was old enough to see which way the wind was blowing, I tried to be a Science Boy too. But with an nine-year head start, Dave was far too advanced for me to catch up. Russians, Shmussians: I had fallen behind in my own house.

Dave was intimidatingly smart, and in all the right ways. He built radios from scratch, carefully pouring hot paraffin to anchor the circuits; he assembled intricate models without so much as a glance at the instructions; he drew star charts and tracked the planets, always on the lookout for the sudden appearance of a new comet; he launched water-powered rockets and gas-propelled airplanes; he collected rocks and fossils, checking his finds against official-looking "field guides"; he sketched plans for labor-saving devices on graph paper; he gave his chemistry set such hard use that he frequently went to the hobby shop to replenish his chemicals. You needed *stuff* to do all of this, and our bedroom resembled a laboratory. A map of the solar system and a periodic table of the elements hung on the wall. For a while there was an ant farm, and Dave recorded the ants' comings and goings with scientific rigor. He set up his own radio transmitter, issuing updates on neighborhood news to a four-block radius. His desk was always covered with radio frequency handbooks, logarithmic tables, and precision drafting instruments. One of his prized possessions was a slide rule, which struck me as the key to the future, the indispensable tool for modern times.

A skinny kid with thick glasses, bad skin, and a crew cut, Dave looked the part. His friends were Science Boys too: gangly operators of ham and shortwave radios, designers of tinfoil solar collectors, archivists of back issues of *Popular Science* and *Popular Mechanics* stacked waist high in their garages. My brother and his friends were always going off on "expeditions": fossil hunts, radio reception experiments, still-rare jet sightings, constellation mappings. Wanting to do science too, I begged to tag along, but Dave told me—quite rightly—that I'd get in the way or get bored and want to come home too soon. He would pacify me by giving me a project of my own, usually collecting some form of "data." One night when he and his buddies were going out to chart stars, he told me that they needed to supplement their findings with a faithful map of just those stars which

Dave's birthday, 1956.

could be seen from our bedroom window. He said something about "parallax" and the need for different "angles of observation." I dutifully plotted stars on the sheet of graph paper he left me, checking them against the paperback star guide until sleep overtook me and rendered my data useless.

It was clear that my brother was preparing for Tomorrow with a readiness that I could never hope to achieve. He even had a tomorrow-guy name: "Dave" seemed the perfect name for an engineer or an astronaut. "Jeffrey," by contrast, sounded soft and sluggish, all too appropriate for a chubby kid who spent too much time lying in the grass staring at clouds. Dave was all action and projects; I was all inertia and daydreaming. I tried to undertake projects but could never see them through. I would end up thinking about something else and walking away, or trying to finish things up too fast and then throwing a fit because my squirrel-skull drawing didn't look "scientific" enough. I lacked the patience to chip excess rock away from a trilobite, solder wires to a circuit board, or affix decals in their precise places on a model rocket. My brother assured me that when I got bigger I would be able to do such things, but that was little comfort. All I knew was that I couldn't do the neat stuff *now*.

Dave even showed scientific cool when dealing with our parents. While my sister and I threw tantrums and pleaded dramatically to get our way, he would smile pleasantly and agree with whatever Mom and Dad said—only to go off and do whatever he wanted anyway, later claiming that he had "forgotten" their instructions. I don't remember our parents ever yelling at him: he was simply too bland a presence for that, quietly busying himself with whatever was occupying him at the moment. Asking to be excused from dinner so he could return to a project or slipping silently out of the house for a late-night expedition, Dave was a master at lying low.

As I got older, I began to notice that a Science Boy had to make sacrifices. Dave didn't have much of a social life. The standard teen obsessions that my sister Sue was beginning to cultivate—the friends, the gossip, the dances—simply did not apply to him. He didn't date except for his junior prom, and he hardly spent any time on the phone. By then he was working nights and weekends as a disk jockey at the local radio station, and didn't have time to be a normal teenager. His only school activities were the marching band and, of course, the science club. To be sure, there were several girls at Findlay Senior High in the late 1950s who could talk about probability theory and ultra-high-frequency television, and my brother was good friends with them. But they weren't any more interested in dating than he was. They had projects of their own.

When Dave built a computer in his junior year and entered it in the science fair, he might as well have created life. The only thing about computers that anyone in Findlay, Ohio, knew in 1958 was that NASA used them in the space race. Dave's computer was like a player piano. Instead of using punch cards, it performed its task—multiplying any two numbers up to nine times nine—by taking its instructions from a continuous roll of paper with holes that turned individual circuits on and off at precisely the right times. He easily won first prize and the right to go to the regional fair at Bowling Green State University. Our whole family went along on the big day, but disaster struck minutes after we found a place to park. We had unloaded the computer from the trunk and were carrying its various parts toward the exhibit building when a gust of wind caught the program roll and shredded it to bits. Sue and I scurried around collecting the flapping pieces, and Dad said he would find a drugstore and buy some tape, but Dave just stared at the mess without expression. "Don't bother," he said. "It's ruined."

If it had been *my* handmade computer, I would have howled and kicked the trees, but Dave accepted the risks of science. Hadn't some of his chemistry experiments filled the basement with home-brew tear gas? And didn't storms sometimes knock out his "remotes" for WFIN from the county fair, leaving him to shrug helplessly at the restless crowd peering into the trailer window? The judges at Bowling Green were grownup Science Boys, and they understood: Dave explained how his computer would have worked and won a prize anyway. In the world of science, it was the thought that counted. Good thoughts led to progress, and progress, as the Science Boys at General Electric repeatedly told us, was "our most important product."

. . .

Family psychologists are surely right when they claim that siblings seek their own turf, carving out individual niches to avoid being also-rans. My brother staked out the future, while my sister, constantly on the phone with one of her fifty "best friends," claimed the present. That left me with the past, and I began an unconscious but inexorable drift toward everything old, impractical, and obscure. This move was reinforced by the fact that I had managed to develop an unusual obsession with death. If you spend a lot of time pondering the mysteries of death, your excitement about technological progress will be muted at best. The past, not the future, will feel more like home to you.

The relative merits of the future and the past became a running theme with my brother and me. By now I had become a reader, something he definitely was not, and had developed an interest in things like ancient history, the Bible, and old-time baseball—all of which, he observed, would get me a cup of coffee provided I also had the requisite fifteen cents. Dave often bragged that he had read only two books cover to cover: *Donald Duck Sees South America* and *The Building of the Transcontinental Railroad*.

33

I knew that was a lie, though, because our room contained a third book, a well-thumbed copy of Isaac Asimov's *I, Robot*. Dave was too busy finding things out for himself to read books about made-up stories or "history." I knew he was right. We would all have to live in the future, and if I didn't get with it I'd get left behind.

Dave left for Ohio State just before I turned ten. When our family made Sunday visits to Columbus, the campus seemed like an entire city of big Science Boys and Science Girls. As I gazed at the crew cuts and flips, I assumed that all college students were learning how to make rockets or space food or mechanical brains, things that would make the American Way of Life even better. Strange as it seems, it never occurred to me that people in college studied anything but the future. I knew from my reading that there were "professors" of archaeology and ancient history and biblical studies, but I didn't realize that those professors held classes and taught people—that they actually had *students*.

My brother majored in engineering, and I imagined that he would someday build communications equipment for NASA or design tracking systems to thwart Russian missiles. I was proud of him, of course, but with that pride came self-reproach: what contribution to a Better Life for All was I preparing myself to make? I did things like memorize ancient Egyptian phonetic symbols; was I going to help Keep America First by writing people's names in hieroglyphics? The visits to OSU were both exciting and depressing. While my parents and sister chatted with Dave in the Student Union, I would wander over to the Ohio Historical Museum, which had huge columns that let me pretend I was in ancient Athens or Rome. Although the museum was definitely my kind of place, it seemed at odds with everything else on campus. Here, I thought, was where they gathered all the old stuff to keep it out of the way. I gazed for hours at Indian arrowheads, nineteenth-century farm implements, and what for me was the museum's prize: a genuine Egyptian mummy. As long as I kept peering into those glass cases, I could forget how out of it I was, a loser in my own time.

When Dave started college, he probably figured that he would end up working for NASA or the Pentagon too, but he got sidetracked. To make extra money he took a weekend job at a Columbus radio station, spinning records on the graveyard shift. This move was fully in charac-

34

ter for a Science Boy: after all, rock 'n' roll was part of the future. Drawn to the music and hooked on the thrill of having his voice go out to half a million people—never mind that most of them were sleeping—he began cutting classes and dropping courses to take more shifts at the station. Soon he was no longer a college student with a part-time job but a full-time deejay who took the odd class. This exasperated our parents to no end, but Dave's rational temperament served him well as he patiently explained why changing majors from engineering to speech was a shrewd move. Ever the advocate for the future, he was convinced that the opportunities in broadcasting were limitless. He had considered all the variables, and radio seemed the perfect career for a Science Boy who had discovered a way to reach people—lots of them—while sitting alone in an insulated studio.

• • •

My sister, the Present Person, graduated from Findlay College and became what she had always wanted to be: an elementary school teacher. The youngest child, the Past Person, went to Kent State and discovered that you could indeed major in something besides the future. I drifted into graduate school and eventually became something I didn't even know existed when I was a kid: a literature professor. My brother, the Future Person, finally got his degree after seven years, the last two sweating his way through the Spanish requirement. Donald Duck may have seen South America, but he definitely hadn't learned the language.

Dave was drafted within weeks of graduating and went to Vietnam—as a radio operator, of course. When he returned, somewhat sobered but with his faith in progress intact, he began a fifteen-year career in radio, rising through the ranks as jock and program director and station manager in larger and larger markets. Radio may seem far removed from the laboratory and the drafting table, but Dave never stopped being a Science Boy. He approached flagging ratings as a problem involving variables to be analyzed with scientific precision. He was never comfortable with the people part of the business: the power lunches, the deal making, the promotional events. But he had a real gift for working with the numbers, with listener demographics. His specialty was the "MOR" format—that "middle-of-the-road" mix of accessible acts like Sinatra and Tony Bennett, and later,

35

Jackson Browne and the Eagles. He quickly earned a reputation as someone who could turn around any station in any market. He even once got a small write-up in *Billboard.*

In a volatile business like radio, fifteen years is a good record of longevity, but in the early 1980s it all came to an end. You can't do science if people keep changing the rules on you, and new factors in the radio business were skewing the data beyond recognition. Like many other elements in American popular culture, radio was fragmenting, its audience splitting into a dozen specialized niches: hard rock, soft rock, all talk, easy listening, country. Dave had spent fifteen years programming for the middle market, the average listener, but suddenly there *was* no average listener. What's more, the age of listeners was decreasing, which was bad news for MOR. Jackson Browne might please everyone, after a fashion, but he was definitely not the first love of young consumers who craved David Bowie or Iggy Pop. Middle of the Road radio faced the same problem that the TV networks are facing today with the advent of cable and a hundred splintered choices. Forget trying to be all things to all people; an MOR programmer in the 1980s could no longer be most things to *most* people.

Pittsburgh was the first city where the predicted turnaround failed to materialize. From there my brother quickly descended through a series of smaller markets until he wound up at a station in Greenville, South Carolina. When the old magic didn't happen there either, he was out of a job and out of radio altogether.

. . .

The militantly upbeat world of MOR radio had sheltered my brother from huge cultural changes during the sixties and seventies—changes that made lots of Science Boys feel the squeeze. Science Boys had been too practical to be beatniks. Now they were too practical to be hippies, and far too devoted to detached observation to get caught up in anything so emotional as politics. There weren't many Science Boys at the City Lights bookstore, at Woodstock, in Chicago's Grant Park, at May Day in Washington.

Indeed, the times had not been kind. With strontium 90, napalm, Love Canal, and Malathion, science was no longer good for children and other living things. Aside from the applied chemistry necessary for staying high, science came to be seen as a money rake for soulless industrialists, agribusinessmen, and other denizens of the military-industrial complex. Science Boys found themselves being called "nerds" or "baby killers," depending on how much harm they had managed to do. Research and development, a virtual religion in the fifties, was scaled back as money was diverted to programs with more immediate payoffs. "Progress" was out, "natural" was in, and the ideal for good technology regressed to pre-industrial levels. Why use a gas-powered lawnmower when you can use a reel model and save the earth? Better yet, why mow at all? What did those aphids and deer ticks ever do to you, man? The cult resource for cutting-edge hepcats was no longer the catalog of the Edmund Scientific Company, with its chemicals and prisms and pickled specimens. Now it was the *Whole Earth Catalog*, which talked a futuristic line but seemed, on closer inspection, to have been compiled at the Council of Nicaea. If anyone walking the earth in 1972 had invented a nonelectrical, non-fossil-fuel device for recycling human waste into trail mix, that person would have beaten McGovern *and* Nixon.

Things got so bad that a few prominent Science Boys, shaken by their sudden irrelevance, defected to the other side. Harvard psychologist Richard Alpert, turning to the intuitive East and an impressive array of turbans, transformed himself into Baba Ram Dass. His colleague Timothy Leary dropped acid and transformed himself into, well, Timothy Leary on acid. Tune in, turn on, and forget the quadratic formula. No need to record data and frame a hypothesis when one greedy lungful of hash will suddenly make visible the aura of that girl you're smoking with, answering your every question and even a few you hadn't thought to ask.

The Summer of Love eventually caught up with my brother, ending his radio days in the metallic howl of high-feedback guitars. As he emptied his desk in that Greenville station, he sullenly grasped the most immediate and personal result of the decline and fall of the Science Boy in America: he had become a radio guy who detested the music that sold radio ads.

• • •

I was always the brooder in the family, flinching at anticipated horrors and nursing dark thoughts even in the midst of fun things, like birthday parties. I still struggle with this pessimism: it is a serious handicap for a teacher, and poison in the classroom. True to the child I once was, I still

37

relate uneasily to the future, despite the fact that teaching is supposed to be all *about* the future. Optimism is the province of Science Boys, for whom the universe will always make perfect sense given a viable hypothesis that accounts for all observable phenomena. The Science Boy bases his entire being on hope. It is his best trait.

When my brother hit bottom in Greenville, he was forty, married, and the possessor of a huge mortgage. Even worse, he had suffered the Science Boy's ultimate embarrassment: he had become dated. The times had passed him by, in a paradigm shift sealed by Reagan's election. The American Hero was no longer the scientist but the businessman. And the technology that would prove most relevant to the bottom line of commerce was not radio or even broadcasting in general, but something completely different.

During Dave's fall from radio grace, this new technology was being forged two thousand miles away by young men—boys, really—who would rise to full prominence in the 1990s. West Coast names reminiscent of 1950s science fiction began appearing in the business press: Digital Research, North Star, Intel, Altair, Microsoft, and—bucking the spaceship futurism—the all-American "Apple." Once a more familiar name, International Business Machines, entered the game and the new technology became respectable, things happened fast; by 1983 *Time*'s "Man of the Year" was the personal computer.

A true Science Boy may be down, but he's never out. As Dave scanned the trade papers and the business sections of the *New York Times* and the *Atlanta Constitution*, he read about these magic machines that could race through any task reducible to a series of ones and zeroes, current flowing and current cut. The news struck him like a memory. Although the medium of choice was a floppy plastic diskette rather than a roll of shelf paper, this was a place he had been before.

Dave bought a Heathkit computer and put it together so he could see how the hardware worked. Then he bought an IBM PC and began a noble experiment in retraining, a one-man space race against obsolescence. He gave himself a year to live on his savings while he taught himself to program the machine. If he didn't find a way to make a living in computers by then, he would start all over in radio.

Although our parents thought he was insane, I suspected even at the time that the experiment was less risky than it seemed and that Dave knew it. It was no surprise to me when the mysteries of software awoke powers of the Science Boy that had lain half-dormant during his years in radio, an industry in which the ratio of techno stuff to people stuff had always been too close to fifty-fifty to suit his deeper nature. For a while he had done reasonably well even with those aspects of radio that reached disturbingly into the real world, but it had always been a strain. Now, as he sat up nights with a Basic manual—coding simple routines, compiling them, running them, debugging them, and running them again—he had a feeling that he had come home.

. . .

Dave was not alone in his fall, and he would not be alone in his redemption. Thousands of Science Boys ended up finding a home—and, in many cases, a second chance—staring into the lurid glow of those monitors. It's a lucky thing, too; what other home could they have found? Bill Gates makes the cover of *Time* as America's richest man, but watch him move and listen to him talk. How far would *that* guy have gotten if he had been forced to pick his way through cocktails and golf foursomes, the traditional obstacle course of old-style corporate America? Computing turned out to be the perfect Science Boy sanctuary. A computer is absolutely predictable, the flat opposite of humans with their sudden veerings, their untraceable insincerities. Barring the odd bug or a power surge, a computer will do precisely what you tell it, no more and no less. It is a machine with honor: like the Science Boy, it follows the rules.

In this new industry it didn't matter how unpopular you were in high school or how incapable of small talk you might be. The press now routinely refers to the "computing community," but the term is a misnomer at best, almost an oxymoron. If you doubt this, consider the industry term for someone sitting at a keyboard at the receiving end of the work. Neither a "person" (too sentimental and humanistic) nor a "consumer" (too crass and businesslike, a denial of the Science Boy's delight in *making* rather than selling), he or she is simply a "user"—as reductive a term, socially, as one can imagine. How many teachers, psychologists, and case workers would think to call the people they serve "users"? Or consider the sobering history of computer documentation. I'm not talking about manuals in pidgin English, written by Japanese or Korean engineers whose dissertations at MIT were smoothed out by unemployed English Ph.Ds. I'm talking about documentation written by red-blooded American guys capable of placing accent-free orders for cappuccino in any Starbuck's in California. In the early days "documentation" meant just that: a programmer's logbook of how a program worked. That didn't change much when software went commercial. If "users" weren't smart enough to look over the programmer's shoulder and figure things out for themselves, they were probably unworthy of the technology anyway.

If those buoyant Microsoft ads leave you unconvinced of a persistent unsociability in Cyberland, walk the aisles of a computer store and check out the patrons, especially the ones over forty. There's a silent intensity about them, often the faint scowl of people who haven't spoken to anyone in days. Something is usually a little off—maybe a bit dated—about their clothes and haircuts. As they peer at the specs on software boxes, a hard little gleam in their eyes breaks through a studied facade of ennui. Note how many of their questions to the sales staff are shamelessly performative. You'll hear epic accounts of config-dot-sys and IRQ manipulations, cautionary tales of boards and chips successfully installed after encountering a Big Problem but solving it on their own, no thanks to those cretins in customer support. I don't wish to seem uncharitable, but I would rather eat a bag of that recycled-shit trail mix than be a computer salesman. Imagine how tricky it must be to describe your wares without appearing to know more than the customer does and, as a result, watching him stomp off in a huff.

Cyberland, that last-chance oasis for 1950s Science Boys and their younger counterparts, is a haven for loners. Science Boys—and I'm including Science Girls here—are pathologically uncomfortable with people. They can be brutally unkind even toward each other, their social hermeticism revealed in flaming color on bulletin boards, in Usenet newsgroups, and in those quaintly misnamed "chat" rooms. Even when they're not being arrogant or dismissive, many cyberfolk seem to lack that basic sense that tells us how we are coming across to other people. Visit two or three personal homepages on the Web and you'll see what I mean. Here's my resumé, my dog, my favorite vacation spot, my girlfriend—all presented in the absolute conviction that others will find this material irresistible. "Be sure to bookmark this page," the webmaster gushes. "I'll be posting a new picture of Judy every week!"

Such self-absorption is nothing short of astounding. And yet there is something touching about the webmaster's faith that you, too, will want to download that gigantic jpeg that shows Judy washing the car and smiling like an idiot. What's touching is the unflagging optimism of the Science Boy, the naive expectation that since he has figured out how to make the computer *do* this thing, people will naturally want to see it done. The Science Boy has found his own field of dreams, and it's called the Internet. If you post it, they will download.

. . .

You can probably guess how things turned out in Greenville. My brother found his idea, wrote his program, and made some serious money. He designed a spreadsheet and presentation program that took raw data from the Arbitron radio ratings and broke down the demographics, transforming the numbers into attractive charts and graphs that even a non–Science Boy businessman could understand. Dave sold the program himself until he found a software distributor who not only marketed it but hired him and his wife as salaried consultants. Several job changes later, he is now an "interface" specialist who designs screens—their layout, colors, sequencing—to fit the "users" of other people's programs.

There's irony in the fact that this private, quirky guy gets paid to enhance the user-friendliness of software. Had the social demands of radio not forced Dave out into the world of people, he might have been unable to do what he's doing today. The radio years certainly made him more socially presentable than most Science Boys; if you could hear his pleasant, morning-man voice and feel his hearty handshake, you'd never suspect how weird he is. He can pass for a perfectly normal, affable guy if you don't know what signs to look for, like the glaze that sometimes covers his eyes during conversation—a glaze that tells you he's pondering a work-related problem while Mom asks how his son Timmy is doing in school. You could easily miss the slight pause, the extra beat before he blinks and smiles. "Fine. He's learning Spanish now, you know."

These ironies are not lost on Dave, who has always been more reflective than his placid surface suggests. He knows where his bread is buttered, and like most of the people who have made good with these magic machines, he is a Science Boy who learned to think as if he weren't one. Denizens of the industry have a word for a computer guy's ability—when he has it—to empathize, however minimally, with everyday people: they call it "vision." Steve Jobs had it when he built "a computer for the rest of us," artfully positioning himself against IBM as the last, best hope of the common folk. Gates had it when he transported Apple's point-and-click interface to IBM and its clones. Both cause and product of the rehabilitation of science, Gates has made technology seem downright sociable. How could it *not* be, linked as it is to his nerdy but affable promises of a bright future for all? America is going to stay on top and get even richer. It's like the 1950s all over again, but without the Red Scare.

Meanwhile my brother sits in his home office, a one-man hog heaven for identifying problems and finding solutions, and ponders the arcana of screen design: the size and apparent recession of buttons, the minutely differing effects of background colors, the optimal balance of fullness and brevity for on-screen text, the size and proportion of help screens, the proper mix of alarm and reassurance in error messages. Given the user-friendliness of current software languages, the available libraries of prewritten subroutines, and the conventional "look" of all Windows-based programs, Dave does very little actual coding these days. Instead he makes aesthetic decisions. He does the work of an artist—a commercial artist, to be sure, but an artist nonetheless. I can't resist teasing him about this: a fine thing for a Science Boy to end up doing, meditating on the psychic impact of bright cyan on slate gray. This is artsy stuff, far removed from those scale maps of the moon, meticulously rendered in mechanical pencil on sheets of graph paper taped together with scarcely a seam showing.

· · ·

It's hard for brothers to stay close when they're nine years apart, especially when they have taken opposing paths seemingly predestined from childhood. After I left for college, my visits home never seemed to coincide with Dave's, and we kept in touch only indirectly, mostly through our sister, the People Person. It's not that we disliked each other; it's just that he didn't read and I didn't listen to radio—and on those rare occasions when Past Boy and Future Boy met, we had little to say. Although this was sad, it seemed inevitable. For most old-line humanists, Science Boys are the enemy. In English departments many people—usually the older crowd—curse Cyberland as the beginning of the end for the printed book. I don't disagree with that, and it disturbs me, too. But my concerns about the Decline of the West and the Dumbing of America are tempered by the fact that computers brought a tangible benefit to our family. After years of partial estrangement, they gave my brother and me something to talk about.

Maybe Gates is right when he insists that computers are all about "connectivity." Dave did his part in moving toward such a connection in the early eighties, when he began his pilgrim's progress from a bloodless compiler of code to an aesthetician of screens, a dealer in shapes and colors and the emotional responses of poor forked creatures trying to decide which key to press next. A few years later I started my own crawl toward the center when I succumbed to the hype and bought a gunmetal Kaypro 4 to do my writing with. Terrified that I would mess something up, that I'd see a flash and smell smoke the minute I turned this incredibly expensive machine on, I let it sit in its box for six months. But when Dave and his wife happened to pass through my city on a trip, his first visit to my place in ten years, he plugged in some cables, flipped on a switch, and showed me how to "back up" my master diskettes. "You're gonna love this," he said brightly.

Few things are more boring than conversion stories, so I'll spare you the details of mine. Suffice it to say that I got hooked on these magic boxes, and now, with a little distance, I think I know why. Computers were the first thing from Dave's world that I could actually understand. This felt like discovering a second brain, and I pursued the forbidden knowledge with a vengeance. I mastered the Kaypro's CP/M operating system and dabbled in Basic and Pascal and file conversions until I found myself becoming something of an English department guru, gently leading my fellow humanists into the zip-and-zap beauties of word processing and the confident glow of tomorrow.

For the first time in my life I was a Science Boy too, an unexpected turn that began to strike *me* almost as a memory. The English professor may not be that different from the Science Boy, especially if he has always been drawn to unpopular things: poems rather than novels, old texts rather than new, minor figures rather than major. I've always liked nothing better than a solitary, esoteric pursuit. Writing up the results is secondary, and teaching them is tertiary: simply finding the solution to a problem is what raises the gooseflesh. Maybe this old schism between brothers—our domestic embodiment of C. P. Snow's division between humanists and technicians—was never as acute as we always thought. Maybe it wasn't even real.

Nowadays my brother and I call—or, more frequently, e-mail—each other regularly, chattering like magpies about default settings and memory requirements and software features. During visits to our parents, which now coincide, we open our laptops and put them through their paces. My machine is always one or two platforms behind his, but I don't mind. What he has now I'll probably have in two or three years—and even a Past Person can learn to appreciate a glimpse or two into the future. If you didn't know better, you'd think you were watching *two* Science Boys as we retreat to our parents' utility room and their only three-pronged outlet. Our belated bond has become a standing joke in our family and a minor irritant to our mother. "Boys," she asks, "Why don't you turn off those machines so we can talk? I want to know if you're happy." Several Thanksgivings ago my brother gave the now-classic response, the prototype of all subsequent answers with which we tease her: "Well, Mom, I'm a lot happier now that I've increased my swap file to 300 megabytes." At such moments our mother rolls her eyes, unsure whether to get mad or to be pleased that her night-and-day sons are finally on such good terms.

As we compare mice to trackballs to pointing devices, my brother and I are following a forty-year-old script, one of the earliest I remember. In it, a senior Science Boy initiates a junior Science Boy into a world of wonders. When old walls collapse, they become grist—new variables, perhaps—in the compulsive questioning of identity that plagues midlife guys like me. Maybe I gave up too soon on being a Science Boy when I was a kid. Or maybe I've always really *been* one, but simply spun off into "unscientific" topics because I could make them my own. It's a humbling realization, but the academy is more like Cyberland than I've been willing to admit. Both places can serve as pretty good hideouts for people who might have been done in by life in the mainstream. Humanities professors sometimes get a little snobbish about the high road we took and the humane values we promote. We lament the shoddy ethics of businessmen and the horrors of technology, and a lot of us convince ourselves that we're above all that. But in truth, most of us withdrew from such practical realms because we were too shy, too awkward, or too obsessed with our own interests to join the regular flow. Weirdness, after all, is not confined to people who once knew how to use a slide rule. I walk the aisles of that computer store too, and when I catch my reflection in a mirror next to a stack of upgrades for the latest version of Windows, I'm only mildly surprised to discover that I fit right in.

Don't get me wrong. If you spotted me on my own turf, wandering through the literature shelves in a college library, you would probably think I was as normal as the next guy, just like my brother. That might be the deeper conspiracy that he and I have come to share: a recognition, at once humbling and enabling, of having beaten the odds in a world that seems stacked against us, of managing to convince people that we're not deeply weird and hopelessly lost in our own obsessions. All brothers share secrets. Ours is the relief of two middle-aged guys who know that they've been graced with the social instincts of salamanders and yet have managed, somehow, to get by.

Summer Place

The rhythmic squeaking of the floorboards beneath the living room rug was especially loud in the basement, where I was usually drawing chalk streets on the uneven concrete floor for a miniature town scaled to my toy cars. At first I would try to bring the noise into my play as a marker of miniature time: sixteen squeaks to a day in the town's life, thirty-two if I wanted to slow things down. After a while, though, the squeaking became an irritating reminder that I wasn't laying out a real town, that these thimbles weren't really gas pumps and these blocks cut from two-by-fours weren't really buildings after all, despite their carefully drawn doors and windows.

The squeaks told me that my sister was "on her rocker" again, as my older brother called it. Closer listening always revealed Percy Faith's "Theme from *A Summer Place*" playing in the background. The French horns, which at one point made three downward swoops like elephant calls, shot through the heating ducts with particular clarity.

By the time I was nine and my sister was fourteen, rocking to Percy Faith had become a ritual. Sue would put on the 45, flop into the rocking chair, and go—sometimes, it seemed, for hours at a stretch. This struck me as a waste of time tantamount to self-punishment, like making yourself sit in a corner. As the record grew increasingly scratchy, the song's "Chopsticks" rhythm made it feel as if my breath and heart were trapped in the monotonous, endless beat. What's more, Sue didn't seem to enjoy

Sue and her little brother, 1955.

the endless back-and-forth ride, at least in any obvious way. When she was on her rocker, she sometimes didn't hear anything we said to her, and the fact that she often chewed gum as she rocked only added to her distant spookiness.

I didn't get it: how could a person do *nothing*, and for hours on end? And why "Theme from *A Summer Place*?" What was the mysterious appeal of those endless piano triplets and that sappy melody that kept looping into itself, refusing to end? One time when I was whining about Sue's song, Dad admitted that he had liked it for the first thousand times but that now, after the thousand-and-first time, he wasn't so sure. He did nothing, however, to stop the music. More than once he even ordered me to stop badgering my sister about it.

. . .

I had a sense, even as a kid, that Sue was having a hard time of it. Our house must have been a difficult place to be a girl in the late 1950s. By any standard we were a strange bunch in Findlay, Ohio, a family of loners convinced that the outside world was filled with rampant, arbitrary goofiness. We came by this arrogance honestly. Dad was a New Deal Democrat working for an oil company dominated by the sort of Republicans who cannot imagine anyone *not* being a Republican. His coworkers listened to his political rants with genuine puzzlement, even pity. Anyone who didn't revere the still-fresh memory of Robert Taft—Ohio's "Mr. Republican"—was regarded like a person with a hump. Our mother felt even more out of place in our town; when she questioned the concept of hell in her church discussion group, she might as well have been proposing the slaughter of Findlay's innocents.

My older brother and I reacted to our family's awareness of not fitting in by retreating into private obsessions. Dave rejected the high school social scene to pursue his fervent devotion to science. I took the opposite tack and decided early on that ancient history and archaeology were more interesting than what usually passed for fun among nervous packs of little boys. Neighborhood baseball games were an exception, but even there I came to appreciate the meditative quiet of right field, where nobody else wanted to play. First base was my preferred spot, but right field became bearable once I pretended that I was manning Hadrian's Wall, poised to catch barbarian pop flies.

Sue was the middle child, stuck—in every possible way—in the center of a family so introverted that we bordered on the antisocial. Acutely aware of our weirdness, she was determined to be "normal," as if to show the rest of us that a person could live a perfectly honorable life without being a misfit or a hermit. While she suspected us of *trying* to be weird just to embarrass her, I was equally convinced that her pursuit of normality was a deliberate salvo against the family. It certainly *seemed* deliberate. Dad was reclusive and thrifty; Sue was gregarious and free spending. Mom loved poetry and art; Sue detested poetry and art as retreats from real-life action. Dave worshiped science; Sue scorned it as the touchstone of geeks. I loved to read; Sue saw reading as a loser's time-killer of last resort.

It was a bold choice in our house to chase that elusive, small-town prize known as "popularity." The rest of us had pretty much given up on

49

it, and Sue's decision to embrace what Findlay expected from its young girls made her the odd one at home, the public citizen as private rebel. She entered a kind of limbo: while her quest for popularity set her apart within our family, it also pitted her against the tight little cliques that governed Findlay's teen culture. Rocking to "Theme from *A Summer Place*," I now realize, afforded some respite from the constant, low-grade anxiety that plagues kids who want desperately to fit in. Each rocking session usually began with a social setback—a snub at school, plans that had fallen through, or a phone call from a boy that had ended badly. As Percy Faith and Doublemint worked their magic, the crease above her eyes gradually faded and her face achieved a glazed approximation of repose.

When Dave, who called Sue "the Social Whirl," left for college, I took up the struggle to convince my sister that her energies were misplaced. I undertook that mission with honorable motives, or so I thought. I figured that she was making herself far too vulnerable to what *other* people did—whether they called her back, shared secrets with her, or went along with her Saturday night plans.

Sue didn't exactly welcome the advice. Protesting that "smart" kids never had any fun, she pointed out that I was becoming even weirder than Dave. If I didn't start acting normal, I'd end up like the old men who hung out at the public library and smelled like the catbox. Whenever I accused her of cowtowing to her silly friends, she replied that at least she *had* friends, while creeps like me were doomed to go through life bitter and alone. "Nobody *likes* you!" she shouted during one of these arguments. "When you get to junior high, you're going to be *unpopular!*" She issued this last pronouncement with the wide-eyed solemnity of a death sentence.

On that score, at least, Sue knew what she was talking about. Nobody ever became king of the hop by being able to recite all the pharaohs of the Eighteenth Dynasty. I wound up drifting invisibly through Donnell Junior High until I started to play the drums—an activity, finally, of which my sister approved. When I began playing in bands and acquiring a rudimentary social life, Sue figured there might be hope for me yet and started advising me on ways to mask my innate creepiness. Having just graduated from high school, she dreamed of passing on the social torch. She wasn't convinced that I could carry it, but if I dropped it and remained a creep it wouldn't be *her* fault. One weekend when she was home from Ohio State, she came to a "battle of the bands" where my band defeated one consisting of far more popular guys. She was proud that I was finally doing something normal, but as we launched into "Hang On Sloopy," a puzzled and slightly irked expression crossed her face. How in God's name had her creepy little brother managed to become something as cool as a drummer? She had paid all sorts of dues, but he was getting *his* popularity handed to him on a goddam plate.

She needn't have worried. While I tried to heed her tips on teen behavior, I was already too far gone to get with the program. Besides, I remained unconvinced that Sue's ways had even served *her* all that well. Hadn't she wasted all that energy looking for the next good time because the last one hadn't quite worked out? If there really was a "Summer Place," I never saw that rocking chair take her there.

• • •

My sister inherited our mother's restlessness and our father's shyness, but not the independence that had enabled them to forge uneasy truces with their time and place—to get by in Findlay without giving in. Sue reacted to the pressures of small-town conformity by embracing them fully, and the result was a proactive flurry of activities and endless "plans." She had always possessed an unquiet nature, a habit of easily getting bored that was reflected in another nickname our brother gave her: "Never-Satisfied Sue." When she began her teen odyssey, she plunged into a series of activities only to discover something wrong with each one—and once she did, that was that. She took piano at our mother's encouragement until she botched a tune at a recital and quit her lessons. She marched in the junior high band until she learned that band members were shunned by the popular crowd, and the cornet that Dad had paid for in installments wound up in the back of her closet. For a while her life revolved around the Teen Center, with its ping-pong tables, soft drinks, and dance music. But one night Mrs. Bonhoffer, the Teen Center director and on-site chaperone, called Mom to claim that Sue was hanging out with "the wrong crowd." Hot with indignation, Sue didn't go back to the Teen Center all that year.

She also tried Campfire Girls. Boys like food, don't they? With a merit badge in cooking, a girl could be a good citizen and a cool teen all at once.

Sue and Nancy Schaap planned a full-course dinner, which they cooked and served one night with great ceremony to our two families at the Schaap house. I remember having to wear my white church shirt and sitting at a card table covered with a tablecloth. There was extra, mysterious silverware at each plate, and my parents and the Schaaps made pleasant conversation as we dug into a meatloaf whose outside and inside tasted like two completely different things. The scalloped potatoes were blackened chips, and even though Dad and Mr. Schaap insisted that they liked them that way, nice and crispy, Sue was not fooled. I don't remember what happened to Nancy Schaap, but Sue quit the Campfire Girls and never touched a saucepan again until she got married.

Cooking may have fit the teengirl script, but doing well in school definitely did not. Once the social mandates of junior high kicked in, Sue's teachers began reporting that she wasn't "applying herself." Any fool, I thought, could see that; she did her homework as quickly as possible with her records blaring, clearing the decks for that night's phone calls. I felt some culpability in this, convinced that three years before I had played an unwitting role in Sue's academic slide. One day when the principal heard that I could read in kindergarten, he paraded me around and made me read aloud to all the classes. When I was led into the fourth-grade classroom and began to read from *All about Dinosaurs*, Sue sank behind her desk and covered her face. I found out later that her classmates were laughing at me. Her little brother was a freak! Mercifully, I was concentrating on the long words and didn't notice the snickers. As I prattled on about the "Triassic," "Jurassic," and "Cretaceous," she may have vowed, right then and there, never to get tagged as a smart kid.

Just as Sue was deciding to be normal, against all odds of nature and nurture, the image of the "teenager" was being shaped by the purveyors of youthful consumption: TV, the movies, the fashion industry, the record companies, and those ubiquitous advertisers. It was an onslaught, and Sue could resist none of it. From the moment she first peered at the snowy images of Bob and Justine dancing on *American Bandstand* and heard the eerily smooth Dick Clark intoning the salvific wonders of Clearasil, she was hooked. Out went her obsession with horses and the well-thumbed copies of *Black Beauty* and *National Velvet*. Out went the Ginger and Ginny dolls, the "Royal Wedding" paper dolls in tasteful long johns, and the glassy-eyed horse and tiger that once shared her pillow. In came a portable phonograph, a tiny yellow suitcase with musical notes painted on it, and a slew of 45s by Frankie and Dion and Ricky Nelson and a dozen other guys who I thought resembled curried steers. These weren't the hard-edged rockers that my brother listened to. Indeed, listening seemed to have little to do with it; when you bought one of these records, you bought the guy rather than the music. Sue's new magazines made these teen idols seem more important to the American Way of Life than Wonder Bread and Ovaltine. She devoured revelations of their favorite colors, their favorite foods, their do's and don'ts on dates, their likes and dislikes in a girl. She learned that Tommy Sands likes his girls quiet. Bobby Rydell doesn't date girls who smoke. A sure-fire way to land a boy is to show an interest in his hobbies. Master the basics of football in ten easy steps! Impress the boy of your dreams by learning how a car engine works! Or aim even higher and win a date with Fabian! Just tell us in twenty-five words or less how Max Factor has changed your life!

In my view Sue was being disloyal to the family, dumbing herself down to please a pack of snotty girls at Donnell Junior High. I figured that if Frankie Avalon ever endorsed Feenamint, she'd be chewing the stuff all day. I resented this reduction of my sister to a walking cliché—my sister as Everyteen. Besides, there were consequences for the rest of us. Sue's endless phone calls started getting us in trouble with the Craibells and the Mainses, with whom we shared a party line. Even worse, the endless parade of Sue's friends made our house less private than before, and the constant sleepovers were keeping me awake. One morning after an especially loud night of giggling girls, I drew circles under my eyes with Mom's eyebrow pencil in an attempt to look exhausted so the parties would end and our house could get back to normal. It got to the point where there was peace only when Sue went out, which was every chance she got: to the movies, the roller rink, the bowling alley, the municipal swimming pool, high school basketball games where the score mattered less than who took whom to the game. Sue and her "best friends"—we kept losing track of who they were—began cruising the Main Street circuit, first on bicycles and then, the instant one of them turned sixteen, in a parent's car.

Being popular cost a lot of money. Along with the frenzy of activity came a constant stream of teengirl merchandise: cat's eye glasses, saddle shoes, pedal-pushers, make-up mirrors, diaries—whatever was the latest thing. I had acquired something of Dad's tightness with a buck and could not fathom Sue's constant drive to buy things, especially clothes. Her closet kept filling up with perfectly good clothes that she loathed soon after buying them; Sue eyed these innocent blouses and skirts as if they had turned traitor on her. I was astonished that she actually stopped wearing things before they wore out.

These years saw some terrible arguments, usually when our parents nixed one of Sue's plans. During one of these fights our mother got angrier than I had ever seen her; Sue began a rebuttal with the words "Look, lady—" when Mom's hand shot out like a snake and slapped her. Drama this high, however, was rare. Usually the aftermath was just a sullen grumpiness that pervaded the house. Whenever her plans were curtailed, Sue would sulk for days, especially if she had received the ultimate punishment of being "grounded." The word seemed perfect. Sue was like a restless, fluttery falcon on the lookout for social prey, and it was easy to imagine her feet being tied to a post so she couldn't fly off to the movies or the bowling alley.

. . .

My sister had a fierce sense of fairness when we were little and would not tolerate any cheating at games. If you broke a rule or made one up on the spot, she would quit in protest. Expecting teen life to play by the rules, too, Sue assumed that popularity was a meritocracy based on the fulfillment of certain teen mandates. With the right clothes, the right hair, and the right friends, even a girl from a weird family could be popular. But she possessed the Hammond face, round and pasty, with dull, worried-looking eyes; another family trait showed in her thick eyebrows and the visible hair on her arms, of which she was deeply ashamed. She also inherited the Hammond build, thick-waisted and blocky, and our stubbornly ordinary hair. Sue's straight brown locks proved incapable of assuming much shape beyond a Prince Valiant pageboy, which gave her a severe, helmeted look that ran counter to the delicate, All-American blondes who gazed out from her magazines. The worst of it, though, was the fact that she matured early. She stooped her shoulders in an attempt to downplay large breasts that made junior-high fashions fit badly, and the teen-pixie image she sought was not enhanced by her debilitating periods. Sue was easily embarrassed to begin with; it did not help to get sick to the point of missing school with such revealing regularity.

Sue also underestimated the limits that caste and class in small-town America placed on how popular a lower-middle-class kid could become. Dad was an accountant who had recently been a pipeline worker, but Sue was trying to break into circles that included the daughters of doctors, lawyers, and executives from Marathon Oil and Cooper Tires, whose home offices gave a white-collar cast to our town. Movies, basketball games, and school dances posed few problems, but whenever the country club threw a party, things got uncomfortable. The rich girls knew that they weren't supposed to ask friends from nonmember families to club affairs, and their talk changed to whispers whenever my sister happened by. To Sue, her exclusion seemed merely mean and arbitrary—as did the fact that she had to work after school to earn college money. Saturdays and two or three weeknights she clerked at a pharmacy across the street from the Blanchard Valley Hospital. Most of her friends did not need jobs, and while they cruised Main Street or partied at each other's houses, Sue put up with old men's jokes as she rang up their Pepto-Bismol and Preparation H.

Then there were the dates, the supposed pinnacle of teen experience. By the time she started going out, Sue had developed a powerful sympathy for the underdogs of the world—a trait that revealed itself in the boys on whom she got crushes. I remember them as a sad and unpresentable lot, the sort of boys who would honk their horn and wait in the car because they were incapable of talking to grownups. Some of them had wild reputations, which Sue invariably explained by claiming that they were "misunderstood." She would typically befriend a bad-boy classmate who was astonished to find a girl actually listening to what he had to say. He would pour out his troubles—an alcoholic father, a wild mother, an older brother AWOL from the army and hiding out in Toledo—and start thinking of Sue as a buddy. Meanwhile, of course, Sue would see the boy as a diamond in the rough and get a crush on him. Eventually these mixed motives collided, and she'd go on her rocker again.

Friendships with troubled boys did nothing to further Sue's status among the right girls. She often complained about the snobbishness of this or that girlfriend who had warned her, once again, about her reputation. Ironically, some of these snooty girls wound up missing school because of mysterious two-week "vacations" in Cleveland or Detroit, while Sue, who possessed an almost Victorian sense of morality, found herself the subject of rumors because she had been spotted talking to a "greaser" after school.

Once my sister learned how quickly a teen could get labeled a loser, she grew painfully self-conscious, anticipating embarrassment at every turn. Expectation had a way of becoming reality, and reality prompted more sessions with Percy Faith. When one of Dave's college friends visited for the weekend, Sue fell for the boy and began mincing around the house with an insane, fashion-model smile unrelated to anything that was going on. Naturally, she wound up swallowing the wrong way during the last dinner of his visit, and had to rush from the table with milk spurting out of her nose. Sometimes Sue's nervousness produced bungled phrases that were mistaken, to her mortification, for deliberate crudity. One night she and a friend were on a double date with two popular boys, and as they were deciding where to eat, Sue's date asked if she liked pizza. "Are you kidding?" she replied, "I'm the biggest eatsa peter in town!" Another time, when her civics classmates were complaining about the difficulty of a recent quiz, the male teacher told them to stop whining because it was only a "quizzie." "Oh yeah?" Sue volunteered, "I'd hate to see one of your testies!"

When our parents were planning a two-week vacation in England, Sue was insulted by their decision to hire an elderly woman to stay with us. She figured that a high school senior could be expected to handle things—meaning me—without needing a "babysitter." But our parents insisted, and Mrs. McConnell settled in as they drove to the Cleveland airport. Sue fumed the whole first week about being treated like a kid. During the second week, though, she snuck out one night to attend a keg party at the reservoir. On that particular night Mrs. McConnell thought she heard a prowler and peeked into our rooms, and when Sue crept in at two in the morning, the old woman was waiting for her in the rocking chair.

Sue was always having that kind of luck. One night at the end of a date, the boy's car remained parked in front of our house for about an hour. Suddenly I heard the front door slam and peered out my bedroom window just in time to see our father racing toward the car with his bathrobe flowing behind him like a cape. Sue and I laughed about it later, secretly referring to Dad as "Batman," but when he jerked open the car door and told the boy to leave or he'd kick his royal ass for him, she was hardly amused. It wasn't fair. Other girls stayed out much later than she did and parked on country lanes, sneaky and unobserved. Besides, Sue and her date had only been talking: should the boy go into the army or the Marines? As proof, the next morning she pointed to the dozen or so cigarette butts that were still lying in the street where the car had been parked, beneath the driver's side. Nobody, she told Dad, could make out and smoke at the same time. I had to agree with her on this one; it just wasn't fair.

• • •

It's difficult to remember what my sister was like before Dick Clark grabbed her by the throat. I have always thought that there was a clear-cut before and after, but things aren't that simple. Sue's bike, which pre-dated her teen madness by several years, may have offered a clue to her deeper nature. Dave, the boy scientist, rode a new J. C. Higgins that he assembled himself, a Sears racing bike with sleek tubing and five speeds. My bike, a used one-speed of indeterminate make, was perfectly suited to a junior tightwad; I painted it red because that was the can in the garage with the most paint left in it. Sue's bike, by contrast, was drop-dead fancy, a baroque girl's model with heavy, sculpted lines. It was robin's-egg blue with thin white stripes, large wheel guards, balloon tires, and a delicate wicker basket mounted between the handlebars. This was a Cadillac of a bike, a vehicle of luxury that onlookers would surely notice.

There were other signs that Sue's social impulses were strong from the start. She was always more curious than the rest of us about the neighbors, whom I saw simply as people who were not to be bothered for fear that they would start bothering *me*. Sue often hushed us up in order to overhear the next-door neighbors having one of their legendary fights, which sounded like botched fire drills at the Grand Old Opry. People stuff always perked Sue up. I remember her watching with what struck me as morbid fascination—and talking about it for days afterward—when a ten-year-old neighbor girl climbed out on her roof and refused to come down, screaming and flinging feces at her mother standing in the yard.

I guess Sue was born liking a good time. My earliest memory of her involves the wild, postbath dances when Mom would put on one of her records—"The Poor People of Paris" or the "Hungarian Rhapsody"—and conduct us with her baton. These dances always whipped Sue into a frenzy, and it took her a while to calm down afterward. Maybe I should stop blaming Dick Clark after all. Sue might simply have been born with a deeper capacity for fun than the rest of us—a "people person," as Mom later called her, from the very beginning. Especially prophetic, perhaps, was her sheet-metal dollhouse, in which a tiny, stiff-jointed family constantly alternated the roles of "host" and "guests" for high tea and gossipy conversation. With their happy talk and perpetually smiling faces, Sue's miniature family was a lot more normal than we were.

When the "people person" went off to college, she found herself in paradise. Ohio State was like Findlay, only bigger and with fewer snobs—and no parents around to foil the evening's plans. After she pledged a sorority in her sophomore year, her grades fell to near-lethal levels. She saw something inevitable, almost impersonal, about this; she still describes the sorority debacle as something that simply could not be helped, like an illness. On the verge of flunking out, she transferred to Findlay College, but not before meeting her future husband in one of the bars on North High Street. Sue finished college living at home and working at Findlay's Kodak plant, and soon after graduating she married her Ohio State boyfriend. After two years in a small town on the Lake Erie shore they settled in Columbus, where she taught elementary school.

Four kids and fifteen years later, when the marriage was falling apart, Sue accepted her problems with a sullen stoicism that recalled her sessions with Percy Faith. Once again, she had done her best to fit in, putting up with her husband's temper, his complaints about her housekeeping, and his crazy business schemes, like the franchise that left them with three Pachenko machines lined up like smiley-faced tombstones in their garage. Sue, who never said much when she was on her rocker, was just as reticent this time around, but when the situation became unbearable and she finally told our mother, it was like a dam breaking. Before long she was even asking my brother and me how she would ever get over her anger and shame at staying with her husband for so long. I don't remember what Dave told her, but my advice—it was something stupid like "You'll get through this because everyone does"—was Hallmark at its worst. Sue's brothers did our best, but it was characteristic that we had little wisdom to offer. How, given the stunted social experience to be gleaned from our furtive walks through the world, could Dave and I presume to counsel Sue about people stuff? We felt like two demons trying to give spiritual advice to the pope.

. . .

"Why are you and Dave so weird?" Sue's question, posed several Thanksgivings back, reminded me that if her brothers have always been outsiders to her world, we are equally mysterious to her: two feral guys barely able to get along in a realm where getting along is life itself. If, during our Thanksgiving reunions, we grow restless whenever the conversation turns to her neighbors or coworkers or Findlay people from long ago, Sue assumes that life has lost its savor for us. She's wrong about that, we think, but she's surely right in believing that Dave and I never acquired her ability to move through the world with the robust give-and-take that it demands. The fact is, Sue's forays into public space ended up making her far tougher than we could ever hope to be. It's possible, of course, that Dave and I could have taken the knocks that she did, but we'll never know. We dropped out of the fray too early to tell.

Now in her mid-fifties, the "people person" remains the hub through which all family news circulates. On Thanksgivings Dave and I struggle to make ourselves presentable to the constant stream of visitors—neighbors, teachers at her school, her kids' friends and their parents—who pass through her house. Like the greeter at a suburban Lourdes, Sue introduces us to the throng and provides coffee and Bundtcake for all, repeatedly excusing herself to answer the phone or to tell one of the kids when to be in that night. As I observe her position at the vortex of this constant activity, it occurs to me that she has attained power similar to that wielded by those snooty girls back in Findlay. The ground and anchor of this swirl of people, Sue is now in a position to approve or disapprove, to accept or reject.

She almost never rejects. Those anxious years in Findlay taught her to take people pretty much as they are—and this, in turn, has made her popular beyond her wildest girlhood fantasies. Nowadays she can afford a casual indifference toward popularity. If you're civil to people, she declares in her definitive, no-nonsense way, they'll like you—and if they don't, screw 'em. Such independence could never have been predicted from the old days. It's as if Sue took enough crap in Findlay to last a life-time and vowed never to take it again. In this, too, there may have been early precedent. I remember when she and I sobbed over our cat Snooks, flattened to a furry disk on the highway in front of our house. Sue couldn't have been more than ten, but once she dried her tears, she vowed never to go through that again. She lost all interest in pets and later became ac-tively hostile toward them, claiming during visits that my cat gave her "the creeps" because it kept staring at her. Nor is she shy about attack-ing other forms of creepiness. After shedding the piano, the cornet, and the oven, she finally gave up trying to please snooty, difficult people. As her tirades against her ex-husband, lazy or indifferent teachers, and ad-ministrative paperwork reveal, Sue is nobody's fool.

Sue's materialism faded along with her vulnerability, eventually set-tling into disdain for the one-upmanship that often governs suburban neighborhoods like hers. She is blissfully indifferent toward the furniture, the house, and the dented van—a surprising outcome for a girl who once whined for a month after Dad said that the car coat she wanted was too expensive. But she has not forgotten how badly she wanted that coat. Her firsthand experience of peer pressure produced the kind of mother and teacher who is smart enough to know that this too shall pass. When her nineteen-year-old twin boys, fed up with jobs and school, took the sec-ond car in the middle of the night and drove down to Key West to "think things over," their father wanted to take out a warrant for grand larceny and clap them in jail. Sue, rolling her eyes as he yelled this over the phone, calmly talked him out of it. They'll be back, she told him, when their money runs out. "Remember what *we* were like at their age?"

Fabian may have liked his girls petite, but who cares? Despite the oc-casional diet, Sue has mellowed into a good-humored acceptance of the substantial Hammond body. In contrast to her school-morning keenings about having *absolutely nothing to wear,* she has achieved a regal indiffer-ence to the dogs of fashion, calmly padding around in sweatpants and oversize sweaters, devoid of makeup and equally at ease in her wood-paneled TV room and the aisles of Kroger's, where her eyes adroitly scan the shelves for specials. In contrast to the pre-date frenzy of teasing and curling hair that would not assume the desired shape, Sue keeps her hair, now flecked with white, in a low-maintenance cut that hugs her head, once again, like a helmet. If anyone doesn't like it, screw 'em. And what about her mania for "plans," those endless departures in nervous anticipation only to return in glum silence? Sue now spends her evenings with romance novels, made-for-TV movies, and a widower from the neighborhood whom she's been seeing for several years. You won't find them zipping down High Street looking for fast times. Instead they rent videos, order pizzas, and—if the spirit moves them—pursue more basic pleasures before the kids get home.

Findlay dealt Sue some hard lessons, and I wouldn't blame her for cursing the town and everything we thought it stood for. But she still has lots of friends there whom she visits regularly, and she rarely misses a class reunion. She keeps her senior yearbook up to date, neatly entering notations on marriages, children, divorces, remarriages, and deaths. She tells my brother and me what's happening with Findlay people from the old days. I don't know about Dave, but whenever I hear these stories of time and the changes it brings, I'm mildly ashamed to realize that I don't remember—or never knew—most of the people she is talking about. Sue's Findlay updates force me to recognize that I passed through that town like a watermelon seed. I never really *lived* there in the same way she did.

. . .

For all her nostalgia, Sue lives more solidly in the moment than Dave and I could ever hope to do. And unlike her brothers, who quickly grow antsy during vacations, she still likes her fun. Once a year she spends a week in Florida with three of her college chums. Naples may not have the fast-lane ambiance of Key West, from which the twins sheepishly returned after three weeks, but Naples is as good a Summer Place as any for a quartet of middle-aged women with an annual plan: a week-long escape from the pressures of jobs, families, and everything else that we acquire as we move from youthful dreams to something else.

As Sue and her friends sprawl by the pool and eye the lifeguards, they resume a conversation that began in a freshman dorm at Ohio State thirty-five years ago, when the world lay before them, beautiful and new. The talk comes easily under the Florida sun. One woman suspects that her husband is having an affair. The daughter of another plans to attend a high-powered tennis camp. The husband of another is afraid of losing his job. Celine Dion put on a great show in Columbus last year. The school administrators are tying our hands and letting the kids get away with murder. In three years I can take early retirement at 60 percent pension. Is menopause making your food taste funny? Have you read the latest John Grisham? What did you think of *Titanic?* Sue sips a Diet Coke and listens, leaning in for the details and giving her opinions. She might be more cynical about people than in the old days, but there's no need to be wary here. She knows that these women will listen to her stories too—a fitting reward for making connections and keeping them up, and all the more satisfying now that the old anxieties have vanished.

An outsider pondering his sister's poolside calm might feel relief at her midlife contentment and even a measure of pride at how things turned out. Acutely aware, in his own middle age, of his social inferiority to her, he might appeal to their shared experience by observing that Findlay, Ohio, could be a hard little place in which to grow up. Sue might nod in agreement, and the outsider would think that he was about to win a forty-year-old argument. But then she would say, with the faintest touch of sarcasm in her voice, "Well, I know it was hard for *you,* but I had a great time there."

Republicans and Money

When I was growing up in the 1950s, I learned two indelible lessons. The first was that money was supposed to be saved and not spent. I've spent my whole life compensating for learning this so well, vainly struggling to exorcize a cheapness that runs bone deep. You could say that I have an obsession with *not* obsessing about money. I rush to pick up tabs with feigned glee. I shamelessly overtip. I never grumble about prices. However queasy I might feel while nursing a five-dollar Coke in a hotel lounge, I always find a way to make it right. In Beijing, I remind myself, this Coke would cost even more.

The second lesson was never to trust a Republican. Even today the word conjures up a fat man in a suit putting out a cigar in somebody's face. We all have our quirks, I guess, but mine make paydays almost unbearable. I can't go to the bank to deposit a check—my *money*—without feeling like I've entered a world of Republicans. All the men working there are wearing suits, aren't they? What evil things are they going to do with my money?

The seeds for these habits of mind were planted twenty years before I was born. In our house the Great Depression was one of those events that never seem to have ended, like the first Christmas or the American Revolution. Our family wasn't poor, but like many kids with Depression-hardened parents, I grew up convinced that we could *become* poor—and pretty quickly. My parents weren't trying to scare me with their stories of hoboes and Hoovervilles and Roosevelt closing the banks. It's just that when I heard about the bad old days, I saw no reason why they couldn't return.

When I was eight or nine, it was easy to picture the dust storms wiping out Findlay, Ohio, and reducing everyone to nomads. I had seen the splintered barns and bloated cow corpses that tornadoes left behind; the dust storms, I figured, would be like that but worse. I imagined us living in tents like Bible people, begging our way along a trail of tears that stretched to Cincinnati and back. Nor was nature the only threat. All I knew about the stock market was that it had once "crashed" and that the Republicans had something to do with it. This could happen again, too, turning all the money in the First National Bank into scrap paper; a wheelbarrow of it would buy a loaf of bread. Maybe we could sell apples, like the men in the 1930s newsreels that the Royal Theater ran to fill up its all-day Saturday kid shows. Or maybe we could sell things we had made, though I couldn't imagine what those things might be: paperweights? ashtrays? drawings of our cat?

After the Depression came the War, and with it, more stories: the shock of Pearl Harbor, casualty lists in the newspapers, rationing coupons for milk and butter, drives to collect tires and tinfoil, Victory Gardens in the backyards. Some people, I knew, cracked under the hardship and forgot the collective good. I learned this after asking my parents what Daffy Duck meant when he screamed at the end of a wartime cartoon, "Who's the bulb snatcher?"

My parents, it seemed, had lived through some interesting times. I loved hearing about the old days, but the stories made me feel guilty. No catastrophes were hounding my childhood, and I wondered how I would handle real trouble if it ever came. Most of my friends, egged on by emergency drills at school, worried about the Bomb, but not me. All I knew was that we would all be dead—or else we would live a while without lips and ears and *then* we'd all be dead. The Great Depression was what scared me. Being broke seemed worse, because a kid would have to deal with it and grow up fast. If he survived, though, he would be a better person, no longer an untested boy who had never been forced to cope with worthless money, swirling dust, or godless Nazis.

· · ·

My father had been tested, and it showed. A former pipeline worker, he had taken correspondence courses in accounting and moved from the Marathon Oil tank farm in Lima to the home office in Findlay. A fervent New Dealer, he was a prolabor, blue-collar guy working in a white-collar, nonunion job—a mismatch that constantly put him on the defensive. Dad liked to say that he wasn't rich enough to be a Republican and hoped to Christ he never would be. In the bad old days Roosevelt had helped people, but FDR was dead and we weren't about to see his like again. Eisenhower had been a great general, but hadn't he cast his lot with the rich bastards and run as a Republican? My father, who had been in the navy, took this as an act of personal betrayal by his Allied Supreme Commander. That the hero of D-day could make such a "whore's choice," as Dad called it, made it clear that all this postwar prosperity was just a mirage. Beneath the bright certainties of the new ranch houses, the TV dinners, and the polio vaccine, it was every man for himself.

Findlay had no problem with Ike's choice. Dad always said that the Republicans could run Hitler and Tojo on the national ticket and still get 85 percent of the vote there. I don't guess he was far wrong. The home offices of Marathon Oil and Cooper Tires produced a disproportionate number of executives and middle managers whose families had built a separate world around the country club, which was located not in the "country" at all—a fact that puzzled me—but in a wealthy subdivision on the far side of Riverside Park. Our family should have felt solidarity with the local farmers and factory workers, but they were Republicans too. That mystified my father: had everyone forgotten what the Democrats had done for the common people? His children, at least, would grow up knowing the score. Whenever my older sister and I ran footraces around our house, Dad started us off with magic words that made us run like the wind: "Last one back's a Republican!"

If the town didn't care about the poor, at least our family did, which made me proud of our alien status. Democrats knew something that everybody else seemed to overlook: the hard times might come again. Gradually, my secret desire to be tested made me *expect* to be tested, and I began to see everything as impermanent. Lessons from school seemed to back me up. Weren't all kinds of dead things lying beneath us? And hadn't they had their heyday, just as we were having ours now? Dinosaurs had once grazed where the Elks Club stood; what would replace the Republican businessmen who hatched their schemes there? For a kid who distrusted Republicans and felt vaguely ashamed of the soft life he was leading, such thoughts were not entirely unpleasant.

I was convinced from watching my father that being an adult meant working all the time. Dad wasn't working to get rich and repeat Eisenhower's defection, however, but to prepare for whatever the Republicans might throw at him. "Waste not, want not" and "savings account" were the two mantras of our house. Even as a kid I knew that we lived pretty plainly. Going out to a restaurant was a major affair, and the clothes that my older brother had outgrown were carefully pressed and stored in the hall closet, waiting for me to grow into them. Occasionally, though, Dad would surprise us by buying something fancy to show that he was holding his own against the rich bastards, taking care of his family against all odds. Once I asked him why he worked late so many nights. Without a word he lowered his Findlay *Republican Courier* and nodded toward the new hi-fi, with its thick screening and shiny blond wood, that held pride of place in the front room.

Dad knew how cheap he was and sometimes joked about it. Whenever the fuel gauge was running low, he would announce that gas was two cents cheaper in Lima, thirty-five miles away. "If we don't make it, you kids won't mind pushing the car, will you?" During those rare restaurant visits he would squint and squirm in mock indecision as he studied the menu. "What do you think, kids? Should I get the $2.95 or the $3.95?" When the check came he always had the same line: "Let's see what the damage is." He watched Jack Benny and howled, partly at the absurdity of Benny's cheapness and partly, I think, in bemused self-recognition. Years later, when I got my first checking account, he was stunned to learn that I was rounding off my check record to the nearest five dollars. He shook his head in disbelief as he read out my entries: "about ten dollars," "about twenty dollars," "about fifteen dollars." Where in Christ's sweet name had he gone wrong?

In retrospect, Dad's tightness with a buck took courage. In an era when buying things was a patriotic act, Findlay proudly held the frontier between commerce and communism. It was a place where Joe McCarthy was someone you couldn't joke about even after he lost face, as my father's arguments at work proved. Dad had trouble with the brand of Americanism that the Republicans at the office were promoting. The company ran a strong-arm United Way campaign, which Dad boycotted because he thought too much money went to the "goddam Boy Scouts" and not enough to the League of Women Voters or the NAACP. Our family felt even more isolated once Mom started circulating petitions and meeting with local realtors to demand why they weren't selling houses to any of the "colored" people who were coming down from Toledo to work at Differential Steel and the Cooper Tire plant. Mom's efforts brought occasional phone threats, always anonymous. Whenever Dad answered the phone, he offered to meet the caller face to face in an alley so he could teach him what America really stood for.

My mother gave liberal politics a softer turn. We kids cleaned our plates for Dad because it was a crime to waste food produced and paid for by American labor. With Mom, we cleaned our plates out of respect for the poor people of Poland, Mexico, and Alabama. My mother's natural benevolence got tested once she started her civil rights work. One time our next-door neighbor, a man from Mississippi who had just gotten a job selling Bibles, asked to practice his spiel on us. It was going pretty well until he proudly explained that his company was first-class and didn't sell its Bibles to "nigras." Mom ran him down our front steps with his samples case open and papers flying all over the place.

Mom was a loving liberal, Dad an angry one. When the news showed Vice President Nixon's car being surrounded by an angry mob in Caracas, I remember my father shaking his fist and saying "*Get* the sonovabitch!" Dad wasn't a Democrat because he loved poor people and wanted to save them. He was a Democrat because the Republicans hated poor people and wanted to destroy them. For him, voting Democratic was tantamount to the patriotic duty of keeping at least a minimal check on the rich. You could vote with your pocketbook, too—by refusing to buy all the stuff that the rich were constantly trying to sell you. The cards were stacked against little guys, but if they kept building their nest eggs, they could at least hope to live decently if the Republicans ever gained complete control and things came crashing down again.

My older sister rebelled against our family's politics. Sue, who actually *liked* living in Findlay, wanted to have fun and didn't mind spending a little money along the way. Whenever her face turned hot red at Dad's restaurant jokes, I thought she was being disloyal. I had absorbed his politics totally, and even when Sue managed to save some of her babysitting money, her motives struck me as appallingly shallow. While the rest of us were saving toward some nameless disaster, her goal was a car coat with beer-barrel buttons or a junior high letter jacket. One time she announced that she was saving for a lobster dinner after learning that it was the favorite food of Ricky Nelson or some other teen idol. "What about the poor people in the Congo?" I asked, self-righteously aping our mother. Sue had a ready response: *her* lobster would rot before it reached Africa anyway.

Our family's sole materialist, Sue was an unrepentant lover of immediate pleasures. The rest of us were masters of deferral, our eyes set on future intangibles. My older brother, who had been a militantly unfashionable high schooler, was working weekends as a disk jockey in Columbus and saving for the next term's tuition at Ohio State, where he was studying to become an "electrical engineer," whatever that was. Mom and Dad were just saving—I wasn't sure for what, except I knew it had something to do with an uncertain future. I became a saver too, content to play with friends' toys and not especially desirous to own any of them. By the time I was nine or ten, I had gotten got so good at saving money that I almost forgot about spending it. A passionate seeker of free fun, I wondered whether a kid could go a whole afternoon without spending anything and still have a good time. What about two afternoons? Such tests, I knew, were good preparation for when the Russians—or the Republicans—felt a rush of greed and swept us back to square one. A kid had to get tough if he expected to keep up with a caravan crossing the sand dunes of Ohio.

. . .

Two places in town offered unlimited fun with no spending required. I spent rainy or snowy days at the Findlay Public Library, with its seemingly endless stacks of books that could be read for free. Most other days I spent at the Hancock County fairgrounds. We lived near the fairgrounds at the edge of town, just before East Sandusky Street became State Route 15. If you were heading out of town and looked to your right, you would see a large clearing, some animal barns, and the old grandstand. Beyond that were a few more houses and then nothing but fields—corn, soybeans, sugar beets—until you reached the town of Carey, thirteen miles away. I remember thinking that if anyone really belonged to the "country" club, it was us.

We kids whose houses were squeezed between the fairgrounds and the fields played mostly among ourselves. We prided ourselves on being a little wilder than our school friends who lived "in town"—that is, on the town side of the fairgrounds. Lenny's father was dead, and his mom ran their auto body shop. Carol and Brent's dad was a carpenter, Dick's worked in Marathon's motor pool, and Tommy's was a long-distance truck driver. Gary's dad worked construction, and Cheryl's and Robbie's dads both tended bar. The scruffiness of our neighborhood was visible. The streetlights and sidewalks ended with the fairgrounds. The next block— our block—was dark at night, with a nonregulation sidewalk on one side of the street. Our fathers had mixed the concrete and poured it themselves, and our names and handprints were there to prove it.

The fairgrounds was our year-round private playground. It had empty barns, two grandstands, woods with trails, a creek, and broad fields of wild grass. It was also our shortcut to Whittier Elementary, despite our parents' warnings that hoboes camped out there and that the creek sometimes overflowed the flat concrete bridge. These were not empty warnings. We had to carry our bikes through the two-foot stream of water that sometimes ran across the bridge in the spring. The hoboes were real too. Mom took plates of food out to men who sometimes showed up at our back door, and I had seen their campsites in the woods and in the unlocked animal barns.

Still, hoboes were more mysterious than scary, and a swollen creek merely posed an additional challenge for a kid navigating his bike through intergalactic space or down a streamlined Oregon Trail. The bike paths that we wore down, with banked curves and challenging ruts, made for an exciting ride even if it was just school we were speeding to. On the way home we would dawdle in the fairgrounds, staring into the creek, sitting in the woods, or sliding our bikes through the sawdust that covered the concrete floor of the livestock-judging arena.

The fairgrounds seemed a perfect place to toughen up, to practice the art of being happy without spending a dime. A few plastic armymen transformed the judging arena into Arizona's great Meteor Crater. Put an armyman in a soap dish, and Lye Creek became the Columbia rapids. Tie

Free transportation from the Hancock County Fairgrounds, 1957.

one to a handkerchief and toss him off the grandstand, and the dirt track became a jump site in Normandy. The steel bars that formed the understructure of the new grandstand served as a vast jungle gym.

When my sister turned twelve, she started to get bored with the fairgrounds. Puzzled and hurt by her reluctance to play with us anymore, I noticed that she had also started buying things. Once she stopped going to the fairgrounds and began riding her bike downtown to the stores, I was sure that she had crossed over to the Republicans. By the time she was fourteen her bedroom was filled with makeup kits with French names and stacks of slick magazines that told about Fabian's favorite color and how Annette had become a Mouseketeer. Sue's fascination with these things baffled me. How had *American Bandstand*'s Bob and Justine met? Who cared? You too can draw Frankie Avalon in four easy steps, the first always being a trisected egg. But who would want to do *that*? Tube socks and saddle shoes and pedal-pushers and poodle skirts and cat's-eye glasses came and went, but these objects never disappeared completely; there was all this *stuff* left over.

As I watched my sister collect useless things, I failed to see why a person couldn't get by with two pairs of jeans (one for school), two shirts (ditto), and one pair of "Red-Ball Jets." I knew nothing, of course, about the fashion imperatives of seventh-grade girls. All I knew was that Sue's closet was stuffed with perfectly good clothes that she didn't wear anymore. The things that crammed her room seemed to justify our family's Spartan ways; she could have saved her money for something *really* cool that she didn't even know about yet. Then again, what if our family had to hit the dusty, post-apocalyptic trail? That trail, I figured, would be a lot like the Hancock County fairgrounds, and there would be no place to plug in makeup mirrors with Christmas bulbs all around them. I couldn't understand why Sue wasn't worried. After all, she had heard the same stories—and weren't some men, down on their luck, already sleeping in the fairgrounds as they passed through on their own Bible-like wanderings?

. . .

When the fair came, we neighborhood kids were torn between excitement and resentment. Although our corner of town was center stage for a change, strangers came in with the gall to charge us admission to our own playground. Still, we agreed that the worst thing imaginable was to have no money when the fair started. We collected pop bottles, mowed lawns, and cleaned out garages to get ready for the big week. We also charged the country people to leave their cars in our yards, each of us working feverishly to make the most inviting "Park Here" sign.

Despite this entrepreneurial frenzy, the fair only reinforced my frugality. I soon learned that a couple dollars a day would do quite nicely, provided you played it smart. I was the best in our crowd at what we called the "Fair Game": the challenge of stretching our money to its furthest conceivable limits. Naturally, the game was my invention.

I considered the rides—a big drain on the other kids' budgets—a frivolity, because once they were over they were *over*. The real fun, I insisted, was watching *other* people go on the rides, especially the tilt-a-whirl, where older guys on dates tried not to scream or throw up. As the teenagers pitched and rolled and shrieked, my sister often among them, I jingled my change, smug in the knowledge that another quarter of Fair Money remained unspent.

Lots of people at the fair were out to get your money, even if they didn't look like Republicans. This was especially true on the midway, where mean-looking men ran the "games of skill." The games were all rigged, I told my friends knowingly, and none of us played them but Dick, whose parents simply *gave* him his Fair Money in what seemed an astonishingly generous but somehow misguided act.

For me, the fair was an annual rite of pre-apocalyptic caution, a practice run for the hard times that I was convinced were coming. The trick to having a good time at the fair lay in not being tricked—and that meant watching *other* people getting tricked and learning from their mistakes. To watch was to reconfirm a profound unreliability at the heart of things, to sense chaos lurking beneath placid surfaces. I watched as tough teenagers who were trying to win teddy bears for their girlfriends got only five of the six iron milk bottles to fall, or knocked over only four out of five fuzz-lined "cats." They went crazy when they lost at the basketball shoot. I could tell from the rebounds that the hoop was slightly smaller than normal. When high school guys couldn't ring the high bell by slamming a tread-covered lever with a mallet, they quickly slipped back into the crowd, sometimes leaving their girlfriends behind.

There was also "Dunk the Jaycee," where you threw baseballs at a trigger that plunged a clown-suited businessman—probably a Republican, I thought—into a tub of water. For obvious reasons I was tempted to play that one, but it was plenty of fun just to watch. The Republican clown razzed the losers—"Hey Wimpy, no Wheaties this morning?"— and they always took the bait, coughing up another quarter for three more balls. I studied this drama for hours, adopting a deadpan expression after making the mistake of laughing when a big guy in a cowboy hat got mad and threw his last ball directly at the cage where the clown was sitting. The cowboy, his face bright red, suddenly spun toward me. "What're *you* lookin' at, Four Eyes?"

. . .

The fair promoted immersion in exactly the kind of junk that my sister loved, especially the free stuff that the merchants passed out at the Commerce Building. I collected it all, justifying this frenzy of getting by remembering that no spending was involved. I might take what the Republicans offered, but I wouldn't stoop so low as to pay for it.

We kids would pick up First National Bank shopping bags and fill them with artifacts of small-business promotion: Cooper Tire bottle openers, Cussins & Fern Hardware yardsticks and vinyl floor samples, Marathon Oil sun visors, wallet-sized Findlay College sports schedules, Blanchard Valley Hospital calendars, county maps with all the A&P supermarkets marked with red arrows, B & G Drugs emery boards, State Farm cardboard wheels with windows that showed the mileage between Ohio cities, Isley's Ice Cream cork coasters, and dozens of rulers and pencils stamped with business names. When our bags got full, we stowed them in the woods and replaced our Marathon sun visors with Delco caps. Secure in the belief that all kids look alike to Republican businessmen, we would pick up new bags and go back for more.

It wasn't hard to picture the merchants' stuff blowing across the barren landscape of the future, despite the confident messages of the "literature": glossy brochures for Fords and Frigidaires; Chamber of Commerce pamphlets narrating the history of Findlay ("a thriving center of commerce and transportation," the town where "Down by the Old Mill Stream" was written); church-distributed comic books that showed drunken businessmen (did Republicans get drunk?) turning to Jesus after they had lost their wives and jobs, which Jesus always returned to them; and assorted leaflets like "Your Insurance Planner" ("compliments of" State Farm), "The Story of Smile-Maker Service" (Marathon Oil), and "Keep America Rolling" (Cooper Tires).

Another attraction was the fake food in the refrigerators at the appliance store booth. We imagined fooling our parents with it. "Here's your steak, Mom and Dad!" Then Mom and Dad would get puzzled looks as their knives scraped the plastic meat. This never happened, of course. For one thing, our parents would never have accepted a steak "prepared" by their fourth-grade kids, though that never occurred to us. For another, the fake food was not a giveaway item. Dick, Robbie, and I once snatched some plaster-of-Paris eggs from a refrigerator door and bolted for the exit. As we ran the salesman shouted, "I know who you kids are! I know your parents!" Scared and ashamed, I buried my egg that night in our back yard. In the game of getting free stuff, stealing was breaking the rules. Don't be like a Republican, I told myself; play it straight.

The Commerce Building was best visited on steamy afternoons, when huge industrial fans made breezes so strong that you had to lift rocks and ashtrays to get the free literature. There was also free entertainment. At the Carter's Music booth the salesman would be playing "Alley Cat" or "Patricia" on the organ. Every so often he would let a little kid hit the trumpet, violin, and piano keys, which all sounded alike. An Ohio State Highway Patrol booth, manned by an unsmiling patrolman, featured blown-up photos of accidents, posters of skeletons drag-racing, and glow-in-the-dark decals for your bike. The troopers' pamphlets always contained a "Safety I.Q." quiz: "Should Safety Cat ride his bike facing the traffic or with the traffic?" There were also lots of statistics, like how many minutes passed before someone else died on an American highway or how much money you wasted by making "jackrabbit starts."

The army booth had pictures of blue-eyed young men in snappy uniforms, along with some rifles mounted on a folding partition. The recruiter was usually talking heartily to two or three wide-eyed teenage boys as he showed them the guns. Sometimes he'd stop talking when we younger kids passed by and give us an official-looking salute. We were too scared not to return it. After all, army guys were tough, ready for whatever hard times might come. Dick's father had told him that in the army they gave you only one minute to go to the bathroom and three squares of toilet paper to use. When I asked my father if this was true, he said that Dick's dad was "as full of shit as a Christmas turkey."

. . .

The animal barns yielded other reasons to move cautiously through the world. The cattle were impossibly huge, like those bulls from Crete in my mother's art book, and they seemed to move in slow motion, like Godzilla or those unclassifiable animals that chase you in nightmares. It made me nervous whenever Dick imitated their bellowing and made them roll their eyes at us. Couldn't he see that these beasts could squash a kid without even trying, and that you couldn't make them laugh or talk them out it? The steers, with wavy coats that resembled Red Buttons's hair, provoked special awe. After Dad told me how they became steers, I kept sneaking glances under their back legs, looking for some horrible wound.

The sheep, once sheared, looked like white, wrinkly dogs and seemed embarrassed at their diminishment. But the hogs, huge and bristly and

74

nothing at all like cartoon pigs, were even scarier than the cows. The pigs seemed smarter than the other animals, more self-willed as they peered at you from the corners of their eyes. One time I stuck some hay through a fence, and the mammoth boar inside banged against the wood so hard that a plank fell out. The farmer at the next stall told me to watch myself. "That one's a killer, boy," he said. "Gutted and ate a young man just about your size last month." I knew he was kidding, of course, but was embarrassed by the commotion I had caused.

The rabbits and chickens gave further proof of nature's irrationality. They shared a tent, which I always entered alone so my friends wouldn't see me flinch whenever the chickens jerked and fluttered in their cages. They would all rattle at once, suddenly and for no apparent reason. I liked looking at the bright colors of the different breeds, but their eyes were inhuman and wild, like devils' eyes. The rabbits weren't cute and furry but quick and ratlike. Some of them were huge, and the white ones with pink eyes looked eerie and boneless, less like animals than animal ghosts. Like the pigs, they kept watching me in that sneaky, sidelong way. Trying to look casual, I kept my hands in my pockets to hide the real reason why I wasn't petting them like everybody else. I nervously jingled my change and moved on.

When I talked with the country kids, they seemed to know more than I did. They were bigger and more sure of themselves, and I figured they'd do all right in the bad times, growing their own food and riding out whatever came along. The farm stuff, exotic and powerful, seemed safer when filtered through our imaginations, as it was when we played on the farm machinery on display. We spent hours high in the seats of gleaming red or green John Deere tractors and Massey-Ferguson combines, pretending to drive nuclear-powered tanks into Moscow. We always checked for keys, half-relieved at never finding any. What would we do if we did? Dick once said what *he* would do: he'd mow down everything at the fair that annoyed him. Sucking on a piece of taffy, he described the swath he would cut: through the produce displays, with the outsized pumpkins and their mean-grandmother growers; through the crafts building with its quilts, cherrywood wishing wells, and wood-burnt plaques that read "Bless This Home" and "Your Name Here"; through the fuzzy-cat game tent, which had cheated him that day; and through the police trailer, payback for being kicked out of the fair the year before when a cop caught him hopping the fence.

We also toured the new house trailers. Provided there was no Dust Bowl, this was the world of the future, rife with conveniences and so pristine that you had to walk through it on a plastic strip taped to the floor. It was in one of those trailer kitchens, with appliances and counters and cupboards neatly nested into each other, that I saw my first automatic dishwasher. The trailer salesman got mad whenever we traipsed through. "You kids gonna buy a mobile home?" We learned to wait until some adults started the tour and to stick close to them. It was fun watching the trailer guy being nice when grownups were around.

The old wooden grandstand had booths under the seats that housed a taffy maker, a tobacco shop, a popcorn stand, and an artist who could turn out a Rocky Mountain vista, complete with mountain lake and framing pines, in ten minutes. People would ask for a lake with forests and a cabin, or a scene that was all snow and ice with a glistening mountain peak in the background. They could even order a sunset if they wanted one. The painter, a skinny man in a straw hat, never said much. He would just take ten or twenty dollars, depending on how big the picture was going to be, light up a Camel (the pack lay on the counter where I was leaning), and start coating and dabbing and stippling a prestretched canvas with a house-painting brush.

Inside the grandstand there was always something free going on: pony races, sled pulls, greased pig chases, baton-twirling contests, barbershop quartet sings—everything you could imagine. At night there was usually a "nondenominational" church service and gospel sing. We kids avoided the area around dusk, afraid that someone's parents would spot us and make us go to the service with them.

• • •

We always headed for the midway in early evening, drawn to the danger that we sensed there. Everyone looked sick and greenish under the lights, and big guys in high school letter jackets from Mount Blanchard, Van Lue, and North Baltimore cruised the area in packs or with dates. The pinball tent—the "arcade"—was filled with these tough-looking guys and their girlfriends, and everyone puffed on cigarettes. The change maker, a beefy man with palm trees tattooed on his arms, sometimes came out of his booth and threw a guy out for tilting his machines or jamming them with slugs. Sometimes a teenager would commandeer a game from a kid our age.

You might expect a penny arcade to be one place where you would *have* to spend money to have fun, but I didn't actually play the games very often. Once they were over, what did you have to show for it? Besides, sticking a quarter into a game meant committing yourself to staying in that tent longer than you might want to. You never knew when some bigger kid would materialize and say, "You want yer ass kicked?" Although the question was scary, I always had to suppress a laugh; who would ever answer *yes*? Tact dictated a cool reply—"You gonna try?"—and a casual stroll toward the exit, with an occasional pause to flip the levers on another machine as you moved on. If you resisted the urge to panic and run out, only the hood would know that you had just been given the boot. The hoods fascinated me. Like the cows and the pigs, they seemed motivated by dark impulses that I couldn't understand. I figured that if the Republicans got their way, I'd be fighting guys like this for food. It was good to practice dealing with them, and there was a certain thrill in threading through the arcade without bumping them or catching their eye.

We would hang around in the arcade—or frequently, just outside it— until an announcement blared from the new South Grandstand, the one built from steel bars. Some nights featured the "Hell-Drivers," and we'd race over to claim standing room outside the fence so we could watch the jumps and the crashes for free. After each stunt the announcer said the same thing: "Uh oh! Folks, is Junior Saparelli all right? He's pret-ty slow get-ting out of that car!" Then a helmeted Junior Saparelli would ease himself out through a window and give Churchill's victory sign, and the crowd would go nuts. Other nights featured harness races, hardly tame affairs when you're pressed against the railing as the carts and horses thunder by and fill your nostrils with track dust.

We usually left halfway through the grandstand show so we wouldn't be late getting home. About the only thing still going on was the teen dance, staged on the loading dock at the rear of the Commerce Building. We were too young to take much interest in that, except for the disk jockey who ran it from inside the WFIN MobileRadio trailer. He was broadcasting on the air, too, and we'd watch him cue up the records through the trailer's picture window. Before he left for college, my brother sometimes served as the DJ as part of his job at the station. My friends were impressed, of course, but I found it disturbing. Dave's radio voice, which made him sound years older, was nothing like his nasal mumbling at home. Then too, he seemed to have crossed over to the Republican world of getting and spending as he played records that I knew he hated, like Patti Page's "Que Sera, Sera" or Mitch Miller's "Yellow Rose of Texas," and read announcements that I knew he didn't believe in. "So when your car needs care," he would intone with a nervous grin, "bring it on down to Little's Marathon. That's *Little's* Marathon. You'll be glad you did."

With our ten o'clock curfews, my friends and I never stayed long at the dance. We wanted to end the night at the First Methodist food tent, when the church ladies cut prices to clear out the day's leftovers. While we ate we determined the winner of the Fair Game, comparing notes on who had secured the most fun for the least money. As I recounted my victory I usually had the meatloaf dinner with two vegetables, roll, and dessert—exactly the sort of meal I'd complain about whenever Mom served it at home. I would order it, though, because it seemed like a fittingly grownup meal, an appropriate reward for having lived the day responsibly, and not being a pawn of the carnies and the Republicans. I never spent everything I had on this last meal, even though the next day's fair money was already parceled out at home. Anything could happen, and I didn't want to get caught short.

. . .

Even at the time I understood that I needn't have been so careful. For all my premonitions, life in Findlay was pretty predictable, "safe as a steer," as my father would say. In hindsight, though, I think that Dad shared my resistance to the tranquility all around us. He had helped his parents butcher hogs and put up tomatoes and beans so their family could eat, but now he wore a suit in an air-conditioned office and tracked the flow of corporate money through the coffers of the Marathon Oil Company. Although he had made a good life for us, he may have wondered whether he hadn't made a whore's choice too, maybe no better than Ike's. The good life may even have bored him a little. After all, the rains were regular and gentle, the banks were safe, and the Japs and Nazis had been beaten. Maybe the Republicans were all he had left to fight.

I was seeking trials of my own, even at the Hancock County Fair. But while I kept looking for signs of the apocalypse, I knew that when I got home that night I would find my parents sitting in the front room looking strangely contented, watching something funny on TV while Dad nursed a beer and Mom glanced at a book during commercials. I knew just what they would say: "How was the fair?" I always said "Fine," but if I had been able to say—or even to know—what I really thought, I would have told them that it had been disappointing, another reminder that I had been born too late for the livelier times my parents had seen.

Gradually, this mental swerve toward the past became permanent. Whenever our family drove up to Dearborn to see Greenfield Village, it was the old buildings—Edison's lab, the Wright Brothers' shop—that grabbed my attention, not the nearby Ford Rotunda, with its model City of Tomorrow filled with space-age cars zipping to and fro on elevated tracks. The Rotunda had a decidedly Republican feel to it, with the latest Fords poised on rotating platforms, waiting to be bought by anyone who didn't want to get left behind in the race for new stuff. The Rotunda seemed like those house trailers at the fair: it forecast a world of convenience, but nothing as exciting as the Great Depression or World War II. There was even a whiff of conspiracy. If you bought a new Ford, wouldn't you be making the Republicans even richer? They wanted you to forget that the Great Depression ever happened, but what if you were driving your new Fairlane off the lot just as the dusty winds kicked up, the banks shut down, or a bunch of Republican bosses decided to fire everybody? Soon the whole country would look like something a tornado had left behind. You would have a brand new car and nowhere to drive except a fairgrounds-like landscape of tall grass, gravel, and dust.

When the Ford Rotunda burned to the ground several years later, I was only mildly surprised; wasn't this just the sort of thing I always expected? By now, though, I knew that the Republicans weren't solely responsible for the inevitable sadnesses of life. Cheryl's father had gone to prison for killing a man in a fight, and Tommy's father had died in a truck crash. The natural entropy that fights, fires, and accidents helped along was too pervasive for the Republicans to be behind it all. I wondered when the dark times would hit home—when I'd be living them, with no need to read about them in the newspaper. I kept saving my money as I waited for the other shoe—the personal one—to drop.

It never did. The definitive Bad Thing never happened, at least not to our family. Marathon Oil never went bankrupt and Dad never got fired, despite his water-cooler political debates. He did have a heart attack eight years after the Rotunda burned down and was forced to retire, but pension and disability allowed him and Mom to shake Findlay's Republican dust from their feet and to try several retirement spots before settling on Columbus, where they're doing fairly well, knock wood. My brother never became an electrical engineer, but he did become a software designer. As long as the electricity holds out, he'll be happy. My sister never accumulated enough stuff to be a Republican, as I always feared she would. She finally got her lobster dinner in Toledo after her senior prom but pronounced it a huge disappointment, virtually tasteless except for the melted butter. Sue now spends most of her time and energy trying to talk kids—hers as well other people's—out of buying current versions of the useless junk she used to love.

The Republicans never got me, either, though I finally came to understand that some of them have beating hearts. I even have friends who are Republicans—not many, granted, but enough to signal a somewhat opened mind. An English professor is neither rich nor poor, and I have enough money to smile pleasantly as I treat friends to dinner—though not enough to suppress a churning stomach whenever I do. I suppose it's a shame that I worried so much as a kid and that I still enact countless rituals designed to counter a pessimism so profound that I've learned not to mention it in casual conversation, let alone in class. I know that throwing money around like a guy with a trust fund is a compensatory flip-flop so transparent as to be ludicrous, and it's never pleasant to feel the tug of compulsion doing its work.

Finally, though, we are who we are, and we can't go back and change what made us this way. Even if we tried, we'd fail spectacularly. If I could sit down at the end of a day at the Hancock County Fair with the penny-pinching boy who I was, I'd shake him by the shoulders and peer into his sober little face. I'd tell him that Sue has gotten it at least partly right, that he ought to give up that stupid Fair Game and start having some real fun. Being who he was, he would probably agree to think it over, but only if I bought him a snow cone to top off his meatloaf dinner. Being who I am, I would buy him two of the goddam things and then fume about having been taken for a ride. This miserly kid with the thick glasses, I'd be thinking, must be some kind of junior Republican. I'd try not to hold it against him, but it would be pretty damned hard.

The Time Machine

When I was in high school in the mid-sixties, I became personally acquainted with Frank "Husk" Chance, manager/first baseman for the world champion Chicago Cubs. Never mind that I lived in a small Ohio town, that the Cubs last won a World Series in 1908, or that Frank Chance had been dead for forty years. The fact that I knew him was fully consistent with changes that came to our family when our grandparents moved in.

At first Henry and Susan Weldon stayed with their two daughters only a few weeks each year, usually during summers or at Christmas, always returning to their bungalow in a tiny Illinois town across the border from Terre Haute, Indiana. My mother and her sister began to worry, though, after Grandpa nearly severed a finger with a jigsaw. Grandma hadn't driven for years, and since the nearest hospital was thirteen miles away, she simply bandaged him up and sent him to bed until the bleeding stopped. This was only the latest in a series of misadventures, and after several months of difficult phone calls in which my mother tried to convince her parents that they could no longer manage on their own, they finally agreed to move in with us—so long as it wasn't "permanent." He was eighty-seven, and she was eighty-four.

Henry and Susan Weldon looked like elderly Americans from central casting, benign versions of that stiff farm couple in Grant Wood's *American Gothic*. Grandpa was a rail-thin, dignified man who had made his living selling dry goods and fabrics on the road and in a series of small-town stores in Minnesota and Illinois. On his good days he looked like an older

Henry and Susan Weldon, 1959.

Woodrow Wilson. On bad days, after he hadn't slept well, he looked more like the mummy of Ramses the Great. Good day or bad, he faced each morning with a clean plaid shirt buttoned to the chin, replaced on Sundays with a white shirt and a tie. He smelled like Twenty Mule Team Borax, his favorite soap. Grandma, whom Grandpa always addressed as "Mother," was more even tempered and did not seem to have bad days. Sweet faced and white haired, she was a serious Methodist who dispensed biblical wisdom whenever she deemed it appropriate. She wore floral print dresses, clunky black shoes, and an apron whether she was cooking or not. She smelled like lilacs.

When they moved in, Mom told my sister and me that our customary bouts of teenage sullenness were no longer acceptable. She had no interest in having her mother think that she had raised untutored brutes. For us kids, the burden of having to put on company manners, formerly reserved for rare occasions, expanded to encompass our entire days. Once our grandparents moved in they were inescapably *there*, always watching us with blandly curious expressions that we read as judgmental. My sister, five years older than me and obsessed with dating, complained that their presence gave her the creeps. Despite Mom's assurances that they were only making conversation, Sue felt that they were keeping oppressively close tabs on her when they asked—as they invariably did—where she was going whenever she headed for the door. With my duller social life, I had it easier. My only real sacrifice was having to give up playing my drums after school, because that was when Grandma's "stories"— *The Guiding Light* and *The Edge of Night*—came on. I was the only drummer in the marching band who had calloused knees from practicing cadences on their muted, bony surfaces.

Our parents had to make changes too. My father was forced to curb his long-standing and, I thought, very funny habit of cursing, which he did even when he wasn't mad. He also gave up his customary beer with dinner, settling for a bottle or two downed furtively at night out in the garage, far from Grandma's still-sharp sense of smell. Our mother, I later realized, had to make the most drastic adjustments, forced as she was to relinquish a considerable amount of household control in an uneasy balance of being mother and daughter under one roof. It was clear even to us kids that the power in our house had shifted to Grandma and her Methodist God. It's not that Grandma was tyrannical—quite the opposite. She was simply one of those people who radiates unalloyed goodness. To upset her felt like making a willful *choice* to be bad.

Despite their age and religion, Grandpa and Grandma were pleasant old people who took, respectively, a salesman's and a Methodist's pride in always having a positive attitude. We kids had always looked forward to visiting them at their Illinois house, which I remembered as a dimly lit museum of doilies, lace curtains, antique toys, paper fans, and a genuine icebox—objects so old-fashioned that they were exotic. It seemed strange that people who lived in such a dark, quiet place could be so quick with a joke. When I was five and Grandpa was driving us to the ice cream stand, I announced that by sitting on some books I could fool pedestrians into thinking that I was a grownup. That might work, Grandpa replied, but those people would surely think that I had a strange-looking head for a grownup. When I was in a bad mood, Grandma would always say, to no one in particular, that an ill-mannered Gypsy boy had broken into her house; if she only knew where the Gypsies lived, she would return him to his real family right away.

The Weldons would have been the first to point out the folly of romanticizing the old. Grandpa was stubborn and something of a know-it-all, with an opinion on everything from the gold standard to the best fabric for neckties. Grandma's religion was stern and inflexible, though tempered by an odd sort of softheartedness. She often said it was a real shame that all those Muslims and Jews were going to hell and expressed genuine pity for the terrible suffering they would have to endure. Grandpa wasn't quite as firm in such beliefs. I remember a mildly heated discussion in which he argued that non-Christians could be good people and Christians could be bad. After all, wasn't that big Swede who had cheated him out of his half of the store back in Minnesota a Lutheran? Grandma did not agree that Christians could be bad; Mr. Risberg must not have been a real Lutheran to have done what he did. She finally conceded, though, that non-Christians could sometimes be good, but she insisted that it was a matter of dumb luck—or unusually moral upbringings—if they were. Mahatma Gandhi, she concluded, must have had very good parents.

Our family had fled the Methodist Church years before, and such pronouncements were hard to take. But Sue and I quickly learned not to talk back. Whenever Grandma got upset, she grew quiet except for a barely audible cluck issuing from her cheek, and her face turned either blank or sad. That was a hard thing to watch, so we just didn't risk it. Besides, we understood—with a few sharp reminders from Mom—that it was difficult for old people to change their thinking. It wasn't their job to do that anyway, so it was up to us to adapt if our newly extended family was going to work out.

. . .

And adapt we did. Sue and I gradually got used to living in a house where the day's rhythms were determined by eighty-year-old sensibilities. Although the pace of things slowed down and the house became much quieter once our grandparents moved in, we grew to appreciate the enforced tranquility. Having been in enough friends' homes to realize that we had good parents, we had always seen our house as a kind of sanctuary. Now, we figured, it had the additional feature of actually sounding like one. Nor were peace and quiet the only compensations. Despite the loss of privacy, Sue discovered that Grandma could be a sympathetic confidante, a wise and eager listener to lightly censored tales of crushes and heartbreak. Sue also gained a skilled and patient seamstress capable of hemming and sewing new outfits from old.

My reward for acquiring a lifelong habit of walking softly, developed in response to our grandparents' "stories" and frequent naps, turned out to be less tangible but more lasting. When it dawned on me how long Grandma and Grandpa had been alive, I began to view them with a kind of awe, as if they were living exhibits in a Museum of Mankind. Their very presence seemed to turn Findlay, Ohio, for all its optimistic Republican immediacy, into the tip of a temporal iceberg, merely the visible portion of a vast, unseen realm of time and space. To observe their slow-moving dignity, like that of human mastodons or giant sloths, was to be reminded that this too—regardless of what "this" was—would pass. Grandma and Grandpa were card-carrying citizens of the "olden days," as they called them, but they were also *here*, sitting on our very present couch, with Grandma sewing with very present needles and Grandpa rubbing his chin and staring out of a very present window at a tree that I had climbed when I was younger.

Grandma and Grandpa turned our house into a time machine. They made it seem as if nothing was forever, or else everything was—I could never decide which. "Then" and "now" became two sides of the same coin, and it was easy to gaze at their pale, wrinkled faces and realize that my "now" would someday be a very distant "then." This did not feel the least bit morbid. On the contrary, it was strangely liberating. If I blew a chemistry exam or my voice cracked in front of a girl, maybe the world

87

hadn't ended after all. I knew that Grandma and Grandpa had suffered similar embarrassments when they were young, and to see them now was to realize that in the long run such things didn't matter. Mostly, they confirmed that there *was* a long run to begin with. Once, we learned, when Grandma was about fifteen and a handsome boy was coming her way, she couldn't decide whether to say "Hello" or "How do you do." At the moment they passed she blurted "Hell-do!"—a fine thing indeed, she always added, for a proper Methodist girl to say. Grandpa, in a burst of youthful patriotism, once boarded a troop train heading for the Spanish-American War but got homesick and jumped the train somewhere in Georgia. He never tired of telling this story on himself, though his adventures on the way back home grew more elaborate with each retelling.

"Living history" has become a catch-phrase at theme parks and museums, but in our house it was a palpable reality. Was I studying the Civil War in school? Grandpa was seven years old and Grandma four when General Grant died. Did those grainy pictures of Marshal Foch and Kaiser Wilhelm in my history textbook look like faces from another planet? At thirty-six, Grandpa was already too old to fight in the First World War. When I was assigned to do a report about Hirohito, I learned that Grandma and Grandpa were approaching retirement age when Pearl Harbor was attacked. That FDR speech about the day that would "live in infamy," filled with ghostly static as if broadcast from the Roman forum?—they heard it live on the massive radio that had occupied their front room.

. . .

Before long, Grandpa's mind began to slip. At first he forgot little things, like whether or not he had just told a joke. Occasionally he would call me by the name of my older brother, who was away at college. Once Grandpa's mental state began to darken, we could tell at a glance whether or not he was thinking clearly. When he was confused, a strange dullness fell over his eyes, and his mouth set into a thin, hard line. Bewildered by the inner fog, he became uncharacteristically snappish.

His worst bouts of disorientation came when he happened to wake up in the middle of the night. Every so often we would hear the front door slam at one or two in the morning, and Grandpa would be shuffling down the sidewalk in his bathrobe and a gray homburg. My sister and I, whose bedrooms were closest to the front of the house, were given the charge of bringing him back. "I've got a sales meeting in Chicago," he'd proclaim. "I've got to be at the Palmer House at nine tomorrow morning!" We learned to be careful about what we said to coax him back, or he would become enraged. He had to get moving, by God—and what did a couple of fresh kids know about his business anyway? We soon learned never to call him "Grandpa" when he was walking to Chicago. At those times he wasn't *anybody's* grandfather, and like any reasonable man in his twenties, he took offense at the term. "Mr. Weldon," we learned to say, "they postponed that meeting until *next* week." Grumbling that nobody in the home office ever told him a blessed thing, he would shake his head and let us lead him back to the house.

The odd thing about Grandpa's mental decline was that he could remember everything that happened before World War II as if it were yesterday's news. Kids usually figure out a way to bend such things to their own uses, and I was no exception. When I began asking him about the "olden days," he was more than happy to talk about them. What was uncanny was that his stories had the feel not just of eyewitness accounts but of *recent* eyewitness accounts, told in the present tense and usually ending with barely restrained shouts brought on by a combination of fresh-headline excitement and poor hearing. To hear him talk, his eyes sparkling with one of his then-is-now memories, felt like being there. Why was Lindbergh's plane called *The Spirit of Saint Louis?* "Because," Grandpa would begin, looking shocked that a bright boy would be so ignorant of current affairs, "he's starting out from St. Louis! He's stopping on Long Island, then heading out! He's a handsome man, and he's landing in Paris!"

There was no limit to what you could ask him. Had he ever met a freed slave? "Mother has a woman named Hettie," he shouted from back within his Kentucky boyhood. "Hettie's come up from Tennessee, where she was a slave! She helps out around the house!" What about the Crash of 1929? "What's to tell? Those damn-fool Republicans have been buying up everything you can imagine, and they don't know a blessed thing about what they're getting! Now they're trying to get their money back, and there'll be no end to it until Roosevelt closes the banks!"

. . .

Not all my interests were as lofty as American history. I was, for instance, a baseball fanatic who had read every history of the game in the public library. The book that had started it all, which I discovered in the third grade, was *My Greatest Day in Baseball*, a collection of old-timers' first-person accounts "as told to Bob Considine," a phrase whose full import I missed. When I read the book, an unadorned wartime paperback, I marveled at what great storytellers all these old-time ballplayers were—a trait even more appealing than their athletic skills.

My father had played semi-pro ball in the late thirties and early forties, and I pumped him for everything he could remember about the old-time players. But Dad had seen very few of them in person. A farm boy in downstate Illinois, he rarely got to St. Louis to see major league games. He knew the players through radio and the newspapers, and when he grew older he went beyond being a mere fan to become a player himself. In 1938 he went to an open tryout with the Cardinals, but like most boys who get the chance, he couldn't handle big-league pitching. Still, he played in industrial leagues for many years, once hitting two doubles off of Detroit's Dizzy Trout in an exhibition game in Terre Haute.

Although I was proud of my ballplaying father, his athletic skill took on darker overtones when it became clear that I was too awkward and nearsighted to follow in his footsteps as a slick-fielding second baseman. Dad may have terrorized Dizzy Trout for a day, but I flinched through thick glasses at Little League pitching and was, to my relief, cut from the Kodak Processing Plant Pirates during the tryouts. *My* baseball, I realized, would have to come from books, and the older the stories I found in those books, the less troubling it was that I couldn't play the game as well as my father could even as an "old" man, as all fathers seem to their sons. I ended up beating a temporal retreat, staking out my own baseball time in the safely distant days of Ty Cobb, Honus Wagner, and Nap Lajoie. There were turf issues here. These men had been in their primes long before Dad's baseball days, so they seemed fair game for me.

Once Grandpa's mind started to go, my baseball time coincided precisely with his. As a traveling salesman in his twenties, before settling down in a small Minnesota town and opening that dry goods store with

90

Mr. Risberg, he had taken plenty of real-world business trips to Chicago. He often saw the Cubs play at the West Side Grounds, their home park until their 1916 move into Wrigley Field, which had been built two years earlier for the Whales of the old Federal League. My books told me such facts, along with other things that I learned not to share with Grandpa for fear of confusing or upsetting him. I knew that Frank Chance had died at the age of forty-seven in 1924 and that Joe Tinker and Johnny Evers had been old men when they died, three years before I was born. One day, when I mentioned that they were dead, Grandpa's face grew dark and confused. To Henry Weldon, "Tinker to Evers to Chance" was not a piece of faded newspaper doggerel but a double-play combination made up of flesh-and-blood contemporaries who were still tearing up the National League.

Grandpa had attended some White Sox games too, which pleased me, because I was an American League fan, Detroit and Cleveland being our nearest big-league cities. He had seen—indeed, he still saw—Shoeless Joe Jackson and the seven other players who would be banned for life in the 1919 Black Sox scandal. When I asked about it, Grandpa couldn't remember this blot on his personal golden age; it simply did not square with the old salesman's insistence on fair play. Once, during a White Sox–Tigers game, he saw Ty Cobb—my personal hero—hit an inside-the-park homer. The implications were almost mystical. Ty Cobb and Henry Weldon had once breathed the same air, and now I was breathing the same air as Henry Weldon. With Grandpa around, my fascination with the past, which sometimes made me the butt of friends' jokes, could be fully and freely indulged. Ty Cobb, Theodore Roosevelt, and Harry Houdini seemed as real as—and more interesting than—my teachers and even most of my friends at school.

Grandpa had a salesman's eye for detail, for sizing things up, and I was always asking him to describe the old-time players. Frank Chance? "He's a big man—a tough cookie!" Joe Tinker and Johnny Evers? "Tinker's always got a five o'clock shadow! Evers has a ratlike face, but he moves like a cat!" At first Mom got angry because she thought I was teasing him, but her attitude changed once she saw how much he enjoyed these talks. Although he got frustrated whenever World War II and later times came up, the fog dispersed when he lurched back to his heyday, our mutual baseball era. Immersed in my own turmoil of high school anxieties, I enjoyed these time travels too. When the present became too complicated for either of us to handle, Grandpa and I sought refuge in the old West Side Grounds, its bleachers smelling of peanuts, beer, and Twenty Mule Team Borax.

. . .

Grandma Weldon brought the past to life, too, though in a completely different way. Despite a long and painful struggle with cancer, she managed to fight off senility to the very end. Well or sick, she always knew exactly who and where she was and relished being at the center—and solidly in the present—of our household. "There he goes again," she'd say whenever Grandpa put down the newspaper and complained that President Taft hadn't done a blessed thing all week. Scornful of nostalgia, she got mildly impatient whenever the olden days came up. Why would anyone be interested in all those babies diapered, meals cooked, beds made, wars fought, friends buried, and presidents coming and going? That was then, and this was now.

Jesus was forever, though, and while Grandma lived solidly in the present, she did so in a timeless sort of way. She had seen too much to get worked up over what was in the newspaper, which she saw as offering little more than an endless recycling of the same old stories. Even Kennedy's assassination, which happened two years before she and Grandpa moved in, had left her unruffled, though saddened. She and Grandpa had already shed their tears for FDR. What happened in Dallas was tragic, she said, but can you show me a time when God *isn't* testing us for our own good? If you read your Bible, you won't be surprised when this world breaks your heart. That's what this world does.

For Grandma, the only thing worth keeping from the past was her faith, which she considered to be far more current than anything in the Findlay *Republican Courier* or the Toledo *Blade*. Her midwestern Methodism brought with it all of the prohibitions that are, for most of us, the stuff of religious and cultural history. It was her smug contempt for alcohol—"Many a life has been ruined by the bottle!"—that prompted my father to drink his beer warm while gazing silently at the moon through the garage window. It also prompted one of our cousins, who was in the army, to send her a box of rum-centered chocolates from Germany one Christmas in an act of pure mischief. The print detailing the ingredients was too small for her to read, and she tore into the box before anyone could tell her what they were made of. She loved them, of course, and her response passed into family lore. "These have such a nice, smoky taste!"

Grandma's unwitting zeal for rum chocolates wasn't all that surprising. She had a natural affinity for fun that didn't seem to fit with her staunchly biblical beliefs. She never got over the novelty of television and loved talking back to the characters in her soap operas, warning them that he's married or she's a golddigger or he hasn't gotten over his *first* wife yet. She and Grandpa watched their "stories" on a portable TV in private, behind a big folding screen in the dining room, which now served as their bedroom. From behind the screen we could hear Grandma's good-natured, theatrical "uh-oh!" whenever a character was about to do something stupid. We wondered how she could watch these shows in complete composure, unflapped by their depictions of lust and infidelity, until we realized that she saw them as morality plays. Those "television people" acted godlessly enough, but didn't they always end up stewing in their own juices? Her stories seemed to reconfirm biblical verities in contemporary dress—Samson and Delilah as a doctor and a nurse, piped into the house by God's grace every afternoon from Toledo.

Grandma treated us kids as if we were much younger than we were, teasing us by kissing the "souse" from our ears or demonstrating the "bottomless jar" trick, where she would manically scrape the last vestiges of peanut butter or jam from a seemingly empty jar, the fat on her arms shaking in great wattles. She loved Protestant hymns and always made my brother play a few on the piano whenever he was home from Ohio State. She didn't mind when he teased her by setting them to a rock 'n' roll beat. My brother made "The Old Rugged Cross" and "Rock of Ages" sound as if they had been written by Huey "Piano" Smith, but Grandma sang along anyway. Musical styles changed, like presidents and hemlines and the other ephemera of this world, but those words were forever—and they could save you.

With Grandpa listening quietly, though not always attentively, Grandma read two Bible chapters aloud each day, one from the Old Testament after breakfast and one from the New just before they went to bed. To the rest of us, for whom Christianity had acquired the spooky overtones of a ghost story, hearing these readings was like eavesdropping on an alien ritual—a thing to respect though it lay beyond our understanding. Struggling to square Grandma's no-nonsense religion with her cheerful personality, Sue and I finally concluded that if you really thought you were saved, as she clearly did, you would probably be happy. Grandma didn't push her beliefs except to announce every so often that she was praying for us, and that she was certain that someday we would come around. It was probably harder for her to imagine us in hell than to imagine Gandhi there.

There was a lot that Grandma did not see—or more likely, chose not to see—in the normal course of a day. Whenever Sue argued with our parents about her Saturday night plans, or I tried to skip school by pretending to be sick, or my father let slip a "Jesus H. Christ," Grandma would clam up and leave the room. Dad kept his beer under a tarp in the garage not because Grandma would yell at him, but because, like the rest of us, he couldn't bear to upset her. We learned to conduct family fights in stage whispers with frequent glances over our shoulders, like actors trying to perform *Hamlet* without waking up a bunch of infants napping in the front row. "Watch it! There's Grandma!"

It has become fashionable to deride the kind of faith that Susan Weldon had, but one fact is undeniable: when the end came, it certainly did its job. Through months of agonizing pain, during which she kept her medication at a minimum because it made it hard for her to read her Bible, she never uttered a word of anger or bitterness. She just kept moaning that her peace was coming. When the pain subsided she seemed almost radiant, already a happy ghost—or maybe a Methodist angel—eager to move on. Finally she did.

Grandpa's religious beliefs had always been tempered by a salesman's easygoing worldliness, a bemused tolerance in the face of life's variety. We suspected that it would be harder for him to leave the world, and we were right. When he died a few months later, he went out ranting, confused, and frightened—suspicious that our parents were cheating him and angry at the darkness that was closing in. I remember thinking, somewhat grimly, that Grandpa died the way I could imagine myself dying. Although his mind was stuck more deeply in the past than Grandma's, he had definitely achieved the more modern sensibility. Grandma's passing, by contrast, seemed to illustrate what my Sunday

School teachers had said years earlier about "dying in Jesus." Although she was adamant about living in the here and now, her death was a message from the past, a final reminder of things older and larger than the immediate and the everyday. When she died it wasn't sad at all, not even to my mother, who was at her bedside at the end. When Mom came home from the hospital, she announced that she would never again be afraid to die. She had witnessed a death from the olden days. This was how it used to be done.

. . .

Even though Grandma would be sad to know that I never "got religion," as she always prayed I would, I did gain something else from her—and from Grandpa—that seems almost as mysterious, especially in an era obsessed with what's happening now. Living with old people will give you an unshakeable feeling that past lives are somehow tangled up with yours, that you are one small part of a single, timeless stream of people who have all breathed the same air. To be sure, our house returned to an approximation of its former state after Grandma and Grandpa died. The folding screen was put away, the heavy drapes came down, and things got brighter and noisier and quicker of pace. My sister and I could now bring friends over without asking them to talk in whispers, and the pervasive smell of urine that accompanied the final months eventually faded. But this strangely flexible sense of time never went away. How could it? If it took just one Grandpa to take me back to Frank Chance and Ulysses S. Grant, it wouldn't take that many Grandpas to get back to Galileo, Grandma's Jesus, or even Ramses the Great, Grandpa's bad-day twin.

Spending two years of your youth in a time machine is not a bad resource to draw on if you've just turned fifty and time is starting to rush by a little too quickly for comfort. Susan Weldon's religion would surely be useful for dealing with the alarming acceleration of things, and in darker moments I can't help regretting that her faith never became mine. As it turns out, those loopy excursions in time travel with Henry Weldon, the wild shifts from this morning's breakfast to turn-of-the-century Chicago and back again, are providing the more helpful legacy for coping with middle age and the nagging feeling that everything is starting to wind down. After all, Grandpa was almost fifty when those Republicans tried to unload everything they had snapped up and the stock market crashed. Those bad old days came and went, and Grandpa weathered them, trusting to FDR and counting himself lucky to be in a relatively depression-free line of work. People will always need dry goods and clothes, he reasoned. Something—maybe the Methodist Jesus—might bring the world to an end, but it sure wouldn't be Calvin Coolidge or Herbert Hoover.

Faced with wisdom like that, I can only agree. Coolidge went, and Hoover went, and Roosevelt indeed closed the banks—and Grandpa still had almost four decades of Grandma's Bible readings to go. That kind of continuity will remind you that fifty is a little early to get overcome by intimations of mortality. Besides, such intimations don't seem quite so grim when you realize that even when the world *does* end, it doesn't end.

If this sounds improbable, try talking to a salesman who has just that day returned from the Chicago World's Exposition and is complaining, a little too loudly, about the packed trolleys and the blessed heat. You know full well, of course, that the famed White City is long gone and that the only Chicago trolleys still around are roped off in transportation museums. But Chicagoans still complain that the summers are unbearable, and even though the West Side Grounds are gone, that new place—they called it the North Side Ballpark, then Weeghman Park, then Cubs' Park, and finally, in 1926, Wrigley Field—is still there. If you told Henry Weldon that the Cubs were struggling as usual, he would answer in a barely controlled shout that it hasn't always been that way. Susan Weldon might even glance up from her sewing and agree. Presidents and world's fairs and ballparks come and go, and given the endless cycles of this world, the Cubs will be champions again. I'll take Grandma's word for it. There will probably be sufficient time before Jesus returns for the Cubs to win, even if my old acquaintance, that tough cookie Frank Chance, is no longer playing first base.

The Bible Tells Me So

I've just finished working my slow way through the fourteenth chapter of the Gospel of John in a 1916 issue of Westcott and Hort's Greek New Testament. It's a schoolbook edition, with "Hickie's Greek-English Lexicon" bound in the back. Only four inches by six, with a sturdy black cover, this book was meant to be hauled around during a busy school day—to stand up to the hard use of boys likely to flop it down with their coats for an impromptu game of baseball. On the flyleaf is inscribed, with Palmer Penmanship flourish, "St. Mary's Seminary, Baltimore, Md." On the rear endpapers, the same hand has recorded the bill of fare for a "Saturday Evening" banquet: blue point oysters on the half shell, consommé of tomato, roast Vermont turkey, mashed potatoes with cranberry sauce, and something called "Fruit Salad à la Baltimore."

This was a meal to remember, and probably longer than whatever Greek the book's original owner managed to absorb. The evidence for that is pretty clear. The text is clean except for eight pages in the Gospel of Mark. There, the English equivalent for every word has been painstakingly entered in tiny script between the lines, a class-recitation pony so massively insecure that the boy might as well have smuggled in a Douay-Rheims to read from when asked to translate.

If the study of Greek discouraged him, at least he ate well. And if Greek was hard for an active boy dutifully paying the family tithe to God's service, it's even harder for people working with middle-aged brain cells. I found that boy's Greek Testament in a used bookstore an hour's drive from Baltimore. New, it cost him $1.90. Eighty years later I paid $7.50 for it and would gladly have paid twice as much. If you're learning a language, you can't beat having a dictionary right at hand, especially if your vocabulary is still small. It has taken me the better part of two weeks, reading in spare moments, to get this far in John.

Unlike my young predecessor, I'm not being forced to do this. When friends ask why I am learning a dead language whose principal text is the most widely translated book in history, their concerned looks tell me that they fear the sort of midlife conversion that makes people quit their jobs to search for Noah's ark. I quickly reassure them that I'm the same liberal humanist—the typical English professor—that they've always known. It's just that I've become fascinated with the Bible.

I say that to keep things simple. The truth is, I've *always* been fascinated with the Bible. Learning this old language feels like coming home, and trying to explain why is not exactly the stuff of office small talk. How, leaning against a copying machine or munching on some microwaved popcorn, could I possibly explain how moving it is to be reading these stories in their oldest extant form?

• • •

How I got into this, at least, is easily told. Like a middle-management Thoreau, I took up Greek because I wished to live deliberately. Halfway through a two-year term as chair of my department, I realized that the job was destroying my ability to think. For my second year I vowed to find something to do that would keep my mind active, something that could be tucked into the spare moments of hectic days. It also had to be something that would stick with me, permanent evidence that my time as chair had not been completely wasted.

I found what I was looking for early that summer in a bookstore, where I spotted an invitingly slim paperback called *Teach Yourself New Testament Greek*, by D. F. Hudson. I already knew some Latin; why not learn a little Greek to go with it? This decision seemed wonderfully practical, especially when I noticed that Hudson's book was half as thick as its neighbor on the shelf, *Teach Yourself Ancient Greek*. This confirmed what I had already heard: biblical Greek was much easier than Homeric or Attic. Better to start with the New Testament, then work back to the older stuff.

I began a ritual of memorizing that took me back to high school Latin. There was something soothing about learning case endings, as if they were chants to keep the dark away: *anthropos, anthropou, anthropō, anthropon, anthropoi, anthropōn, anthropois, anthropous*. Given the parallels to Latin, the basics of Greek grammar came pretty quickly, and by the time classes started I was inching through the three Johannine letters. By midsemester I could read Mark fairly easily. Now, as the second semester draws to an end, I'm working through John, more difficult because it has fewer sections of straightforward narrative and more of those long speeches that have prompted centuries of theological debate.

As an escape from administrative flurry, Greek has certainly done its office. But the payoff has not been quite what I expected. The Gospel narrative, so familiar from my youth as the very essence of "religion," has started to break over me fresh. As I piece the old story together, word by word and clause by clause, it almost feels as if I'm hearing it for the first time. I rush through the day's business—classes, chats with colleagues, a meeting with the dean, run-ins with a jammed photocopier—so I can return to my office and close the door. There's always another irregular verb to learn or another verse or two to crawl through.

My New Testament odyssey has become obsessive, and I have had to consider whether the pressures of this job have driven me back, kicking and screaming, to my Protestant roots. When I was a kid I certainly "had religion," as my grandmother used to put it, but it's probably more accurate to say that religion had *me.* In our small Ohio town there were lots of people who found Jesus and weren't much fun to be around afterward. I remember the signs, and at odd moments I find myself worrying how I'll react to the Passion narrative, only a few pages ahead. That's always the great fear, isn't it?—that one day we'll round a corner and collide with our sad former selves. Mostly, though, I plod through John's Gospel with calm deliberateness, reasonably certain that I won't be swept away by its terrifying climax and dénouement. Remembering a faith and rekindling it, I remind myself, are very different things.

Still, these old words have power, and I'm reacting to them in ways I would not have predicted. This might stem from my snail's-pace reading. Reduced, like all language learners, to the level of a child, I can't help taking in the story as a child would. But I'm not taking it in the way I did when I actually *was* a child. This time around, the old threat—believe this or be damned—is gone. Maybe that's why, as I struggle to match up subjects with verbs and try to figure out what all these participles are agreeing with, I can see John's narrative as a *story*. As the plot thickens, word building upon word and clause upon clause, it seems more immediate—an urgent message from one person to another—than it ever seemed before. The words are so fragile, their tone so breathless.

As a child I knew the Gospels in the King James Version. The narrative was stately and confident, like a John Huston voice-over in a wide-screen movie. In Greek the story feels direct and rushed, slapped together like the speech of someone bartering for eggs. In the King's English it seemed inevitable that this new faith would prevail—that it would eventually spread, as Luke wrote in Acts, from Jerusalem to Judea to Samaria and finally "unto the uttermost part of the earth"—a fair description, I remember thinking, of Findlay, Ohio, where it reached me two thousand years later. In the Greek it is easier to imagine that the outcome is still in doubt. Subject, participle, prepositional phrase, object, verb: one sentence comes together. But here's another sentence, and what happens *here?*

In John 14 the disciples are baffled as usual, and I'm right there with them. "Lord, we don't know where you are going," Thomas complains, "How are we to know the way?" "Lord, show us the Father," begs Philip, "and it will be sufficient to us." As I work through these heartbreaking requests, I can almost forget that a Resurrection lies ahead. You see, I'm not *there* yet—not in this language. For now, uncertainty and fear predominate. I'm still assembling the puzzle, just as the variant readings cited in the textual notes remind me that this particular retelling—the most philosophical of the four—was itself pieced together from hundreds of manuscripts. It doesn't take much nudging to imagine that I've just come across a dusty papyrus and am trying to figure out what it means.

· · ·

I have always loved Bibles as physical objects—their heft and size, their impossibly thin pages and neat columns of tiny type. Years before I could read the Bible for myself, I was told that it was God's Word; everything you really needed to know lay between its covers. This gave God a specific place and shape. I knew, of course, that God was an old man in the sky, like Santa Claus but not nearly so jovial and dressed in white instead of red. I also knew that you couldn't see him in that form until you died. When I tried to picture him in the here and now, what I mostly saw was a book.

In the summer our family would visit my grandparents in downstate Illinois. Grandma's was the first Bible I remember. Big and floppy, with a black-pebbled cover and flaps that zipped shut, it was thumb-indexed, with red page-edges and four or five colored-ribbon bookmarks sewn into the binding. When Grandma showed it to me, she told its basic story as Christians see it: Jesus died and rose from the dead so we could go to heaven. Some of the words were printed in red letters. Those, she said, were Jesus' actual words. The pages were wilted and soft and sweet smelling, and Grandma's notes and underlinings were everywhere. It was fun to flip through the cutouts of the thumb index and watch the black half-moons run up and down the page. If you gently bent the book, the red page-edges fanned out into pink.

My parents had Bibles too, but theirs had no underlining. That worried me. If Grandma was right and this was the book that got you into heaven, I couldn't understand why Mom and Dad weren't reading it every waking minute of every day. I even wondered how Grandma could spend hours at a time *not* reading it. And another thing: if The Book was so holy, why was Grandma always so cheerful? Several times I tried to read a little in my father's Bible, but none of it made any sense. That worried me, too.

My first Bible was one of those tiny green New Testaments with Psalms and Proverbs in the back. Miss Grimes, a bubbly woman who looked like Eleanor Roosevelt, passed them out one day in school, where she came every other week to provide an hour of "religious education." Although this was public school, none of our teachers objected to this cheerful muddling of Church and State. I certainly had no complaints; now, I thought, I'd learn to read the one book that really mattered—and what more important subject could you possibly study, in school or out? But after Miss Grimes passed out the Testaments and had us print our names on the "Presented To" line inside the front cover, she forgot all about them. At her next visit we went back to drawing smiling Jesuses and singing children's hymns. One of those hymns had the line, "Yes, Jesus loves me: the Bible tells me so." Well, I wondered, *where* does it tell me that? I tried to find out but kept bogging down in incomprehensible sentences and tripping over names like Lazarus and Cephas. Some of the people, like John and Mark, had regular Ohio-boy names; why didn't everybody?

I received my first complete Bible when I was eight years old, as our Sunday school class was welcomed with moderate ceremony into full membership in the Howard Methodist Church on Cherry Street. My new Bible had a hard blue cover with my name stamped in small gold letters on the front. That night, as I flipped through it, I found more strange names: Zerubbabel, Melchizedek, Absalom. Still, I had high hopes. Now that I was an officially designated Methodist with my own set of personalized pledge envelopes, someone would surely start teaching me about The Book.

To my dismay, Sunday school was no different after the ceremony than before. Although we heard a few Bible stories, mostly we read about boys who drank and girls who ruined their reputations. The stories always

After church, 1955.

ended the same: after the teenagers prayed, Jesus got them out of whatever jam they were in. Sunday school revealed few mysteries. Would Jesus approve if you found a hundred-dollar bill on the sidewalk and didn't try to find its rightful owner? That was a no-brainer for a bunch of straight-arrow midwestern kids. But what, the teacher asked, if it was a twenty-dollar bill? What about twenty cents? "That one's a little tougher, isn't it, kids?" Well, yes it was—but not as tough as a man coming back from the dead. *That's* what I wanted to hear about.

I finally asked my parents if I could skip Sunday school and stay with them for the adult service, where I figured I'd get the real story. Mom had told me that there was always a Bible text at the beginning of the sermon, which was true. But the sermons seemed to be about everything *but* the Bible. Make time for your wife and kids, don't cheat on your taxes, support the school bond issue, run your business the way Jesus would run it. I remember lots of golfing metaphors. "Strait is the gate," the Bible says, "and narrow is the way, which leadeth unto life." Sometimes you're going to hook and sometimes you're going to slice, but only Jesus can take you straight down the middle of life's fairway. What did that mean, exactly? I knew that Reverend Detweiler meant well, but I didn't play golf. Besides, I had a scary feeling that the Bible wasn't a game—that it wasn't even remotely *like* a game. Only one thing seemed clear: if you believed what the Bible said, you'd go to heaven; if you didn't, you'd go to hell.

When I started to nag my parents with Bible questions, I discovered that they knew quite a lot. They could even recite entire passages by heart, though I had to goad them into doing it. What I couldn't know was that they had spent their entire adult lives trying to recover from fundamentalist upbringings. The mainstream Protestantism of the 1950s—in particular, the easygoing Christianity of the Howard Methodist Church—had been their compromise. Too wounded to believe but too responsible to rebel, they went to church in order to do right by their kids. We would learn about Jesus, but without the fire and brimstone.

Relative to our town, of course, my parents were freethinking radicals. I vaguely understood that Mom was active in efforts to integrate the country club and the local churches, organizing boycotts of local realtors who refused to sell houses to "colored" people. Later I learned that Miss Grimes had stopped coming to our school because a petition drive had run her out.

My mother had helped circulate the petition. Now she was facing her worst nightmare: her youngest child was begging to learn about the Bible.

Mom answered my Bible questions with patience but not much enthusiasm. My father was more direct. One day, when I was bothering him with more questions, he lowered his newspaper and said, very softly, "You know, son, a lot of what's in the Bible is horseshit." That night at dinner, when I told Mom what Dad had said, she gave him a dirty look and said I'd have to make up my *own* mind about it.

After dinner she went to a closet, took down a box from the top shelf, and gave me what turned out to be my key to the Bible. It was her childhood copy of *Hurlbut's Story of the Bible for Young and Old*, by Jesse Lyman Hurlbut, D.D. A big blue book with a stamped cover, it broke the Bible down into nearly two hundred stories, each three to five pages long and fairly easy to read. It was filled with pictures, mostly of *Arabian Nights* people striking dramatic poses. I must have read that book at least fifty times over the next few years. I stared at the pictures for hours on end, peering into an alien world of domed houses, flowing robes, beams of celestial light, and patient-looking donkeys. This was a world far older— and a lot holier—than Findlay, Ohio.

The Old Testament stories were my favorites: the Garden of Eden, Noah's ark, Abraham almost sacrificing Isaac, Joseph and his brothers, the flight from Egypt, David and Goliath. They were less scary than the New Testament stories, which Grandma said were the ones that really counted as far as heaven and hell were concerned. You weren't supposed to read the Jesus stories just for fun. Then too, some of the Jesus stories were pretty unsettling. The two scariest were the ones that Hurlbut called "The Darkest Day of All the World" and "The Brightest Day of All the World." Naturally, they were about the Crucifixion and the Resurrection. The illustrations were hard to look at; the first story showed Jesus as a dead body, the second as a pitiless ghost. I tried to avoid the post-Resurrection pictures but couldn't resist an impulse to peek. The picture of the Ascension showed Jesus hovering in the air with an eerie glow and an expressionless face. I had nightmares about it.

By now I knew that being afraid of the Savior was not a good sign. I tried to compensate by focusing on the other Jesus in the book, the one who healed people and fed hungry crowds and told stories to children.

He looked like the Jesus on the covers of *The Upper Room*, the meditation-a-day magazine that Grandma sent to our house. Whether sleeping through a storm at sea or knocking on a door or carrying a lamb on his shoulders, this Jesus seemed too gentle to send a kid to hell. I knew, though, that the risen Jesus—that ghostly figure who could appear and disappear without warning—was the one you had to believe in.

What if I couldn't really believe in him? Grandma was too sweet to say much about hell, but it was easy to fill in the blanks. Then again, what if I *did* believe? A kid might wake up in the middle of the night and actually *see* him, all bright and terrifying, and be forced to change his life forever when all he wanted was to be normal and fit in. The glowing figure I definitely did *not* want to find standing at the foot of my bed might be calling me out of that bed for the last time.

· · ·

The Bible was like a car crash that I couldn't turn away from. Caught between attraction and fear, I gradually worked out a solution that I could not have articulated at the time. I knew that the Bible was old and sacred; maybe a kid could avoid the sacred part by concentrating on the old part. With ancient history serving as a buffer between me and that scary business about heaven and hell, I began to find out as much as I could about Bible times, and the older the better—or at least, the older the safer. The New Testament, I figured, could wait.

Hurlbut's Story of the Bible listed the Bible passages on which each story was based, and I began reading the Bible itself, comparing its stories—in my mind, the "real" versions—with Hurlbut's retellings. Although this was hard going, I soon discovered that the town library had lots of books that helped: atlases, handbooks, dictionaries, and books on archaeology and ancient history. Some of these books I could already read; more of them taught me *how* to read.

The Findlay Public Library had everything an earnest young Methodist could want. I peered through the library's stereoscope at sepia Victorian photographs of the pyramids, "Joseph's Granary," and a rubble ziggurat labeled "The Tower of Babel." I ran across Bishop Ussher's chronology and neatly entered dates on the appropriate pages in my presentation Bible, from 4004 B.C. for the Creation through 586 B.C. for the

Babylonian Captivity. When I learned that some Old Testament laws had been borrowed from the Babylonians, I checked out a book that contained Hammurabi's Code and copied selections from it into a notebook. I gazed at pictures of Mesopotamian silt deposits that "proved" the Flood. I read Sir Leonard Wooley's description of "Ur of the Chaldees" and was amazed to find that Abraham's hometown seemed even smaller than Findlay. I learned that Moses had an Egyptian name—the same name borne by Pharaohs like Ramses (Ra-Moses) and Thutmose (Thoth-Moses). I traced the Exodus through Sinai, somewhat disturbed to find that two different routes were proposed, along with two sites for the Red Sea crossing and two locations for Mount Sinai—or was it Mount Horeb? I studied maps of Jerusalem and floor plans of Solomon's Temple, and wondered what became of the Ark of the Covenant and the Tables of the Law. I read about the fall of the Northern Kingdom and tried to sound out the mesmerizing names (Adad-Nirari, Assur-Banipal) of the Assyrian kings who conquered it. The citizens of Judah in the south had it better than the northerners: if you had to go into exile, better to do it in a great city that boasted the Hanging Gardens, one of the Seven Wonders of the World. I supposed that the Captivity was like being carried off to Cleveland.

It was the Bible—and books about it—that turned me into what my father called "a reader." He was puzzled, and maybe a little concerned, that his son would just as soon curl up with a library book about biblical archaeology as play catch. But I did normal things too. I studied the Tigers' box score each day, for instance, to check the performances of Al Kaline, Frank Lary ("the Yankee Killer"), and my favorite, the pudgy outfielder Charlie "Paw Paw" Maxwell. But I had another set of heroes that Dad found strange: Wooley of Ur; Henry Rawlinson, breaker of the cuneiform code; Sir William Flinders Petrie, father of modern Egyptology; James Breasted and John Wilson, old-time and current Egyptologists at Chicago's Oriental Institute; W. F. Albright, dean of Old Testament archaeologists; E. A. Wallace Budge, who published the Egyptian *Book of the Dead* and a hieroglyphic dictionary; James Pritchard, editor of *Ancient Near Eastern Texts*, where I had found the Code of Hammurabi.

As it turned out, those two routes for the Exodus prompted the first stirrings of a ten-year-old skeptic. I soon learned that there were two Creation stories and two Flood stories. No boat could possibly hold two—or was it seven?—of every animal I had seen at the Toledo Zoo. The Red Sea crossing probably took place in the "Sea of Reeds," more a marsh than a sea. The manna from heaven might have been nothing more mysterious than secretions from a desert plant. It didn't make sense that at the end of Deuteronomy Moses could write about his own death and close by saying that nobody knew where he was buried. There were two and maybe three separate Isaiahs, hundreds of years apart. And the world could not possibly have been created in 4004 B.C. Now that I knew that the gravel in our driveway was older than that, I sheepishly crossed out the dates that I had entered into my presentation Bible.

Serious men—scientists, no less—had discovered facts that rushed into my head like Joshua's army sweeping across the Jordan. Now I knew, though, that Jericho's walls had already come tumbling down, apparently in an earthquake, centuries before the conquest of Canaan. No Canaanite writings mentioned a sudden invasion; it was probably a long-term migration instead. No Egyptian records suggested that the Hebrews had ever been in the Delta. Moses may not only have had an Egyptian name: he may actually have *been* an Egyptian, perhaps a follower of Akhenaten, the monotheist Pharaoh whose hymn to the Sun Disk ended up as Psalm 104. The story of Joseph sounded suspiciously like the Egyptian "Tale of Two Brothers." Those silt deposits in the Tigris-Euphrates Valley were probably laid down at different times by a number of small floods. The flood story in the *Epic of Gilgamesh* predated the Genesis version by centuries. Some of the psalms referred to events that happened hundreds of years after David's death.

Most shocking of all, there were Bibles completely different from the King James Version. My neighborhood pal Lenny, whose family went to our town's only Catholic church, showed me his mother's Bible. It contained books I had never heard of: Tobit, Judith, the Wisdom of Solomon, Ecclesiasticus, the books of the Maccabees. How could The Book be telling the truth when there was disagreement even over what was *in* it?

It took a while to absorb all this, but by the time I was twelve I was convinced that the Bible wasn't all "true," at least not in the way that Grandma claimed. I didn't stop believing in God, but my forays into biblical history and archaeology assured me that he would not willingly violate small-town Ohio ethics. It was a scary God who commanded Abraham to kill his son, or drowned Pharaoh's charioteers—weren't they just following orders?—as the Red Sea rushed back in upon itself, or struck a man dead just for keeping the Ark of the Covenant from sliding out of an oxcart and hitting the ground. Surely there were natural explanations here. Maybe Abraham just *thought* he had to sacrifice Isaac but then stopped because a loving God gave him a conscience. Chariots could easily bog down in a marsh while chasing people who were crossing it on foot; wouldn't it be natural for their descendants to claim that the Egyptians had drowned and that God had done it? And what about poor old Uzzah, struck dead for touching the Ark? A man trudging beside a cart in the desert sun could easily have a heart attack, couldn't he? It wasn't necessarily God who killed him.

I'm sure the Deity was grateful for whatever moral rehabilitation I was able to offer. Jesus, however, was another story. I still rarely looked at the New Testament. I was probably holding off until I could face it, until I could be positive that the Bible sometimes exaggerated things and even made stuff up. A man coming back from the dead was a much bigger miracle than the Red Sea parting. What natural explanation could possibly exist for it? What's more, the stakes were infinitely higher. You wouldn't go to hell for not believing that Moses led his people out of Egypt between towering walls of water, but if you doubted the Resurrection, you were in big trouble.

Around this time our family made our own exodus: out of the Howard Methodist Church. One Sunday morning my sister and I feigned sickness in order to avoid going. It was not the first time, and my father lost his patience. After a huge fight, during which Dad ordered us to go to that "goddam church" and immediately found his anger sapped by the irony of the phrase, we all faced the horrible truth of our family's godlessness. As we drank hot chocolate around the kitchen table, my sister and I still sniffling, our parents admitted that they had been going to church for our benefit, convinced that we should learn something about religion. My sister and I admitted that we had been going for *them*, hating every minute but trying to believe because we thought *they* did. Mom said that the time had come for a family vote. Should we attend church or not? The vote was unanimous. I went up to my room, brought down my stack of empty pledge envelopes, and dumped them into the wastebasket under the sink. "It's all horseshit," I announced as Mom shot Dad another one of her stern looks.

That's what I thought about church, but not about the Bible. Only parts of it seemed untrue: the trick was picking out which ones. The Old Testament seemed to contain a kernel of actual things said and done, but it also had all this other stuff that was unreasonable, unscientific, and just plain scary. By now I was pretty sure, for instance, that there had been no Universal Flood and no Noah—but there *had* been periodic floods in the Tigris-Euphrates Valley, and it made sense that ancient people would condense them into one big story to tell the kids. The New Testament, however, was different. It wasn't so easy to dismiss the Big Question it posed: did Jesus really rise from the dead? Once our family left the Howard Methodist congregation, faith no longer had anything to do with church. Would I end up believing or not? The Bible would have to tell me so.

• • •

Sometimes faith seemed more complicated than simply believing or not believing. Maybe you could "sort of" believe in Jesus, as I would have phrased it then. Other times faith seemed far simpler, maybe even a matter of dumb luck. When I shot baskets after school, I sometimes told myself that if I made the next one, I believed—not that I would *try* to believe but that I *did* believe. If I missed the shot, I didn't believe—as simple as that. I always made sure I ended the day by making one.

Most people, I suspect, first read the New Testament in order to believe. It now seems clear that I first read it in order *not* to believe, though I would never have admitted this to anyone. As I worked through it, I looked for the same historical core that I thought I had found in the Old Testament. What seemed comfortably "true" were the stories about a wise and gentle teacher who preached repentance and forgiveness. Maybe, I thought, this was the "real" Jesus, who had been covered over by the scarier parts: the tempted Christ being whisked by Satan up to the pinnacle of the Temple, the snarling demons and the exorcisms, Lazarus stumbling from the tomb in burial wrappings, graves opening at the Crucifixion, and most of all, the Resurrection itself and those frightening appearances of the risen Christ, an unpredictable ghost who made people touch his horrible wounds.

Wanting to make the Gospels less threatening, I closed one eye so I could read them that way. Many years later I learned that Jefferson snipped out the supernatural parts of the Gospels to create a Jesus fit for a rationalist. An unwitting deist at twelve and thirteen, I tried to do the same—and went back to the library to learn what science could teach me. Out came the dictionaries, the handbooks, the commentaries, and the gospel "harmonies." Once I learned that John's Gospel was late and that his Jesus was the ghostliest, I became a no-nonsense Synoptic Boy. I was looking for a Jesus who wouldn't threaten me with nighttime appearances or eternal damnation, someone too reasonable to send a kid to hell just because he wasn't sure that a man could rise from the dead.

I kept my New Testament probings secret whenever our grandparents came to visit. Grandma read Grandpa two chapters from the Bible every day, one in the morning and one at night. He was nearly deaf, and whenever she read we had to quiet down. Her voice was calm and musical as it floated out from behind the folding screen that walled off the dining room, where they slept. The evening reading always took place just before they went to bed at nine o'clock—usually during the fourth or fifth inning if a Tigers game was on TV. When Grandma started reading, Dad would turn down the sound and slip out to the garage for his first beer of the night. I'd keep watching as she read, gazing at Jim Bunning's noiseless delivery and perking up if the chapter was from the Gospels. I remember noticing that Grandma's voice sounded exactly the same whether she read a "natural" part or a "ghostly" part. That distinction, I knew, was mine and not hers: she believed every word.

Sometimes I wished I did too. I'd be reading along and everything would be fine: a healing here, a commonsense moral lesson there, a theological debate, a rebuke, an exorcism. I learned to rationalize these things. Miraculous healings? The mind can affect the body, can't it? I knew that if I stared at the clouds and tried to find shapes in them, a skinned knee didn't hurt so bad. Loving your neighbor "as yourself" made perfect sense. It made sense, too, that the different kinds of Jews—Pharisees, Sadducees, scribes, elders, high priests—would lock horns and that Jesus would be right in the thick of it. And if people really believed in unclean spirits, they could surely imagine that they were possessed by one.

Before long, though, one of those rough spots would come along—and what was worse, many of them were printed in red in Grandma's Bible. Since John's Gospel contained more of that red print than any other book, I knew I had to read it. And there, of course, was that disturbing Lazarus story. The practical sister Martha worries that the corpse will stink after four days in the tomb. That seemed "real"—I could imagine my sister saying something like that. But then comes that terrifying scene where Jesus cries out, "with a loud voice," for Lazarus to "come forth" from the grave. Why a loud voice, like a werewolf's bellow? There was also that strange story at the very end of the book, where Jesus seems to torture Peter by asking him three times: "Simon, son of Jonas, lovest thou me?" If someone asked me the same question three times, I'd know that he was accusing me of lying. Peter's grilling comes just after Jesus causes a miraculous catch of fish. The disciples' nets may have been full that night, but what about the other poor fishermen of Galilee? Did they go to bed hungry just so this wizard could show off? And if you've just come back from the dead, why would you need to make fish jump into a net anyway? Hadn't the Resurrection already proved the point?

God may dwell in the details, but fear resides there too. Red-type evidence against the comfortable Jesus was everywhere, and not just in John. Humility is a good thing, right? Yet Jesus explicitly claimed special kinship—virtual identity—with God. Honor your father and your mother? No gentle philosopher would scold his mother at a wedding, as Jesus did at Cana, or renounce his family in favor of his followers. Turn the other cheek? Forgive those who trespass against you? Jesus said that it would be better for Judas never to have been born, even though someone had to betray him for the Resurrection to take place. Love everybody? In all four Gospels Jesus promised that nonbelievers would be cast into the fire like dead branches. And what about the Resurrection itself? I was hoping to convince myself that it was the biggest of those superstitious overlays, but Jesus predicted—again, in all four Gospels—that he would die and come back on the third day. There was no getting around it: it was right there in red and white.

The two Jesuses—the kind one and the ghostly one—kept fusing and separating, blurring the clear-cut line I sought between history and superstition. God was all right: I had softened him enough to go about my business without too much worry, but Jesus remained dangerously out of focus. He had become a kind of embarrassment, like a math problem I was too stupid to solve. Most of all, he seemed an affront to historical reality, which was something I *did* believe in. He practiced a kind of magic that the educated people of his day had long since outgrown. The Romans had bridges, highways, aqueducts, and indoor plumbing. Caesar was a shrewd general, Cicero a practical moralist. After two years studying Latin in school, I had encountered nothing particularly ghostly in the Roman world. But in one corner of that world, people were claiming that a man had come back from the dead.

When I was fourteen I gave up looking for a comfortable Jesus, and the New Testament became a kind of no-man's land. I never lost my fascination with the Bible and the ancient world. But because the banks of the Nile and the Tigris-Euphrates had proved friendlier territory than the shores of Galilee, I froze the Holy Land in time. In Jerusalem, the Second Temple still stood as Zerubbabel had rebuilt it, not yet refurbished by Herod the Great, because Herod hadn't been born yet. I was perfectly comfortable moving *back* in time: to the desolate city during the Babylonian Captivity; to Zion, David's capital; or even farther, to preconquest Salem, where the Canaanites still offered up sacrifices to Baal. But I refused to move forward. I told myself that the Jerusalem of Jesus' day was too "recent" to be of much interest. In truth, it was just too scary, a haunted city where a dead man may have walked the streets.

• • •

Very early in my Bible days, our family went to the Millstream Drive-In to see *War of the Worlds.* I had nightmares for weeks afterward. The scene that got to me, of course, was when the clergyman walks calmly toward the monster, praying as he goes. He gets zapped anyway. At that point I had seen enough and hid under a blanket for the rest of the movie.

Several months ago, *War of the Worlds* popped up on late-night TV. Safely embedded in adulthood, I thoroughly enjoyed it. It was as if I had reclaimed something. That's what my recent forays into the Gospels feel

like. It's exhilarating to revisit an old fear and to find myself unafraid—
to be bowled over by the sheer pleasure of a measured, grown-up response. As I work through John's Greek, it feels as if I'm returning to a
battlefield that has been transformed, after thirty-five years, into a pleasant meadow; here is beauty where I don't remember it being, where I
never expected to find it. There's danger here, too. Every so often an old
landmine turns up, as it did last week when I translated a passage in
which Jesus, preaching in the synagogue at Capernaum, proclaims that
whoever eats his flesh and drinks his blood will have eternal life. I remembered these red-type words as one of those ghostly spots that sent
me reeling as a kid. What I had forgotten, though, was that Jesus' followers found them ghostly, too. "Therefore, many of his disciples, upon hearing this, said: 'This is a hard saying; who can hear it?'"

I've since learned that entire theologies have been based on "hard say-
ings," some of which were attributed to Jesus years after the fact in order
to make his words conform to beliefs and liturgies that had developed
among early Christians. The speech about flesh and blood, for instance,
likely represents one of several retrojections of a primitive Eucharist. At
twelve or thirteen, I tried to pin down such words according to a simple
formula: were they true or were they false? Now deep into middle age, I've
learned that "truth" is usually more complicated than that. Nobody was
"lying" in that flesh-and-blood passage: the Johannine community was
merely expressing the belief that their central rite had been inaugurated
by their Lord. That's an understandable, human thing, something that a
young deist might have found useful had he known about it. But the whole
story is a human thing, isn't it? As a child I didn't know that a story can be
compelling without being literally true. I couldn't see that having more
questions than answers doesn't necessarily get you tossed into the fire.

This time around it strikes me that the Jesus story leaves ample room
for doubt, or at least discomfort, as one way to stay engaged with it, to
keep yourself in the mix. This, finally, might be what John's Greek is telling me with peculiar force. To be sure, the Gospels themselves present
their message in a believe-it-or-not manner, and that's certainly how most
of us first experienced them. But the choice of accepting or rejecting is
pretty reductive. The story and its claims are far too evocative to be treated like binary code, on or off, yes or no. Maybe it's more a matter of on

and off, yes *and* no. Sometimes you make the basket and sometimes you don't. Maybe I was never as good a Methodist as I was at twelve or thirteen on the basketball court behind Donnell Junior High. Such insight, though, would have been lost on me then. It was still lost on me in my mid-twenties, when I asked my dissertation advisor, a former minister with the Disciples of Christ, how smart, educated people could believe that the Resurrection actually happened. Couldn't they see that it was just a hoax or a fable, and didn't such knowledge shake their faith? "Well," he said, "whether or not it actually happened might be the least interesting thing about it."

It took the study of Greek to pound it into my head, but I finally understand what he meant. There's mystery here, and I'm feeling something of it, though in a mundane, distanced manner appropriate to the kind of person I am. Grammar, as it happens, is a little like history: checking tenses and matching subjects with verbs is a good buffer, a vehicle for keeping things manageable. Even though my youthful probings into the New Testament led to a dead end, people don't transform utterly when they grow up. I realize that reading the story in Greek is yet another homage to history, another attempt to return to first versions. This time, though, I'm not in such a hurry to pin things down. This time it's not the tale but the excitement of telling it—not the historical truth that the story might contain, but the imaginative possibilities that it opens up.

These ancient texts might not be leading me to the figure at the center of it all, as I once thought I was supposed to be led, but they are certainly giving me a sense of the wonder with which first-century believers spread the news. And who can blame them? This is a story about a man who rose from the dead. Even if I never believed it the way my grandmother did, its powerful mix of fear and hope makes it as fundamental to the human spirit as a story can be. Although there are a hundred logical reasons to dismiss it, I simply cannot put it down—in either sense of the phrase. After all, this is a mystery story, the first one I remember hearing. As a kid I assumed that you could investigate it and then you'd *know.* I didn't understand that the deepest mysteries are the ones that refuse to reveal their secrets, the ones that, once recovered, will not exhaust themselves even in the midst of midlife torpor. You may think that you've outgrown such things, but sooner or later you'll find yourself going back and confronting those old questions, like how to live and why we die, and the stories that first posed them to you. If those stories had any power over your childhood, an occasional twinge of nostalgia might make you wish that they were true. But then it will hit you—as it hit me somewhere in the Gospel of John—that their fascination does not hinge on whether they are true or false, but on their capacity to take you beyond the simple dichotomies of truth and falsity that you embraced as a child. You'll discover, to your considerable relief, that you can watch the whole movie and not look away. Of that, at least, I've got all the proof I need: the Bible tells me so.

Drummer Man

It's late afternoon on a hot Friday in early June, and I am sitting in a plaza in a close-in Maryland suburb of Washington, D.C. I'm working, without much energy, on a typical summer project for an English professor: a study of the funeral elegies of Puritan New England. I always write my scholarship in public places like this. Writing is lonely work even when your subject isn't seventeenth-century funerary poems, and it's a comfort to look up and see people going about their business.

A swing band is setting up for the weekly dance here in Bethesda Square. The musicians are adjusting their music stands, donning their outfits—loud Hawaiian shirts—and warming up. They have a familiar look about them, a hip goofiness: big guys with beatnik goatees and little guys with thick glasses and anachronistic, *American Bandstand* hair. In the midst of the beeps and honks and scales, I hear the drummer tuning his snare drum. I can't see him, but his tentative tapping tells me exactly what he's doing as he works his way around the rim, pausing to adjust a lug here and there with his drum key. From the rising pitch of the taps I can tell that he's "tuning up," tightening the drumhead and the snares stretched across the bottom. You do that when you're playing with a big group and you want the drum crisp enough to cut through a lot of noise. If this were a small combo he would be "tuning down," loosening the head and snares for a mushier sound.

By now a crowd has gathered, and the leader kicks things off with a bouncy rendition of "In the Mood." I collect my papers and wander over to watch the drummer. He is about my age, fiftyish, with thinning sandy hair. He might be new to this band, because he is keeping his eyes glued to the charts. New or not, he's a real pro, with a light foot on the bass drum and hi-hat afterbeats as regular as a clock. His accents on the snare are precisely where they should be, punching up section work from the brass. He has long since learned the secret of driving a big band: rushing the beat slightly. Good drummers constantly fight entropy. Most musicians tend to drag the beat, and a sluggish, lead-footed drummer only makes things worse.

This is tasteful, workmanlike drumming, the kind you *feel* more than hear, and at the band's first break I consider going up and telling him how good he is. In the end I decide against it. After all, he's just doing his job, and besides, I've always known that my appreciation of good drumming is borderline obsessive. What if I started babbling, unable to conceal a degree of enthusiasm that middle-aged guys are supposed to have outgrown? And what if the conversation took its inevitable turn and he asked, "Do you play?" I'd have to say "I used to," but that response would leave so much untold that it would feel like a lie.

. . .

There's a joke that band directors tell, and it goes like this: *God created the world in three days. On the first day He created singers and said that it was good. On the second day He created musicians and said that it was good. On the third day He created drummers and said, "Two out of three ain't bad."* I heard that joke a lot when I was in high school, always with a twinge of self-righteous indignation. After all, *I* was a drummer.

Until ninth grade I hadn't been much of anything except what grown-ups called "a nice young man," the kind who got paid for babysitting other kids only a year or two younger than I was. Parents were always pleased when I hung out with their sons, because they figured there would be no trouble. Naturally, I was embarrassed by this reputation, in part because it wasn't something I had set out to achieve. It seemed a pure product of my round, bland face. One look at me and you knew that I wasn't about to down a six-pack of low Stroh's and piss into your gas tank. Since grownups "knew" this, I figured I had no choice but to go along with it.

In ninth grade I decided to cultivate a cooler image and began neglecting my homework and making wisecracks in class. But I couldn't manage to get myself into any real trouble; instead of getting mad, my teachers just got concerned. It was unfair. Scott Carlson could tell the civics teacher to kiss his ass and get sent to detention, like a regular guy. Whenever I acted up, the teacher would look troubled and call my parents that night to set up a conference.

Mom and Dad were bewildered. How could their nice, bookish son be making Bs and Cs? James Dean was dead but not forgotten, and with all the talk about juvenile delinquency, they probably figured that midnight heroin runs to Cleveland were coming next. My father, an intuitive behavioralist, said he didn't give a damn *what* the problem was, as long as I fixed it: "Shape up this summer or there's going to be world news made in this house." My mother, a committed believer in Dr. Spock, took me to an adolescent psychologist in Toledo, forty-five miles away. I must not have posed much of a diagnostic challenge. The psychologist said I was acting up because I didn't have any interests that involved other people. The interests that I *did* have—Bible history and ancient Egypt, for instance—were all quirky, private things. Fifteen years later he probably would have said "get a life." He could work me into his schedule, but before my next session I had to come up with five school activities that I would be willing to try.

It was sad watching Mom fumble with her checkbook as she paid for the session, and on the drive home I promised to get involved in school activities like a normal kid. Scrambling for something concrete, I remembered that my older brother, now at college, had been in the marching band. Wasn't some of his drum stuff—a pair of marching sticks, a rubber drum pad, some old lesson books—still in the closet of the room we had shared? If I started taking drum lessons, could we cancel next week's appointment?

· · ·

My teacher was a jazz drummer named Bill Sims, who drove over from Lima on Thursday afternoons to give lessons in one of the soundproof booths at the back of Carter's Music Store. An immense black man in his early thirties, Bill had a goatee, an easy smile, and huge arms that made his hands look too small to be a drummer's hands. He was a passionate believer in solid foundations and meticulous technique. Don't get lazy;

maintain the correct grip, and turn those wrists until it hurts. No sloppy buzz rolls; keep those rolls clean and open, so you can hear every stroke. Learn to sight-read; don't play anything until you can count it out. Above all, get the fundamentals, which meant learning the twenty-six standard "rudiments" for the snare drum: the five-stroke roll, the flam-tap, the paradiddle, and all the rest.

I learned quickly, working through books 1 and 2 of *Haskell Harr's Method for Snare Drum* in six weeks. Then Bill started teaching me how to play a drum set, using a mock-up consisting of drum pads bolted together. He worked me through the basic rhythms: jazz, blues, swing, rock, country, polka, and Latin. Bill stressed "independence," the ability to play different rhythms simultaneously. This purposeful devolution of the body's inclination toward symmetry was just strange enough to be fun. Learning to play straight eighth notes with one hand and triplets with the other felt like unlearning how to walk.

I rapped out my exercises on my brother's rubber Gladstone pad and a practice "set" assembled from coffee cans, tin pie-plates, and imaginary foot pedals. Before long I developed a drummer's hands, with leathery calluses and thickened muscles in the joint between thumb and forefinger. All the practice kept me from noticing something else I was acquiring: a drummer's heart. I discovered *that* one day in mid-August. I was Bill's last student of the day, and Carter's had already closed when we finished our lessons. This time Bill took me to the front of the empty store, sat me down at one of the new drum sets on display, and ran me through some of the standard rhythms I had been learning. The tinks and clunks and thumps of the mock drums I'd been practicing on had not prepared me for the depth and range of the sounds I was getting from these real drums, these shimmering red swirl Slingerlands with shiny chrome hoops and genuine Avedis Zildjian cymbals.

Bill peeled the cellophane from a Count Basie album and placed the record carefully on the turntable of one of the display hi-fi's. Then he cranked up the volume and mouthed, "Swing it, man!" Astonished to find that I actually could, I swung it, man, meshing with "Night Train" as the late afternoon sunlight streamed through the storefront window.

· · ·

I left ninth grade and Donnell Junior High an amiable goof. When I entered tenth grade at Findlay Senior High, I was an amiable goof who could play the drums. I joined every musical activity available: marching band, concert band, orchestra, swing band, pep band, pit bands for school musicals. That Christmas I got my own drums, a used set of Ludwigs that Bill had spotted in the classifieds. The set was minimal but solid: a twenty-inch silver sparkle bass drum and one matching tom-tom, a high-hat with sixteen-inch cymbals, a single eighteen-inch ride cymbal, and a gleaming chrome-shell snare.

Drumming brought an immediate social payoff, especially after I joined a rock band and started playing at sock hops in the school cafeteria and at the local teen center. I learned, to my amazement, that even barely competent three-chord rock bands attracted groupies. I felt awkward when girls came up to talk to me during breaks, but it was a pleasant awkwardness for a change.

Now that I had a social identity I stopped acting up, to my parents' great relief. On a deeper level, though, the psychologist's plan to turn me into a more normal kid backfired. The fact was, drumming simply became my newest obsession. I pored over textbooks on orchestral percussion, studying the proper techniques for tympani, tambourine, wood blocks, cymbals, and the deceptively simple triangle. Important percussive controversies emerged at every turn. Should a triangle be struck on its inside surface or on the outside? Should the fulcrum for a tympani roll be the thumb and forefinger or the thumb and second finger? Is it acceptable to tune tympani with a pitch pipe, or should you be a purist and work from a single tuning fork? More questions emerged from those sock hops. Which were better: regular sticks or those new, metal-tipped models? Should the bass drum beater strike the drum slightly above center or slightly below? Should the snare be tuned up or down, crisp or mushy?

The deeper into drumming I went, the more I felt that something was wrong. I began to see that what I really wanted wasn't popularity but respect. Remember that joke about singers, musicians, and drummers? Drummers have always had a reputation as the dim bulbs of the music world. Imagine being in that row of guys—there weren't many girl drummers in those days—standing stiffly in the back of the orchestra, poised to pick up an object every so often and strike it. There you are, counting

121

rests for ten minutes and trying not to move your lips as you wait to execute a single "ping" on the triangle, which the conductor cues with the theatrical exaggeration of a man signaling a dog to sit up. By the time you finally hit that triangle, you'll *feel* like a dog sitting up.

Playing in the rock band brought more problems. Rock drummers in the sixties were expected to be either feral shit-kickers or dead-eyed zombies—icons, in either case, of blood-beat intuition. Charlie Watts had the proper look, but it's hard to achieve that look if you're pudgy and pasty faced, with Steve Allen glasses that keep slipping down your nose. I never figured out what to do with my face when I played rock. There I sat, a whirl of sticks and pedals—and a useless, balloonlike face at the center of it all. I had to check a natural impulse to glance around with a wide-eyed lucidity that just didn't go with the Stones' "Satisfaction." Forcing myself to stare at an arbitrary spot in the middle distance, I chewed gum in an attempt to keep my face safely occupied.

Then there were the drum solos. Convinced that drums were meant to be accompanying instruments, I always hoped to get through the night without having to assume sole responsibility for a gymful of sweaty teenagers jumping up and down. Sooner or later, though, some idiot would cup his hands and yell "Wipe Out!" and immediately the lead guitarist would launch into that mindless Surfaris hit, with its drone of monotonous sixteenth notes on the tom-toms. The crowd wanted the solo to sound just like the record, of course, and whenever I tried to make things interesting by syncopating the accents or slipping out of the old four/four throb, the dancers would buck and start like confused cattle and shoot wounded looks in my direction.

It seemed to me that only an exhibitionist could truly enjoy playing rock 'n' roll. But I wasn't drumming for glory; I didn't even like being *looked* at when I played. A junior scientist of percussion, I was a firm believer in taste and technique. My heroes were Brubeck's Joe Morello, light of touch and able to shift time signatures in a flash; that nameless, rock-steady drummer and ultimate sideman who backed James Brown; Ed Thigpen, whose subtle brushwork backed Oscar Peterson; even the oft-derided Ringo, whose simple beats and understated fills I defended as appropriately minimalist. I was convinced that Buddy Rich shamelessly overplayed, with every arrangement a drum solo thinly disguised as a song. Dino Danelli of the Young Rascals had excellent technique but stooped for the cheap thrill by twirling his sticks at almost every beat. The worst offender was Ginger Baker, who was just starting to hit it big—and loud—with Cream. Ginger Baker seemed the quintessential rock drummer, a fortissimo monster who abhorred even a split second's vacuum because he failed to grasp the power of silence. But rock is a repudiation of silence, and for no one more than a drummer wedged helplessly between screaming amplifiers. It was hard even to think with the fuzzy howl of a guitar boring into my head, my spine vibrating with the buzz of the electric bass.

. . .

Of course, a rock drummer shouldn't be *trying* to think, and that was my whole problem. The real cause of my discontent soon became clear: I was an embryonic jazz guy trapped in a rock 'n' roll world. The beat that came naturally to my head as I walked was not the staccato eighth notes of rock but an easy shuffle, the triplets and the dotted eighths and sixteenths of the standard "ride" rhythm of jazz. Rock's endless two and four on the snare just couldn't compare with the tasty, erratic tappings of a jazz drummer's left hand.

Fortunately for me, Findlay High had the Swinging Trojans, a seventeen-piece dance band led by assistant band director Dale Rivers. Although the band, like the school's sports teams, was named after history's first losers (students routinely acknowledged the more modern connotation by tossing condoms onto the basketball court to protest fouls called against our guys), the Swinging Trojans at least played my kind of music. What's more, Dale Rivers tried to create my kind of atmosphere, a jazzy space where even big, goofy kids could feel like hepcats.

A trombone player in his thirties with black, slicked-back hair, Mr. Rivers called every playing job a "gig," even PTA open houses and the Sadie Hawkins Dance. When a set went badly he called us "you people," like any other teacher, and spent the break alone outside, chain-smoking and gazing in exasperated silence at the stars. When a set went well, he called us "cats." Then we could call him "Dale" and join him during breaks for some jazz-guy talk about whether the piano was properly miked or which girl in the crowd was the sexiest. When we were "cats," Dale even let us bum cigarettes, glancing nervously around to make sure no adults saw him passing them out.

One night the Swinging Trojans played the prom at Mount Blanchard, Dale's old high school. While were setting up he chatted with his former teachers, his face bright red as he fumbled with the cardboard music stands. You *can* go home again, it seems, but the stakes of doing so surely get raised when the success of your homecoming hinges on the performance of seventeen rabbity kids. But we had done some extra rehearsing that week and were "cats" all night, outplaying ourselves as we worked through "Hawaiian War Chant," "Sing Sing Sing," "Stars Fell on Alabama," "My Funny Valentine," "String of Pearls," and everything else in our book with scarcely a blat or miscue.

The earnings of the Swinging Trojans were supposed to go toward new uniforms for the marching band. That night, though, Dale split up the money and gave each of us a share—twenty dollars, I think. He said he was breaking the rules, just this once, because he wanted to teach us an important lesson: a true cat always gets paid. I was making better money than that from rock jobs, but this was different. This was *jazz*. After we got back to town, a bunch of us stopped at the White Castle for bags of fifteen-cent hamburgers, sweet reward for budding jazzmen. I had trouble getting to sleep that night because "Take the A Train" kept running through my head. We had really wailed on that one.

• • •

I arrived on the threshold of the jazz world just as it was starting to shrink. Bill Sims soon moved to Toledo, where there were more playing jobs, and turned his students—a dozen kids whose ages ranged from six to fifteen—over to me. Between playing rock two or three nights a week and teaching on Saturday afternoons, I was saving decent money toward college. But the would-be jazz drummer will always play "Wild Thing" with a heavy heart.

One day Phil McKenna, the store manager at Carter's, got a call from Johnny James and the Crowns. They were looking for a drummer. I was so excited I could hardly call them back. The Crowns were the real thing: professional, adult musicians. I think they even had a listing under "Entertainment" in Findlay's Yellow Pages. When I finally called, Johnny

James said that their regular drummer had suddenly left town. They had two gigs that weekend and needed a replacement fast. Did I have reliable wheels? Would I be available weeknights, too? Did I have the "chops"— that is, could I play something besides rock 'n' roll?

My audition took place at Johnny James's apartment, upstairs from James's TV Sales and Repair on West Main Cross. The bass player couldn't make it, but the pianist, Eddie Plotz, was there, and of course so was Johnny James, who came upstairs after closing his shop and immediately asked me never to call him Johnny, which was "just for publicity purposes." Mrs. James brought John and Eddie beers and gave me a Coke. I couldn't stop staring at her. The first adult woman I had ever seen wearing blue jeans, she was beautiful in that spooky way of beatnik folksingers. After twenty minutes of playing a few bars from different kinds of songs, John announced that I would do. He wouldn't ordinarily use a sixteen-year-old drummer, but he was in a jam. Then we rehearsed in earnest, with John and Eddie running me through their trickier numbers, including their signature tune, "What a Difference a Day Makes," which they took into a weird, odd-time breakdown at the end. They closed their eyes and cocked their heads as we played, as if they were trying to concentrate on how I *sounded* rather than on how goofy I looked. I was grateful for that.

Afterward John went into a back room and returned with a silver sparkle tuxedo jacket, which he handed to me along with a phone number for the musician's union. He had been blackballed several years back for using a nonunion kid drummer and wasn't taking any chances. He also told me that I wasn't, under any circumstances, to drink on a job. The kid drummer had a rum and Coke perched on his floor tom-tom the night the union busted the Crowns. John had almost gone to jail, and escaped only by having the kid swear that it was Eddie's drink and not his. The next morning I called the American Federation of Musicians, Fostoria Local 121, and asked about auditioning for membership. A woman's tired-sounding voice told me that no audition was necessary; if I just sent a check for twenty-five dollars, my union card and a list of clubs to boycott would arrive by return mail.

John and Eddie were representatives of a dying breed: the small-town hipster. So was Bill Sims, with his Dizzy Gillespie goatee and his wide-eyed "Oh, Man!" So was Phil at the music store, who called everything a "gas," except when he was dealing with parents shopping for band instruments. The era of Jack Kerouac, John Coltrane, Jackson Pollock had pretty much ended in cultural centers like New York and San Francisco, but an ideal of hipness hung on at the margins, in little towns like mine where small battles against the squares were still being fought. It was a losing effort, and a sense of being in the wrong place at the wrong time made it hard for some small-town hipsters to stay sober. The guitar teacher at the store, a thin, tattooed guy in his late twenties with a classic duck's-ass haircut, said he had played with Johnny and the Hurricanes until they fired him for smoking pot. He was a jazz guy at heart, and if you remember Johnny and the Hurricanes—they put old chestnuts like "Red River Valley" and "Reveille" to a saxophone-and-guitar surfer beat—you might begrudge him the occasional toke. The hipster's drug of choice, however, was booze. Bill worried that he drank too much on jobs and kept talking about cutting back. The ex-Hurricane sometimes seemed mildly drunk even on Saturday afternoons at the store. I would soon learn that Eddie Plotz drank a lot too. This puzzled me; why would anyone who got paid to play music, especially jazz, ever need to get drunk?

John James, by contrast, was a jazzman in complete control. By day he was Mr. James who ran a TV repair shop, but by night he was Johnny James, a cat of the trumpet and saxophone who also sang, very occasionally, in a nondescript, lounge-guy voice. Somewhere in his late thirties, he was rail thin and pockmarked, with blond hair combed up and flipped in an Edd "Kookie" Byrnes wave. Cool in the way that rocket scientists had been cool a decade earlier, he wore thick black-rimmed glasses with a slight maroon tint. He could make wisecracks in an absolute deadpan, perfect for firing under-the-breath insults at audience members. Whenever we were playing something slow and corny, like "Laura" or the "Tennessee Waltz," he would turn away from the crowd and stick a finger down his throat. He had a collection of obscene titles with which he called up the songs he hated: "Nude River," "Nude Indigo," "Love Is a Long and Slender Thing," "I'm in the Nude for Love," "Fuck-a-Me Mucho." I thought he was the ultimate jazz guy, surviving in these soybean hinterlands on raw talent and thick hipster irony.

John was a solid musician, but I was amazed at how little he actually played in the course of some of our jobs. On a given night he either "had it" or he didn't. On off nights he would play just enough to get a song started—the first sixteen or thirty-two bars—and then drop out altogether, slackly "conducting" us with those straight jabs that Louis Prima used to make. On these nights he got moody, nervously blowing into his mouthpiece or licking his reed, endlessly moistening his lips and putting the horn to his face, only to lower it again as a signal for us to cover until the next time around. On good nights, though, he could hardly wait in each song to get through the obligatory setup, when he had to play the melody fairly straight, so he could take off. Whenever he finished a solid solo, he smiled thinly and cracked "Close enough for jazz," or "Where's that advance man from Decca?"

Eddie was a hipster, too. Around John's age, he taught piano and worked in his family's hardware store. Sometimes he drank too much on our dates. For the first few sets he was fine, but after a while his chording got sloppy and he started to play too loud. He would get a particular riff in his head and begin doing it to death, working it into every song and giggling until John told him to knock it off. The only unmarried Crown (besides the kid drummer, of course), Eddie occasionally tried to pick up women in the audience, always without success. John told me that Eddie once nearly cost the band a night's pay by walking up to a tall brunette and saying, "How would you like to fuck a really good piano player?" I believed it. Eddie cursed a lot, mostly when John told us that we had to stick to slow tunes because everybody was dancing.

Like a crisply tuned snare drum, the word "fuck" cuts through all manner of noise, and nobody wants to get kicked out of the Knights of Columbus Hall because the piano player has started saying it repeatedly. It usually took a fatherly frown from the bassist to lower Eddie's voice. Herman Klein was the moral center of the Crowns. In his mid-fifties, Herm worked at the Cooper Tire plant and was the father of a shy girl in my French class. He had only three fingers on his plucking hand, the result of an industrial accident years before, but the bony stubs got a rich, full sound even in the upper registers. John gave Herm lots of solos, and he could get fancy when he had to. Unlike flashy bass players, though, he never played a run when he should simply be "walking." His strong, steady beat freed my right foot from thumping out the old four/four on the bass drum; consequently, I could play it like a real instrument, saving it for accents and varying its dynamics. A drummer may make or break a band, but it's the bass player who makes or breaks a drummer.

We played a lot, and at all kinds of places: the K of C, the Armory, the Elks Club, the VFW Hall, the Fort Findlay Lounge, Petti's Alpine Village, the Dark Horse Tavern, the Findlay Country Club, and the Eye-75 Lounge at the Holiday Inn out at the bypass, where we had a standing gig one night a week. Sometimes we ventured out of town, to jobs in North Baltimore, Tiffin, Fremont, and Fostoria. Once we had a New Year's Eve gig beside an indoor pool at a yacht club up on Lake Erie, a five-hour job at double scale because of the holiday. That night, under the appreciative gaze of the corporate leadership of Sandusky, Ohio, I played the best drum solo of my life. Playing with the Crowns had changed my attitude toward drum solos. I now played them willingly, even eagerly. In a jazz solo you can explore any rhythm and texture that comes into your head, and you can even go soft, pulling the audience in with barely audible clicks and taps and hisses. I played a ten-minute solo that night, and for part of it the Crowns wandered off to the bathroom like rock bands did. When they returned and I cued them to fall in, the crowd applauded wildly. After John flashed me a thumbs-up and said something to Eddie, they kicked into "Drummer Man," the old Krupa standard.

With tips and double scale, I made over a hundred dollars that night. On the trip home I kept dozing off in Herm's station wagon, replaying tunes in my head and thinking that a guy might be perfectly happy doing this forever, living his life as Drummer Man. On good nights with the Crowns, the drumming felt almost entirely mental; I needed only to imagine rhythms and my hands and feet would simply *do* them. I got so I could guess where John was taking a solo and could echo the rhythms with which Eddie comped chords. I could anticipate Herm, too, calculating the perfect angle at which to ride the cymbal so that his bassline and my sizzle sounded like the bottom and top of a single instrument.

There is no way to describe what this felt like without sounding corny or religious, maybe both. When you're playing drums in a band that's clicking, you realize that music really *can* take you places where you wouldn't otherwise go. You can even forget, for the moment, that your skin isn't clearing up, that you are still awkward on dates, that your grades in English are slipping, and that you'll graduate from high school in six months, with more things to worry about than you think you'll be able to handle.

. . .

The inevitable slide from novelty to routine is one of life's first and most frequent lessons. The longer I played with the Crowns, the more clearly I saw that they had been forced into practical choices that most working musicians must sooner or later make. There were around fifty songs in their repertoire, plenty for even the longest jobs, and instead of working up anything new, they played the classic jazzman's game of ringing changes on the old tunes. After a few months even those changes sounded stale. I began to notice that John's wildest-sounding improvisations combined patterns that I had heard before—in some cases, many times before.

The Crowns were tired, partly from their day jobs but mostly from fighting a losing battle to retain a sense of hipness in a place that kept beating it down. They had caught the jazz bug, but it had doomed them to irrelevance, to connecting with no one in particular. They found themselves playing either for oldsters who wanted to foxtrot and waltz or for youngsters who wanted to twist and shout. The Crowns coped with the older crowd by indulging in musical in-jokes, like sticking two bars of "Malagueña" in the middle of "Sentimental Journey." With the young crowd, the people my age or a little older, they barely coped at all. Their closest approximation to rock 'n' roll was "Mississippi Mud," which Eddie played with a schmaltzy chop that was really sped-up ragtime. Herm fell in with a calypso rhythm, while John issued spitty blats on the trumpet or flatulent growls on the sax. I tried to merge Herm's calypso with Eddie's ragtime, but the young crowd always snickered. On such nights the Crowns did not do much talking during breaks. To be considered square, even by antijazz Luddites, was the worst fate that a small-town hipster could imagine. John tried to keep his dignity by calling the audience "bovines."

Then there were the drunks, for which Bill Sims's meticulous instruction had not prepared me. You've just turned seventeen. You're playing a class reunion, and a beefy, red-faced man in a 1957 letter jacket grabs one of your extra sticks and starts pounding on your tom-tom. You ask him to stop, but he tells you that he was a Marine and could kick your ass good. What do you do? Suppose a watery-eyed guy at a wedding reception leans into your ear and shouts that he was once a drummer and begs to sit in. What if you finally let him, only to watch in horror while he jabs the sticks downward as if he's *trying* to break a drumhead? Or what if a woman in her fifties, so drunk that she has been blowing kisses to John for the past half-hour, wobbles up to the stage and insists on hearing that idiotic "Mairzy Doats" song? What if John tells her that we don't know it and she looks right at you—the kid drummer—and orders *you* to play it? When you laugh and say that you can't play a melody on a set of drums, she narrows her eyes and says, "Fuck you!"

The older Crowns took this sort of thing in stride, but their kid drummer was made of softer stuff. Such incidents, though rare, made me darkly philosophical, and a truth slowly dawned on me: a drummer might have his moments of onstage transcendence, but the odds were good that he would wind up as a small-town hipster, struggling to practice an art he loved but constantly hitting the unyielding wall of business, as John did whenever a club owner or, more sadly, a bride's father tried to shortchange the band at the end of a gig. With a strange flatness in his voice, John patiently reviewed the fee and the number of hours of music that had been agreed upon. It was probably the same voice he used whenever someone complained about the repair bill on an old Philco.

Whoever said "Be careful what you wish for, because you might get it" must have played in a small jazz combo somewhere in the Midwest. My life as Drummer Man was petering out in disillusionment. By now I had gotten my college acceptance, and I was surprised at how natural the thought seemed when it hit me: drumming would probably end up being just "something I did in high school." When I graduated and had to make some real money for tuition at Kent State, I gave the Crowns three weeks' notice so I could take a summer job at the local Whirlpool plant. I brought my best student, a tall red-headed boy who had just turned sixteen, to a few of our gigs in order to break him in. Once he joined the union, he became John James's new kid drummer. I felt more than a little sad when I gave him the silver sparkle tux, but at least the end was amicable. The Crowns were grateful that I hadn't left them in a jam, and at my last job with them, a wedding reception at the Armory, John pulled me aside and gave me a hipster's blessing: "Get some college and get out of this hole, man."

• • •

Three years later I was back in Findlay for another summer at Whirlpool. Four students had just been killed at Kent State, and I was scared and depressed. I had spent the spring term at Southern Illinois University in an exchange program with Kent's anthropology department. The Carbondale campus shut down soon after the shootings, and I was home three weeks before Whirlpool was taking on summer help. My high school friends were either in the army or at schools that hadn't closed, and there was nothing to do.

One afternoon I stopped in at Carter's and found Phil leaning back in a swivel chair with his feet on his desk, reading the latest issue of *Downbeat*. I asked whether anyone from the old music crowd was still around. Most were gone—to college, to Cleveland, to Vietnam. When a well dressed man came in and started to tinkle the high keys of the grand piano at the front of the store, Phil straightened his tie. "This could make my month," he said with an exaggerated wink. As he approached the man at the piano, he suddenly turned back to me. "Hey, I almost forgot. Simsie's back in town. He's teaching up at the college."

When I arrived at the Arts Building at Findlay College I found Bill Sims in one of the practice rooms, dozing in a metal folding chair that faced an old upright piano. I rapped on the window, and as soon as he looked up I knew that something was wrong. He waved me in and tried to smile as I sat on the piano bench, but he looked terrible. His skin, formerly a rich brown, was yellow with greenish shadows. He slurred his words and seemed to have a hard time keeping his eyes open. I asked if he was okay, and he said he was just tired. He was teaching more and playing less because nobody wanted to hear jazz anymore. He asked how school was going and we made some small talk, but after a while he cleared his throat and said that he had to prepare for a percussion class. As I stood up he stayed in his chair and took my hand, looking up with a sleepy smile and slowly turning his head from side to side, like he did when he played. I said that we would have to get together and jam, like in the old days. He squeezed my hand and told me that I had to go because of his class.

The next week I started what would be my last gig. A woman from Columbus had called Phil at the store. Her name was Maria, and she needed a drummer to back her on Saturday nights. Although I hadn't played much since high school, I was desperate to fill up my time. Phil told me to show up at the Dark Horse Tavern at seven-thirty that Saturday with my set and a dark sport coat. The job paid thirty dollars a night plus tips, if Maria was willing to share them.

The Crowns had played the Dark Horse several times. It was one of those wood-paneled, vaguely Alpine restaurants that once could be found in every small midwestern town. Findlay College kids sometimes went there on dates, but the crowd mostly consisted of middle-aged office workers from Marathon Oil and Cooper Tires treating their wives to a special dinner. There was a salad bar, a novelty for Findlay in those days; the best-selling item was the prime rib, which always came medium when you ordered it rare. The lighting was a little dimmer than was comfortable for eating. Once your eyes got used to the darkness, you could make out a faded painting behind the bar: a black horse rearing up next to a beer stein.

Maria, a large woman in a spangly cocktail dress and an immense bluish wig, was sitting at the bar when I showed up. Like John James, she immediately asked how old I was and whether I was in the union. Not yet willing to relinquish my drumming identity completely, I had kept up my dues. As I handed her my card she said she didn't like working with kids and she didn't play rock 'n' roll. Could I deal with that? I would have to use brushes most of the time. Could I deal with *that?* Remembering this drill from my grilling by the Crowns, I told her that I loved brushes because you could play like shit and nobody would notice. She took a deep drag from her cigarette—it was in a holder—and glared at me. "Uh-huh."

When I said I had taken lessons from Bill Sims, her mouth dropped open in exaggerated surprise. "Honey, why didn't you *say* so? Bill Sims and me go way back." In fact they had played together in a small combo in Columbus when Bill was fresh out of high school. I told her how awful he had looked at the college, and she vowed to drive up early some Saturday to see him. Smiling now, she removed her cigarette from the

holder and stubbed it out. "Go set yourself up." As I got up from the bar-
stool she took my elbow. "Honey, I'm a sideman's dream. You back me
good, the tips go fifty-fifty. Maria never stiffed nobody." Within a half
hour she was easing into that old Crowns' favorite, "What a Difference
a Day Makes," in front of my steady—and very soft—brushwork.

I backed Maria every Saturday night that summer. Thirty years of
playing lounges had hardened her to the wearisome task of entertaining
people whose tastes were not hers. She knew how to work a room, how
to stack and pace a set, and how to make music that would not intrude
on table conversations. She had developed a sizable repertoire of snappy
patter that grew increasingly risqué as the evening wore on and the din-
ers were replaced by the drinkers. But Maria had drawn one uncrossable
line: whenever a Findlay College student requested a rock song, she
leaned into the mike and said, "I got a better idea, Honey—how about
some *music?*" In her sole concession to the times, she had worked up a
few of the softer Beatles numbers, which came out sounding more like
Errol Garner than Lennon/McCartney.

Between Saturday nights at the Dark Horse and the graveyard shift
at Whirlpool, I saw almost no one all summer, no mean feat in a close little place like Findlay. That was fine with me. After the Kent shootings,
what I needed more than anything else was the privacy to work things
out without being watched. That Toledo psychologist might not have approved, but I wanted to be invisible. A small spotlight shining down on
Maria threw everything around her into deep shadows. That's where I
sat, with only the outer edge of my ride cymbal protruding into the light.
I could not recall being in a safer place.

The only time anyone I knew came into the Dark Horse was one night
when I recognized one of my high school gym teachers, Tony Antolini,
making his unsteady way toward the bathroom. He was so drunk his eyes
weren't focused. As he passed the stage he stopped and peered into the
darkness behind the cymbal. "I know you, man," he said, "don't tell me."
After snapping his fingers a few times, he convinced himself that I was
an old fraternity brother from Bowling Green whose name he couldn't
remember. When it became clear that there was no telling him otherwise,
I finally said that he was right and that my name was Jerry Hamilton.
"That's right! Shit, man, I knew it!" He yelled back at a table of beefy guys

that this was his "frat brother Jerry here, playin' the fuckin' drums and everything." Maria smiled and said that these hick towns bring out the best in all of us. "Those dear hearts and gentle people, Honey."

· · ·

Not long after the "Tony A" episode, I read in the paper that Bill Sims had died of liver failure. That Saturday, when I told Maria the news, she marched to the bar and bought two shots of bourbon. Since I was still underage, I followed her as she carried the drinks through the kitchen and out the back door. Standing next to a dumpster in the golden light of early evening, we drank to Bill's memory. When we went back inside and were about to start the first set, she switched on her mike and announced that tonight's music would be dedicated to Bill Sims. Then she turned to me and whispered, "Give me a good drummer song." I thought for a few seconds. "Caravan?"

She nodded, and as we started into it the patrons—still mostly the dinner crowd—looked up from their conversations. As was proper for a song like "Caravan" and a farewell to Bill Sims, I had abandoned my brushes for sticks, which thumped on the tom-tom and filled the room with sounds that could not, by any stretch of the imagination, be called "dinner music." A few of the younger people on dates began calling for their checks. But several older, married-looking couples got up and started an easy jitterbug, urged on by Maria's patter but driven more deeply by an impulse that I never really understood until many years later, long after I had given up drumming for other things.

On the Pipeline

That my father never went to college was not unusual for Depression-era boys, especially farm boys from downstate Illinois. Like all his friends, he started working right out of high school, first as a postal clerk and then as a pipeliner at the local tank farm. After taking a job at a tank farm in Ohio, he did a stint in the navy. A few years after his discharge he took correspondence courses in accounting; in his late thirties he became an accountant in the home office of the oil company for which he had once laid pipe.

My father's rise from the field to the office was a real accomplishment, but to his children it seemed no big deal. Like most kids in the 1950s, we assumed that moving from blue collar to white was what was *supposed* to happen in America, the inevitable result of hard work and relentless self-improvement. We didn't understand that Dad's progress involved far more than exchanging hip-boots and coveralls for coat, tie, and company pin. Neither did he, fully, until eighteen years later, when a severe heart attack forced him to retire at fifty-five.

This is no parable, I'm happy to say, of another good man sacrificed on the altar of American Success. For one thing, my father is too complicated to be reduced to a Marxist icon. For another, it's hard to wrest edifying tragedy from a story that turned out well. Not only did he survive his illness, but he realized during his recovery how relieved he was to get out of that office. He missed working, of course. True to his GI Generation,

Evan "Sam" Hammond, circa 1950.

he saw idleness, enforced or otherwise, as a soft, unmanly beast to be beaten down at all cost. Once he began preparing friends' income taxes and manning an H & R Block booth part-time at a Sears store, he adjusted to retirement fairly well.

What my father did *not* miss about office life, however, was the stress of spending nearly two decades astride a fault line defined by social class, a line that made it difficult to reconcile who he was with who he had been. The class system—its power and rigidity—is not a comfortable topic among believers in the American Dream, as he surely was, and for that reason he tried to ignore the strain at work until the chest pains made it impossible to do so. Although he had a gift for numbers and was good at his job, his deep self-consciousness kept him from becoming adept at being *in* his job. After he moved into the office, his "little Dixie" dialect, with its nasal tones, dropped *g*s, and the occasional "ain't" and double negative, began to sound rough to his ears. He could not break the habit of speaking in the easygoing banter of working men sharing a task. He feared that his speech, so natural in the open air of the tank farm, sounded crude under the fluorescent lights of the accounting department.

There were other signs of a fault line that did not exist solely, or even chiefly, in his own mind. Hands-on experience with keeping the books proved no match for a formal education, as he learned after being passed over for several promotions in favor of "golden boys," his term for younger men with college degrees in management and accounting and, toward the end, the first wave of MBAs. When these men were hired or promoted, Dad was routinely asked to teach them their jobs.

My father was naive about office politics. Because he couldn't shake a deferential shyness in executive meetings, he would mention his ideas to coworkers, who sometimes took the credit and moved up the ladder. And when he filled in as "acting" supervisor while college men were being interviewed for the job, he was not comfortable with giving orders and evaluating employees. Although he was bitter at being passed over, he never enjoyed being anyone's boss. Once he was finally named permanent supervisor, a decade or so behind the usual career schedule, the stress became palpable: four years later he became too sick to work.

His three children followed his lead and became "professionals": a software designer, an elementary school teacher, a college literature professor. I'm the college teacher, and my father's resentment toward those "golden boys" makes me deeply ambivalent about what I do for a living. For one thing, I feel guilty about making more money for working less hard than he did. For another, my education and profession reinforced an estrangement from my father—the sense of separation that Richard Rodriguez describes so eloquently in *The Hunger of Memory*. Although this gulf was years in the making, it seemed unbridgeable by the time I entered graduate school. While I was writing my dissertation, Dad's constant, puzzled question was "How's that paper comin' along?" When I called home, ecstatic at having landed a tenure-track position despite the terrible academic job market of the late seventies, he asked how many hours a week I would be in the classroom. When I answered nine, he hesitated a moment. "You mean it's only part-time?"

I don't mean to patronize my father, who is in fact one of the most intelligent and reflective people I've ever known, in or out of the academy. It's just that we inhabited antithetical working worlds. Naiveté, as the people in my world say, is always positioned. Twain stated this idea in terms closer to Dad's world when he remarked that we're all ignorant—just about different things. I know something about seventeenth-century literature, but what do I know about depreciation and inventories, let alone arc-welding or pipe dope? I realize how easily things could have gone the other way. If my mother's inclinations hadn't led me to become what Dad called "a reader," I might have ended up knowing a great deal about steel-toed boots and heavy lifting—or worse, daily doses of office anxiety. Academic politics can be plenty vicious, but off campus, where there's no tenure, the stakes of winning or losing are far higher.

Until stress took him out of the race, my father survived and prospered in that unsheltered world, even to the point of changing the external markers of social class. Although he paid a steep price, he accomplished exactly what he had set out to do. Self-knowledge is always suspect, but given similar circumstances, I don't think I would have done as well.

· · ·

My father was perplexed by his youngest son, the one he teased because he was always reading. It was clear from the beginning that I was going to be more like my mother, a lover of poetry and opera, active in book clubs and politics. There was baseball, of course, but while Dad taught me to love the game, he couldn't do much to improve the skills of a chubby, nearsighted boy who kept flinching away from pitched balls. Still, play strengthened a tentative bond that work—the indispensable glue of Man-Talk—would eventually weaken.

For all our differences, our working lives have had one thing in common: I have never felt any more at ease in the academy than he did in the office. Outwardly I do all right, coping with the social demands of a profession in which the male ideal has always seemed to be, at least to me, some variation on David Niven. Inwardly, though, I realize that a son of my father cannot *be* David Niven—and in fact has no desire to. To a son of my father, an English department can seem like a strange place. Even after a quarter-century I'm not completely at home here, and all too often it shows.

I have never been able to shake the feeling that I'm somewhere I don't really belong—that I've been fooling people with this long-standing masquerade as an English professor. There is serious doubleness here. To the degree that I remain my father's son, I am not at ease with how I make my living. To the degree that I've managed to internalize a "professional" identity, I feel rootless, disturbingly alienated from large chunks of my past and, perhaps especially, from him.

We Americans like to see ourselves as self-created individuals, captains of our fate and all that. That's why confronting the impact on our lives of class origins is such a revelation—and not often a pleasant one. My father's legacy lives on in the fact that I have always had trouble thinking of what I do as a "career," a term that still strikes me as pretentious. I certainly enjoy teaching literature and feel lucky to be doing it, but I've always seen it as something I do to support myself. It is my "job." This attitude puts me at odds, from time to time, with colleagues for whom a professor's life, with its quasi-pastoral setting, seasonal rhythms, and genteel decorum, is more an extension of their upbringing than a break with it.

Like my father, I don't talk like most of my coworkers, and like him, I let it bother me. I know that colleagues don't always find me a comfortable presence. My jokes are sometimes too raw and are usually aimed at targets that academics don't find funny, like professional self-importance and the sanctity of "the work." I cannot pay the usual deference to creative "genius," whether in a Norton anthology or a visiting poet; I don't see literature as a religion or teaching it as a moral mission; I distrust theoretical dogmatisms and thus can't get fashionably angry at people whose scholarship differs from mine; my remarks in meetings often sound deflating and cynical; I sometimes seem irreverent toward "the profession" and perhaps stubbornly uncommitted to it. Most of all, I cannot tolerate the pretentiousness that constitutes our chief occupational hazard, especially when it gets directed my way. Whenever someone starts doing David Niven to me, I find myself exaggerating my midwestern accent, snapping off a few working-class locutions and leaning in for the reaction. I know it sounds petty, but if I don't do this I feel like I'm being erased.

· · ·

When I was in college, reading books and talking about them seemed like soft work compared to my father's. I looked forward to summer jobs in part because they felt like atonement for the good life I was living at school. These jobs kept alive my increasingly tenuous connection with my father, because they took place in his world, a demanding realm of problems and solutions and the need to get along. It's a world that's still out there, and according to its rules, reading for pleasure—and certainly reading "critically"—is a form of malingering, an indulgence of people with too much time on their hands. It has become fashionable for those of us who inhabit English departments to lament the elitist underpinnings of "literature" as a set of practices performed by and supportive of the leisure class. Many of us salve our consciences by doing "political" criticism, but only the narrowest ideologue sees such work as sufficient payback for the soft lives we lead, whether we teach Milton or Marxism or both. No matter how radical we think we are, the continuing, unstated assumption of *free time*—the sheer leisure to read and think—makes possible virtually everything we do. Our relative isolation from pressures in the larger society makes it easy to forget this. In our annual merit reports we say we're working hard, and we cite progress on this or that manuscript and new class preparations to prove it. But from the perspective of most Americans, we're hardly working.

One summer job put me in touch with my father's roots in the most literal sense possible. After two summers working at the Whirlpool plant in our small Ohio town, I wanted to do something different, preferably out of town. Most of my high school friends had moved on, and I didn't want to be the last guy in the old crowd to be still hanging around. Dad came up with a solution. He pulled some strings and got me a job at the Illinois tank farm where he had started out nearly twenty-five years before. At first I felt sheepish about taking a job that my father had lined up for me; wasn't I able to make my own way *yet?* After a few weeks of indecision, Whirlpool's deadline for signing up came and went. I had no choice but to leave for Illinois.

Thus it was that in the summer of 1969 I actually *did* know something about arc-welding and pipe dope. My grandfather—Dad's dad—still lived in the small town where the tank farm was located, and I arranged to stay with him in his run-down, shingled bungalow. I took Sunday dinners with my uncle Haven and his family, who lived down the street. Although I didn't know anyone else in town, it soon became apparent that everyone knew *me*. All that summer I was stopped by strangers: "You're Evan's boy, aren't you?" I felt as if I had entered a Living Museum of Dad's past. While Americans first walked on the moon, I was confronting the ghost of my father's younger self.

I soon learned that Dad had prospered on the pipeline. On my first day at work, the tank farm supervisor told me how pleased he was to meet Sam's boy: "We always knew Sammy was going places." My father wasn't "Evan" to the pipeliners. They had called him "Singin' Sam," later just "Sam" or "Sammy," because he liked to sing while he worked. Consequently, the older workers called me "Little Sammy," then just "Sammy" or "Sam." At first, an adolescent concern with identity made me resent this. But I soon realized that the pipeliners, like the townspeople, needed to *place* me—and once they did, there was no getting around it. They had done the same thing, after all, to my father: "Sam" wasn't his name, either.

It's hard to describe the unsettling oscillation between strangeness and familiarity, between fitting in and *not* fitting in, that I felt on the pipeline. Because of my father I was immediately accepted by the older workers. The other college boys' fathers were high-level executives, and it was a novelty to have the son of a former pipeliner coming on for the summer. I suspect that the "lifers," as we called them, saw me as a democratic token—living proof, like my father, that the American Dream was alive and kicking. But even though it pleased them that Sammy's boy was in college, I was still summer help, and they treated me with the bemused tolerance that they directed toward all the kids who were just passing through. Squeezed into a liminal position as part "regular guy" and part "college boy," I found myself mediating between the lifers and the students, cracking jokes to ease tense moments, calming down the other kids after a savage bawling-out from the boss, and convincing the lifers that the peace-sign decals we pasted on our hard hats weren't anything to get worked up about.

There were two crews of about ten workers each, including the college help. The summer hires almost doubled the staff; we were needed because summer was when the bulk of the maintenance and construction work for the whole year was scheduled. There were five lifers in my crew: Al, Ira,

Tommy, Bob, and Dave. Al Lawrence, a small, sun-dried man who was fifty-five but looked ten years older, was our foreman. Al, who had worked with my father after the war, looked like a mummy in a khaki work uniform and a wide-brimmed straw hat. He could curse like nobody I had ever heard; in Al-Speak, "fuckin'" became a free-floating linguistic catch-all capable of assuming every grammatical function conceivable. As Al saw it, college boys were bosses-in-embryo who needed to be brought down a peg or two, and he used language to shock us out of our privileged skins. He routinely addressed us as "you girls," sometimes with absurd results. "Any of you girls man enough to fuck that?" he'd ask, pointing to a section of pipe two feet in diameter. At first we just laughed nervously, but it soon became clear that Al wanted a reaction—that he expected us to give as good as we got. Once we caught on, most of us enjoyed trying to out-do him. "I'm man enough, Al, but I'm afraid I'd get stuck and *you'd* try to free me with your mouth." If you had a good comeback like that—and on the pipeline, that *was* a good comeback—Al would walk away smiling and lay off of you for a day or two. Another of Al's tricks was to launch into graphic descriptions of cunnilingus with "the wife" while we ate lunch. You could see his eyes twinkle as he probed his mind for more and better images: how would these pampered boys with soft hands react to *this?*

Nowadays, of course, we would be seeing Al in court—but this was a different era. Today we wouldn't hesitate to define Al's speech as sexual harassment or employee abuse and trundle him off to a workshop before the end of the shift. In that time and place, however, his profanity seemed to hold a different and more obvious meaning as thinly veiled class warfare, social resentment recast as workplace fun. Al wanted to show that he was someone to reckon with, even for a bunch of college boys headed for easy lives and big money. He was merciless whenever we messed up, cursing and shaking his fist in our soft, sullen faces. With me it was worse, because his anger was mingled with genuine puzzlement. How could Sammy's boy forget something as simple as strapping the ice-water canister to the back of the truck that morning? In the old days Sammy showed no fear; why was Sammy's boy so rabbity as he inched the backhoe up ramps onto a truck-bed?

During one of Al's lunchtime sex narratives, a tall, serious boy who was studying at Eastern Illinois University to be a minister—we all called him "Preacher"—announced to Al that he didn't "appreciate that kind of language." Al's reaction said it all. "You fuckin' pussy!" he roared, "Did Jesus make you better than me?" After that, Al's verbal routines grew even more elaborate, and a few days later I witnessed what people in my working world would call the full power of discourse: during one of Al's stories, Preacher threw up in his "Jesus Saves" lunch bucket. Preacher had apparently run out of other cheeks to turn, and after washing his face, he stalked out of the bathroom with a balled-up towel and hurled it straight at Al's head. Then, in a quiet but shaky voice he said, "I'm gonna pray for you, you Nazi weasel." What kind of man was hiding behind Al's profanity? We never knew for sure, though there were hints—and we saw one now. After dodging the towel, Al rose dramatically from his chair, apologized to Preacher, and shook his hand. From then on, the lunchroom stories stopped whenever Preacher was around.

There were other signs that Al's verbal savagery concealed a soft heart. Whenever he yelled at one of us for screwing up, he would wait ten or fifteen minutes and then describe something boneheaded that he had done when *he* was just starting out. Obsessive about seeing that we took water and salt tablets, he got furious whenever he saw a college kid doing one of the more dangerous jobs: "Get that girl out of there!" When a student cut his hand on a piece of sheet metal, Al drove him to the emergency room in Marshall, thirteen miles away. And one Saturday night late in the summer, I received a private revelation of the hidden Al when I ran into him and his wife at the local county fair, the only time I ever saw him away from the tank farm. Dressed in a crisp white shirt and a string tie, he introduced me, very stiffly, to his wife as "Sammy's boy." After some awkward small talk he said, "Well, I don't guess you want to waste time visiting with us. The fair's a great place for you young people." Astounded, I watched as Mr. and Mrs. Albert Lawrence made their way, arm in arm, toward the Baptist Church food tent.

One of the backhoe operators, a dark-haired man in his late thirties who looked like the young Nixon, was the crew's prima donna. He wouldn't answer to any of the college boys unless we addressed him as "Ira T. Williams, World's Greatest Heavy Equipment Operator." If we omitted even the *T* he would gaze at the sky or across the fields, pretending not to hear. Although Ira didn't work very hard, he was always recounting Herculean

143

feats he had performed in the old days, before his back stiffened up on him. His heroics had saved countless lives and spared entire landscapes from gas-fed fires—or so he said. Like my father, Ira had plenty of ambition, but because he didn't have the energy to go with it, he was always trying to look good without breaking a sweat. What was endearing about him, though, was the fact that his tactics weren't terribly subtle. One steamy afternoon I was hip-deep in an undrained hole, shoveling out muck so the welder could get started on the exposed joint. Ira sat nearby in the shade of the backhoe, absently watching me dig as he sipped from a bottle of RC Cola and wondered aloud why the Cubs had allowed Ron Santo to get so fat. After fifteen or twenty minutes he suddenly stood up, jumped into the hole, and handed me the near-empty bottle. Grabbing the shovel, he said "Get out of this shit and finish the pop, Sammy. You're workin' too hard here." Touched by Ira's generosity, I climbed out—only to see some bosses from the office approaching in a company car. As the bosses cruised by, Ira straightened up, mopped his brow, and flashed them a wide grin and a thumbs-up. Like all his tricks, though, this one probably backfired. I could imagine the executives' response: "Can't that damn-fool Ira get those college boys to do his digging for him?"

Our welder was Tommy, a thin man, about thirty, who wore his baseball cap backward to accommodate his welder's mask. He was what midwesterners call "salt of the earth," as honest as Ira was shifty. A devout Christian, he would quietly walk out of the lunchroom whenever Al began one of his sex-act narratives. Even at moments when anyone human would swear—when a pipe pinched his thumb or a spark got under his mask—his strongest phrase was a childish euphemism, the cussword of a good Baptist: "Slung-in-a-ditch!" Unlike the other lifers, who would sometimes let us screw up a job so we'd look dumb and they could have a laugh, Tommy always explained things fully and patiently. He was pleasant and easygoing but took immense pride in his welding and was fussy about anything connected with it, insisting that the joint be brushed beforehand to a particular shine; that the hole be sufficiently wide for him to assume the same crouch every time; that the hole be drained dry but not too dry, so there would be moist clay to scoop up if he got burnt; that the plywood platform on which he knelt be perfectly level; that we slap the welding bits into his glove in precisely the right position and with just enough firmness for him to feel them without looking up. Tommy never got snappish when he explained his requirements. Knowing how demanding he was, he defended his methodical ways by constantly saying, "If something's worth doing, it's worth doing well." Everyone always mouthed the words in unison with him.

Bob, the other backhoe operator, was a plump man in his fifties with a round, creased face and a silvery brush-cut that made him look like an old Marine. He remembered my father and was always telling me what a good worker Dad had been. Bob talked about his wife and kids a lot and showed all the college boys their pictures within our first few weeks there. As it turned out, Bob actually *was* an old Marine, and the political turmoil of the late sixties drove a wedge even deeper than usual between a lifer and the summer help. Obsessed with defending the war in Vietnam, he was the chief complainer about those peace signs on our hard hats. Whenever he pulled me aside to talk politics, he appealed to the common ground my father gave us. "I know one thing," he'd say, "I'll bet Big Sam didn't raise you to go along with all this flag-burning shit." Out of affection for my father, Bob felt responsible for me—and he was on me a lot. One day when I couldn't take it any more, I told him a hard truth: Big Sam was against the war, too. It almost broke Bob's heart to hear that, and he didn't say much to me for the next few weeks.

Bob's broader mission, however, was not deterred. He was always telling us what it would be like to "live under communism"—and the first thing to go, he always said, would be those scraggly-ass hippy beards. He brought in statistics, newspaper clippings, and pro-war editorials to pass around at lunch. Gradually, though, we stopped taking the bait. Bob was patient with our screw-ups, easy with a laugh, and generous with breaks when he supervised us. It was painful to watch his face redden as he got so worked up that he couldn't eat the bologna sandwiches his wife had packed. It took a blow-up from Al to make the war off-limits for lunchroom conversation. Bob was going over the Domino Theory one more time, to a roomful of groans, when Al finally snapped. "Jesus Christ!" he shouted, "You pussies ain't gonna end the fuckin' war on a fuckin' tank farm!"

After that, the Generation Gap found more limited expression—in music. Heated debates over whether to play country or rock on Ira's transistor radio finally made Al tell him to leave it at home. But the Music

Wars continued whenever we went out on road trips to fix leaks. We all stopped and ate together, usually at places with jukeboxes, and as soon as we went inside the college kids would shove in our dimes to rack up a solid hour of Led Zeppelin, Hendrix, or Iron Butterfly. Al, Bob, and Ira always tried to get to the machine first so they could load it up with Sinatra, Al Martino, or worse, Merle Haggard. One morning at five o'clock, as we groggily assembled for breakfast, I made it to the jukebox first. The lifers groaned, especially Bob, who announced that he couldn't face his eggs at this hour of the day with that hippy crap blaring. Still feeling bad about our last Vietnam conversation, I had an idea. Hamming it up to the cheers of the other students, I theatrically pushed in my dime, pressed some buttons, and sat down next to Bob at the counter. "Aw damn," he muttered as he pushed the menu away. Then my selection started up: "Cab Driver," by the Mills Brothers. As the song's goofy, shuffly beat began to fill the restaurant, Bob slowly shook his head and grinned. "The kid got me good that time!" he yelled to the other lifers. "That's Sammy's boy!"

· · ·

Well, I *was* Sammy's boy—and still am, although I grew up to become something else as well. The fact that I'm now a college professor makes it tellingly hard to avoid looking down when I'm just trying to look back. In describing Al, Ira, Tommy, and Bob, I am uncomfortably aware that the results are caricature, like those sketches in seventeenth-century character books: the Crude Man, the Sneaky Man, the Careful Man, the Patriotic Man, labels imposed nearly thirty years later by a middle-aged academic who went on to inhabit another world. But they also describe roles that the pipeliners themselves embraced, playing them to the hilt because they helped the day go by and because they gave order to the workplace. Everyone, in other words, was at home on the pipeline—even Ira, who sometimes joked about his get-ahead schemes. The fifth lifer, though, was definitely *not* at home on the pipeline. He would not have been at home anywhere, and the reason was a war that would not go away just because of Al's lunchroom fit.

Dave Hochstettler—everyone called him Crazy Dave—was a Vietnam vet, and only two or three years older than us college boys. Whatever he had actually seen and done during his tour—and his wild stories made it impossible to tell what was real and what wasn't—he dealt with it by embracing it with manic glee, absorbing it into tough talk and a dangerous presence that kept everyone off balance. Whenever Bob ranted about the war, he turned to Crazy Dave for support. "This man was there, boys," Bob would say. "He'll tell you all about it." But Dave had no interest in debating politics. He'd just issue a grunt or a "Fucking-A" and keep eating his lunch. For him, the war wasn't something to argue about. It was simply *there,* like the sky or the trees or the welding truck.

Whenever the really dangerous jobs came up, Crazy Dave threw himself into the middle of them. He hopped onto huge sections of pipe to steady them as cranes lowered them in place; he waded into unknown currents without a safety line to rake oil spills downstream with a two-by-four; he crept backhoes the half-mile down U.S. 40 to the motor pool as tractor-trailers blew by just inches away. We all knew that Crazy Dave was trying to prove something, but we couldn't figure out what. We knew only that he worked in open defiance of the code of the crew. In contrast to the languid rhythms of the workday, Dave was all staccato: quick movements, violent speech, sudden appearances at moments of real work and aggressive leaps into the center of it. Nobody could relax around him, and he seemed to like it that way. Every so often he would come up to someone, lifer and college boy alike, and proclaim out of the blue: "I could shut down your kidneys with two blows." The lifers didn't say much to Dave and avoided working with him whenever possible. He was a hard worker but a scary one, the kind of guy who could get you hurt—who would say "fuck this" because sweat was in his eyes and suddenly let go of his end of a two-hundred-pound section of pipe.

One day Al told Dave to grab one of the "girls" and take a truck back to the scrap yard to find a section of pipe suitable for a repair job. Dave pointed to me—"You're up, Slick!"—and told me to climb in. The scrap yard lay hidden from view, across a field and behind some trees in the rear corner of the tank farm. "This is good duty," Dave said as he gunned the flat-bed down the dusty road. "Pure R 'n' R for an hour at least." When we got to the yard he shut off the truck, pulled out a bag of grass, and rolled a joint. I didn't want to seem unsociable but declined when he passed it to me. After a while I started to get nervous. Won't Al get mad if we take too long? Dave told me to shut up or I'd break his mood. Then he started to talk: about this chicken-shit job and how things weren't fun anymore—how everything had gone downhill since his discharge and how he was thinking of reenlisting. "I know the ropes now, man," he said, "I'd be hell on fucking wheels."

Then he grew quiet, and after a few minutes he started to cry. We sat in silence until I finally mumbled something about how things usually have a way of working out. I have always regretted that I couldn't come up with something more helpful than that. After several minutes I climbed out of the truck and started looking for a section of pipe that was the size we needed. When I found it and shouted toward the truck, Dave came over without a word and helped me carry it back and load it up. As we drove back he said only one thing: "You tell anyone about this, I'll rip out your fucking windpipe. I know how to do it, too." Not long after I returned to school, Dad heard through the company grapevine that Dave had gotten into a shouting match with Al and quit his job. By Christmas rumor had it that he was on his way back to Vietnam.

Gossip is every bit as common on the pipeline as in a faculty lounge, and it's hard not to get caught up in it. What went on in Dave's head was a favorite topic of hushed conversations, and the scrap yard incident had given me something I could add. But I felt an uneasy mix of fear and loyalty, and I did not betray him. News travels fast when there's nothing to do but work and talk, and after a few days Dave knew I hadn't told. He never acted crazy with me again for the rest of the summer. He didn't talk to me that much either, but when he did, he talked reasonably and quietly about everyday things. He stayed his old crazy self with the other guys, threatening to punch them out and challenging them to kick-boxing matches or games of chicken with a lit cigarette between bare arms. Now, though, whenever he acted up he would look at me and wink.

• • •

Most people who have never done manual labor imagine it in starkly cinematic terms, a faceless movement of arms, legs, and backs, silent except for the occasional grunt. Manual labor on a tank farm, at least, is not like that at all. The fact is, a tank farm is a fairly pleasant place most of the time. At worst, there would usually be one really hard or nasty job per day— one leaden thing to lift or one vile thing to clean. It wasn't always you who had to do it either, and if it *was* you, by unspoken rule you were "covered" and could coast for the rest of the shift. Like football, pipelining consisted of lots of standing around punctuated by a few moments of agony. Every task required a huge temporal buffer. There was the task itself, which was performed quickly and wordlessly. But there was also all this other time spent figuring out the best way to do the task, gathering tools for the task, waiting for parts or extra guys needed for the task, cleaning up after the task, assessing how the task had gone, and debating what would have made the task go better. Then came the wait, usually a generous one, for instructions on what to do next, along with the inevitable discussion about whether it was getting too close to quitting time to start something new.

All this downtime was filled with unhurried, continuous talk—episodic, unfocused, playful. There were stories about long-dead pipeliners and long-done jobs; speculations about whether there would be new welding equipment, and when; arguments over how long the new welding equipment had been on order; accounts, with spirited commentary, of items seen in the papers or on the news; discussions of who had been on *Hee-Haw* that weekend and whether they'd been any good; guesses about where the economy was going and doubts whether the company "suits" had the brains to handle things; assorted human stories of infidelity, poker hands, fistfights, gas explosions, close calls, and—in Tommy's case—religious conversion. Al, Ira, and Crazy Dave augmented these topics with endless talk about sex, talk so vivid and animated that I felt sleazy just hearing it. They would talk about things they had done with women, things they would like to do with women, things they *wouldn't* do with women under any circumstances. The timing of this talk was all off, though, as I found out on our first road trip. When we were in the field, Al, Ira, and Dave couldn't say enough about the sexual feats they would perform if given the opportunity. But at the end of the workday, as we ate dinner in a motel bar just outside Indianapolis, freshly showered and changed, a hundred miles from wives and girlfriends and with a free evening before us, all they could talk about was how tough it had been to plug that leak today and whether we could finish the clean-up tomorrow.

Occasionally the talk got serious. Aside from Bob's war debates, the serious talk happened only in private conversations, carried on in quiet voices so nobody would overhear. These talks revealed that while the pipeliners felt at home in their work, they knew that it was an imperfect home. Al and Bob, in particular, could see the limits of their lives. They understood the lengths to which they went in order to keep those limits at bay—to keep things moving and to avoid boredom.

All the lifers, even Dave, talked soberly about the value of an education and how they wished they had gotten better ones. Sometimes they would ask a kid what subject he was studying and what he planned to do with it. These were uneasy conversations, because they underscored the fact that one talker was going somewhere and the other wasn't. For me there was an added discomfort: these talks made it clear that if I didn't feel completely at home studying literature, I wasn't at home on the pipeline either. Most of the kids were studying business or engineering, subjects that offered clear witness to educational opportunity being used wisely. Even becoming a minister made sense to the pipeliners, though it wasn't for them. If Preacher seemed a bit stiff—well, ministers were like that, weren't they? But when the lifers learned that Sammy's boy was majoring in anthropology and English, they were genuinely confused. I told them I hoped to teach literature someday, but that didn't do much to clear things up. Their high school English teachers didn't include any big, goofy guys with beards. Teaching English was something that women did, and if a man did it he must be "that way," as Al quietly said as he flapped his wrist up and down, conveying the idea as politely as he knew how.

Maybe I should have gotten angry at the stereotyping, but I didn't. After all, the lifers were only drawing on what they knew, as my father had done when he teased his Reading Son by announcing that our "repast" would be ready at six, or when he got up from watching a Tigers game and said that he had to perform some "ablutions." For him in the late 1950s, as for the pipeliners a decade later, an English teacher was someone who looked down on you if you used contractions or didn't sound vaguely British when you talked. Ira kept doing a barely competent English accent for several days after learning what my career plans were. "Wroite me a pohem, Sammy." That might sound like a cruel taunt, but it was actually pretty funny. Even at nineteen I understood that not fitting in isn't *all* the stuff of Young Werther tragedy—an insight that I still try to keep in mind.

And here, with Ira's bad Cockney, is where this rambling circle begins to close. We're all on one pipeline or another. Or as the people in my work-

150

ing world say, we are all socially constructed, acting out templates that feel comfortable to us. But sometimes we crave change, and if we pursue it we discover that the old stories we have lived by simply don't fit our lives anymore. Of course, that doesn't make those stories easy to give up. Raised on a fault line of my own, a line halfway between my father's world and the world of books, I still cannot convince myself that my work is entirely appropriate for who I am. Clearly, I'm my father's son in feeling that way. But like Dad, I wasn't at home on the pipeline either. My father also knows that liminality is seldom fun—that when you make choices, you have to live with the inner fissures they create. When he left the security of the tank farm, Dad chose a life of unease, one in which he would have to guess the answers to questions that most of his coworkers didn't even need to ask. In a strange way his having left—and my belated recognition, in the summer of 1969, of how big a step that was—gave me permission to make my own break from *him* and to enter a realm where I would have to deal with my own discomfort.

. . .

Six months after I returned from Illinois, my father had his heart attack: his working life ended just when I had seen how it began. Although my summer on the pipeline reinforced the rightness of continuing down my mother's path, a "reader's" path, it also showed me how much my father had done to let me follow it. I now understood how much he had grown in his life—how far he had gone in order to reach the point where he could have a Reading Son without feeling threatened.

When Dad got off the pipeline, he entered a world of strange new possibilities: that a son of his would spend most of his allowance in used-book stores; that a son of his would get cut from Little League and feel mostly relief; or much later, that a son of his would enter a working world in which a father's help, a lifetime of hard-won lessons, would be of little use. Dad didn't fully realize what was happening to him in the accounting department until he left it. But he always knew that his search for a better life carried with it the risk that his son might grow into a stranger. Dad resented the "golden boys" who brought their college degrees into the office, but that resentment did not keep him from allowing one of them to grow up under his roof and to feel loved there.

151

My father still believes in the American Dream. I cannot look at his life—or, to a far less dramatic degree, at mine—and not believe in it too. After retiring he kept chasing that dream, though the old lust for hard work and self-improvement took a turn that required a final step—a giant one—away from the tank farm: Dad began to indulge a growing habit of reading, and reading for fun. My father is still too much himself to waste his time on novels and other things that aren't "true." Poetry, his old buddy Al would be relieved to hear, leaves him utterly cold. Mostly Dad reads popular histories and biographies, big books that bravely tell sweeping, complicated stories in the classic manner of another era: Toynbee, Tuchman, Morison, Bishop, the Durants. Spending his afternoons absorbed in Lincoln's presidency or the Black Plague or the landing at Normandy, he pursues a pleasure that once belonged mainly to his book-club wife and nearsighted son.

My father has come to see reading as a fitting reward for retirees. It's hard for him to imagine it as somebody's work—that someone could actually get paid to read books and talk about them. To him, that's also beginning to sound like a dream, and he admits that he envies such a person, that he envies me. When I visit my parents and ask Dad what he's been reading lately, I am aware of yet another doubleness, this time in him. As he tells me what he has learned about Alexander the Great, Disraeli, or Eisenhower, it always occurs to me—and always with a shock—that my father would have loved being a college professor. Unlike me, he would have shunned the impracticalities of literature in favor of the more solid lessons of history. Like me, though, he would have been a poor navigator through the murkier waters of an academic career: the departmental politics, the coded talk in committee meetings, the forced niceties and sometimes unbearable pretensions. The career might even have done him in. Still, he would have been good at the job.

Six Flags Over Findlay

My brother, my sister, and I are heading south on U.S. 68 in northwest Ohio, with Dave at the wheel of Sue's Ford Aerostar. Sue sits in the back seat, staring glumly out at the fields as she sips an oversized Diet Coke. I'm up front, idly watching the utility poles as they click by. Suddenly the engine begins to sputter, and as the van spurts and lurches, Dave pulls onto the shoulder of high grass and brings us to a stop. He turns the key a few times, but the problem is obvious.

You don't want to run out of gas late in the afternoon on the day after Thanksgiving in the flattest, loneliest part of Ohio. We climb out into a sharp wind whipping across wheat stubble stretching away for miles in all directions and gaze stupidly around as if we're expecting to spot a Sohio sign among the distant barns. Naturally, the old highway is empty. The serious travelers on the nearby interstate have abandoned the road to three grown children in a van, sated nostalgists who chose the "scenic route" for a gentler reentry into the present.

Some things—and families are high on the list—never change. Always the wisecracking kid of this group, I comment that the barn with the "Mail Pouch" tobacco sign off to the right has considerably less appeal now that it's no longer zipping by on our cruise back to civilization. My brother and sister do not warm to the joke. "I don't believe this," Sue mutters as she pours ice cubes into the weeds.

Guessing that Arlington can't be more than three or four miles ahead, we decide that I will hitchhike there to seek a can of gas while Dave and

Sue stay with the van. After ten minutes with no cars in sight, I give up on hitchhiking and start down the road humming a tune for a walking rhythm. The last time I look back, the van is a dot on the horizon.

. . .

Everyone knows that you can't go home again, but that never stops a few gauzy fools from trying. The Hammond children, now in our fifties, attempted our own nostalgic pilgrimage during a recent Thanksgiving gathering in Columbus. Our hometown was only ninety miles away: why not take a day and drive up? Sue, who still had friends in Findlay, went back fairly often, but Dave and I had not seen the town since our parents moved away nearly thirty years before.

"What came ye out into the desert to see?" I wasn't sure. All that time I had carried a set of mental postcards of Findlay, Ohio, and far from fading over the years, these images had actually grown sharper. Sue warned us that the town had changed, but how different could it be? I knew where I came from and was reasonably certain what I would find there.

At our first glimpse of Findlay, comforting signs of homecoming slowly emerged from beyond a far-off clump of trees: the water tower, the WFIN transmitter, the Marathon Oil building. But there was little time to savor the view. As we approached on U.S. 15, a dual-lane highway built after Dave and I had left, we seemed to be moving at warp speed. Landmarks to the south and east of town, former destinations of all-day bike trips, were passing by much too quickly. We zipped by the reservoir, the public golf course, the sugar beet plant—and before we knew it we were *there*, looping around town on what for us was still the "new" I-75 bypass, now forty years old. The quarry careened by, as did the Imperial Crown Holiday Inn (now, we noted, a Day's Inn), the West Main Cross exit near the cemetery, and the Whirlpool plant on the far north end. Even at a leisurely fifty-five, the town was already behind us.

This was too small to be the Findlay I remembered. A boy could ride his bike all day in *that* place, especially up and down Main Street, the straight spine of a town that was far longer than it was wide. Covering that ground remained a popular time-killer even in high school, after the bike had been exchanged for a 1959 Rambler and the object was to drive the circuit between the Marathon Oil parking lot in the south and the still-new

Big Boy in the north. For Sue, Findlay's three-decade transformation had been incremental. This was not the case with her long-gone brothers, who began to spin a fantasy that would account for the tiny place that lay before us. An entrepreneur responding to the lackluster Ohio economy must have decided to create a *replica* of Findlay, a theme park catering to the town's grown-up children and their MasterCards. The potential profits were vast. Didn't nearly everyone who grew up there wind up living somewhere else? Findlay's middle-aged sons and daughters would surely flock back in droves, eager to relive the past as they remembered it.

Or almost as they remembered it. For some reason, probably budgetary, our entrepreneur had been forced to build his theme park at two-thirds scale. He figured that visitors basking in the soft light of yesteryear would not notice the shrinkage—and besides, isn't America a place where dreams always come true, even if in diminished form? But Dave and I noticed. This was not Findlay; this was "Six Flags Over Findlay."

We amused ourselves with our "Six Flags" routine until Sue told us to knock it off. Still, the fantasy had a certain rightness to it. The Findlay I remembered, rife with schemes for prosperity, had exuded that nervous optimism common to small midwestern towns run by Republicans. When I was still there, a businessman bought a wooded tract a few miles south of town, moved the Wilson's Sandwich Shop diner and some other old buildings there, added a pony ride and some Western curio shops, and christened the place "Ghost Town." At the grand opening there was an article in the *Republican Courier* about the anticipated tourist dollars, but I remember thinking that Ghost Town would soon die a quiet death. Why would people who had eaten at Wilson's for years pay good money to see the old diner sitting in some woods out in the country? I now suspect a darker reason behind my assumption that Ghost Town would fail: the concept hit a little too close to home.

• • •

As it happened, Findlay did not shrink at all. Located in the middle of the glacially scoured flats of northwest Ohio, it now has thirty-eight thousand residents, some ten thousand more than when I lived there. I grew up hearing constant affirmations of Findlay's connectedness. We were situated, the phone book proclaimed, "in the center of an excellent highway system" that linked us to Fort Wayne, Toledo, Detroit, Cleveland, Columbus, and Dayton. These links, trumpeted to promote Findlay's ideal location for doing business, unwittingly underscored its isolation. Findlay may have been a hub of sorts, but in order to get anywhere you had to take one of those excellent highways.

Its relative isolation has always given Findlay the feistiness of any place that has to make its own way in the world. Founded as a fort during the War of 1812 and incorporated as a town in 1838, Findlay underwent slow but steady growth despite its location in the Great Black Swamp, whose muck made northwest Ohio the last portion of the state to be settled. In the 1830s Johnny Appleseed passed through and left a few orchards in his wake. In the 1840s the last Indians moved out and Patterson's general store moved in. Stephen A. Douglas, his Illinois debates with Lincoln still ahead of him, once visited a cousin who lived in town. The first Hancock County Fair took place in 1852, and four years later came the "Great Squirrel Migration"; within a year the squirrels disappeared as mysteriously as they had come. At the outbreak of the Civil War, Findlay's population was 2,467 and Hancock County's was 22,866. Of the three thousand county soldiers who fought for the Union, around five hundred died, six of them at Gettysburg.

In the 1880s the town made world news when deposits of oil and natural gas were discovered there. As a schoolboy, Warren G. Harding marched in a parade celebrating the jackpot. During the oil boom the streets got paved, a trolley line went in, three daily newspapers were in circulation, and a succession of Gilded Age presidents—Hayes, Garfield, McKinley, Roosevelt, and Taft—made pilgrimages to the newfound source of wealth. John Jacob Astor, destined to sink with the *Titanic*, stopped by to plan the expansion of his railroad, the Findlay, Fort Wayne & Western. Buffalo Bill's Wild West Show came to town with featured performer Annie Oakley, and Confederate spy Belle Boyd once gave a lecture there. Robert (Bob) Fitzsimmons, world heavyweight boxing champion, starred in a play mounted in Findlay five months before he lost his crown to James J. Jeffries. Montaville Flowers, a player on the Chautauqua circuit who was best known for playing all the parts in a one-man performance of *Ben Hur*, married a local girl and performed several times in the town.

In 1887 Findlay became headquarters of the Ohio Oil Company, originally part of John D. Rockefeller's Cleveland-based conglomerate. From that point on it was a company town. The Donnell family, who owned Ohio Oil, were generous benefactors. Indeed, I owe my existence to Ohio Oil paychecks drawn by my father. In 1962 Ohio Oil changed its name to take advantage of consumer recognition of its "Marathon" brand of gasoline. The Marathon Oil Company mascot was Phidippides, the stalwart who ran to Athens with news that the Greeks had beaten the Persians at Marathon. According to one version of the story, he collapsed and died immediately after delivering the message; we kids always joked, to our father's irritation, that this would happen to your car if you used Marathon gas.

The town had other claims to fame. During the boom years, Findlay took part in northwest Ohio's famed glass industry. When I was a kid, industrial lots and railroad tracks still sparkled with ground shards from the old factories, including the Findlay Flint Glass Company and Bellaire Goblet. "Findlay Toothpick Holders" are still hot items among collectors of antique glass. There is also a modest collection of Findlay celebrities. David Ross Locke, writing in the satirical persona of a know-nothing racist named Petroleum Nasby, first published his abolitionist letters in the old Findlay *Jeffersonian*. Dr. Norman Vincent Peale, celebrity minister and author of *The Power of Positive Thinking*, once worked as a reporter for the rival *Morning Republican*. Russel Crouse, sometime member of the Algonquin Round Table and coauthor of several hit plays, including *Anything Goes* and *Life with Father*, was a local boy, as was the man who in 1950 invented the radiofrequency mass spectrometer. Clare Dwiggins, the newspaper cartoonist nationally known in the 1920s and 1930s as "Dwig," grew up in Findlay. Another resident was the recently deceased Theo "Mandrake" Clafin, legendary member of the International Brotherhood of Magicians.

Most notably, perhaps, the classic Gay Nineties tune "Down by the Old Mill Stream" was written by a local man named Tell Taylor, who got rich from show-biz ventures and built a golf course on the current site of the Hancock County Fairgrounds. When I was growing up, a boulder next to the Blanchard River commemorated the old mill that had inspired him, and his grave was the pride of a cemetery south of town. Findlay establishments have routinely capitalized on the song's fame. The Old Dutch Brewery proclaimed that its beer was "Brewed on the banks of the Old Mill Stream," albeit two miles downstream from the mill site. In my day the mill had long since been replaced by a roller rink, but the tradition lived on in the Millstream Drive-In Theater, the Millstream Motor Speedway, and the Millstream Press. Indeed, it lives still; Findlay is currently home to the Millstream Area Credit Union, Millstream Building Systems, Millstream Electrical Contractors, Millstream Fence and Home Improvement, UniGlobe Millstream Travel, and Millstream Wood Carvers, Incorporated. In 1991 a group of Findlay stargazers founded the Millstream Astronomy Club.

. . .

Although Six Flags Over Findlay appeared to be a more promising enterprise than Ghost Town, we were disappointed with our old neighborhood. Like most Americans, we wanted visual confirmation of our scruffy origins, reassuring witness to how far we had all come. Instead, our exodus seemed to have improved things. The whole block was tidier, with fewer trees and bushes, and the drainage ditch that used to run along East Sandusky Street, sufficiently deep to serve as a trench during neighborhood war games, had been filled in. The empty lot next door—we called it "Angle Park," after the family who lived on its other side—was once a jungle of shabby delights, with a huge weeping willow, a ruined stone fishpond, and an unruly forest of lilacs. All of that was gone, replaced by a manicured, fenced yard. Fishlock Avenue now had curbs. The old blur of street to gravel to grass, as seen by a small boy running with his eyes to the ground, had been sectioned into clean lines and boundaries. East Sandusky Street, which became State Route 15 just beyond our house, had since been demoted to State Route 568.

Our old house, once we realized that this was *it*, was an impossibly tiny bungalow with aluminum siding covering the wood that our father seemed to be constantly scraping and repainting. The yard, once a vast expanse capable of accommodating every manner of game, was a well-tended postage stamp. Of the two pine trees in front, one was gone, and the other—my favorite climbing tree—had shrunk to pitiful proportions.

It was hard to believe that I once felt so lordly in its branches as I surveyed the neighborhood from its dizzying height.

Memory plays tricks—and the sharper the memory, the bigger the tricks. Probably because I had once known every inch of this ground, our neighborhood seemed to have changed more than any other part of town. The empty lot on Osborn Avenue that served as our baseball field now contained a Masonic temple. The stables just off Fishlock Avenue, where I made spending money cleaning out stalls, had been refashioned into someone's Western dream house, all wooden beams and cedar shingles. The mammoth garage that housed Red Miller's trucking company, where neighborhood kids snuck in for Dr. Peppers in exchange for slugs jammed into a still-novel vending machine, stood vacant. Hancock Hybrids, its silos visible through the early morning haze from the upstairs bedroom that my brother and I shared, was still there, but the silos were gone. A sign on the front read "Thermal Transmission."

The Hancock County Fairgrounds was shockingly ill matched to its vastness in memory. Crisp chain-link had replaced the wooden-slat fence that we slipped through during fair week. A new grandstand occupied the site of the old wooden stands, and there were several new animal barns, though it was hard to tell how many, because the fairgrounds passed by so quickly. I looked across the street for the Old Dutch Tavern, the neighborhood bar where my father once faced down three drunken strangers who were razzing him for wearing a coat and tie when we stopped in for a beer and a pop after a PTA night. "Hey," one of them said, "look at the dude!" Dad walked over to where the men were sitting, slammed his fist on the table, and growled, "Don't let these clothes fool you." The site of this triumph was gone, replaced by a tidy ranch house. East Sandusky Street had become less interesting, but it was a good bet that the current residents didn't mind. Theirs had become a respectable neighborhood; they were the "after" to whom we had been the "before."

. . .

The most remarkable thing about Six Flags Over Findlay, apart from the fiendishly clever miniaturization, was its capacity to be different places to different visitors. My brother, sister, and I saw three parallel but distinct

159

towns, their exhibits waxing and waning according to who was doing the looking. There was reason enough for that: Sue is five years older than I am and Dave four years older than Sue—sufficient intervals to produce three separate landscapes of memory. Every so often one of us would point to a tree or a street corner and blurt out a profound reminiscence that drew blank stares from the other two. I began to wonder if we had really grown up in the same place.

I cannot describe Dave's Findlay; Sue and I could barely see it. "There's the old New York Central roadbed," he exclaimed as we passed over a gentle bump in the street, "and that's where Allen Marsh got stuck in the signal tower." Who was Allen Marsh? And why did it matter, as it clearly did to Dave, that this was the New York Central and not the B & O? Sue's Findlay had an equally stubborn exclusivity. She wanted to drive by the house of an old boyfriend named Swank. All I remembered about him was that he smelled like cigarettes, and I saw only a small frame house with a doghouse in the corner of the back yard. I would not presume to say what Sue was seeing as she craned her neck to gaze at the little house as we crept by. Younger siblings are not observed with much intensity, and accordingly, my Findlay was even more mysterious to Sue and Dave. As we crossed the Sandusky Street bridge, I announced that we were passing over the site where I drank my first beer, warm because I had just stolen the bottle from Mr. Sebring's garage. Sue and Dave responded with blank stares; *their* first beers had been consumed elsewhere.

I am responsible for my own Findlay; my brother and sister will have to answer for theirs. For me the trip aroused vague irritation, prompted, ironically enough, by how happy I had been when I lived there. As a child I was convinced that our town had it all, that it was a manageable but perfectly accurate mirror of the larger world. The real-estate agents whose pictures appeared in the paper were important people; didn't their pictures in the paper prove it? Riverside Park, with its swimming pool, merry-go-round, and taffy stand, contained every distraction a park could possibly offer. The WPA band shell, home to summer concerts in which Dave played tympani, provided music that was surely as good and loud as music anywhere. Those vast department stores, Patterson's and LaSalle's, housed an ample and fully representative selection of the world's finery.

They also featured the only elevators in town that were accessible to kids, at least until the elevator operator figured out—the second ride usually did it—that we weren't there to buy anything. I imagined that Bob the barber, who gave me my monthly "pineapple," a butch with a front fringe that was waxed straight up, offered haircuts equal to what Ike or Khrushchev could command if they had hair. I knew, of course, that there were bigger towns, but I assumed that they offered just more of the same stuff. The barbers of Cleveland, Chicago, and New York surely kept the same back issues of *Argosy* and *Field and Stream* on their chrome chairs with red plastic seats. The only difference, I figured, was that big-city barbers had *more* of those chrome chairs.

This conviction that the world at large was just a bigger Findlay remained even after I started reading about things that did not exist there. Such knowledge merely deepened the small-town habit of inflating small things into satisfying proportions. Although I would have liked to see a dinosaur skeleton, my brother's high school biology teacher showed me his collection of trilobites and fossil leaves. I would have liked to see an Egyptian funerary mask, but there was antiquity sufficient unto the day at the courthouse, where some Indian arrowheads were on display in a glass case. Like most children, I accepted what was before me with no sense of deprivation. The public library's stiff, crumbly copy of James Breasted's 1912 *History of Egypt* seemed like an archaeological find all its own. And weren't secrets from the past close at hand in the abandoned Carey-to-Findlay rail line that my brother traced from the fairgrounds all the way out to the reservoir?

Clinging to such satisfactions, I suspect, made me typical among Findlayites, most of whom seemed to agree that this was the best of all possible worlds. Six Flags Over Findlay prompted sharp memories of this childhood complacency, and while they were not bad memories, they made me feel a little sorry for my younger self. That kid never realized that he was growing up in a place where the chief mandate, always unspoken, was learning to make do. If you were going to have fun in such a place, you had to make it yourself—and you had to make it with what was set before you.

. . .

Proclaiming itself "Flag City" during its sesquicentennial, celebrated with fanfare and sidewalk sales when I was twelve, Findlay is one of those places where the American Dream seems as real as the sun. The dream fosters a never-ending flow of small changes in which nearly everything eventually becomes something else. Most of the buildings I remembered along Main, Main Cross, and Sandusky were still there, but their functions had been altered with seeming randomness, as if a whimsical god of commerce had played musical chairs with local businessmen who were trying to make do with what had been set before *them*.

I've checked some facts and learned that Findlayites still believe in "the power of positive thinking." As the former resident who popularized that phrase once said, "Change your thoughts, and you change the world." Bent on accentuating the positive, the local Chamber of Commerce is doing just that, in part by calling Findlay the "fourth best Small City for Corporate Facilities in the U.S." The town has also been designated a "foreign trade zone," the smallest in the country, and a recent survey ranked it as the twenty-second-best place to live out of 219 small cities nationwide. The website of the Findlay/Hancock County Development Foundation proclaims the town Ohio's "top-rated micropolitan community." Of the fifteen "micropolitan" centers in the Buckeye State, Findlay ranks first in per capita income, educational attainment, and manufacturing productivity, and second in per capita retail sales. It is, as the Development Foundation confirms, a community "not ashamed of its roots in the past, but not afraid to look the future squarely in the eye."

A middle-aged ex-Findlayite could do worse than adopt his hometown's upbeat outlook. Those can-do Republicans may not have the warmest social attitudes, but they certainly know how to mind the main chance. The Fort Findlay Village Mall, built to great excitement during the town's sesquicentennial year, currently has seventy-five stores. A large industrial park called Tall Timbers opened in 1988, and in 1995 Best Buy built a "mammoth redistribution facility" in Findlay—780,000 square feet of appliances waiting to go somewhere else. The town fathers, who could hardly have been more accommodating, provided water, sewage, access roads, and a five-million-dollar loan. As Best Buy's chief engineer described the negotiations, "We didn't discuss why we needed a 24-inch water main. We discussed where to put it." Lowe's and Hercules Tire and

Rubber have recently followed suit with new distribution centers of their own. Apparently, Findlay remains an excellent place from which to get to other places.

Such optimism is critical, because nothing lasts forever. In December of 1997, Findlay's OHM Remediation Services Corporation received navy contracts worth five and a half million dollars to perform "environmental remedial action" at Yuma, Arizona, and El Centro, California. A few months later, however, OHM was bought out by Pittsburgh's International Technology Corporation, which laid off Findlay workers and made plans to sell the OHM offices. There was a three-week strike at Cooper Tire and Rubber in 1991 over medical benefits, and Cooper recently had to pay a man 2.5 million dollars for injuries he had suffered in an industrial accident. Due to a slump in the microchips market, Harris Semiconductors recently laid off seventy-nine employees. The worst blow of all, however, came twenty years ago: in 1982 Marathon Oil was taken over by U.S. Steel, which soon became USX. When USX moved Marathon's home offices to Houston in 1990 and left only a branch in Findlay, it was as if the town's heart had been ripped out. It must have seemed like rough justice to more than a few citizens when, three years later, Marathon's pipeline subsidiary was sued over a massive oil spill in Macon County, Illinois.

But as any Findlayite will tell you, life goes on. Cooper still makes tires at its Findlay plant, long after the last tire factory closed in Akron. Despite the strike, Cooper made the 1993 edition of *The One Hundred Best Companies to Work For in America*, and its profits have recently gone up. In 1994 Marathon, semi-gone but not forgotten (today it is known as Marathon Ashland Petroleum), set a drilling record in the Gulf of Mexico: 8,400 feet in twenty-four hours. The Findlex Corporation supplies brake systems to several major auto manufacturers; Findlay Industries makes seats and door panels; and DLM Plastics distributes its pool liners nationally. The technical director of the national Wire Reinforcement Institute, which promotes the welded mesh that strengthens concrete, makes his home in Findlay. Whirlpool has expanded the plant where I worked for three college summers.

The Hammond children were relieved to find that three decades had not effaced Findlay's major institutions, though most of them had been shrunk in accordance with the diminished scale of the Six Flags blueprint.

The Marathon Oil building, now surely the most imposing branch office in the state, was still a study in postwar prosperity. Also unchanged were the Dow Chemical plant, the water works, the Elks Club, and the Armory. We were relieved to find that Whittier Elementary still existed, though it looked small enough to be a private daycare center. The Howard Methodist Church had undergone the same painful shrinkage, as had First Methodist, First Lutheran, and St. Michael's. Although the Hancock County courthouse still had its 1880s gingerbread, it looked ridiculous in its reduced size, like a bungalow with columns.

Six Flag displays that had undergone partial transformation produced an odd mix of familiarity and disorientation. Bob's barber shop was now "The Razor's Edge," a change that I guessed Bob, a tight-lipped veteran with a crew cut, had not lived to endorse. The old Gothic jail, familiar from school tours designed to deter us from lives of crime, had been replaced by an orange-brick and glass "Municipal Building." The public library, a 1906 brick edifice with a gabled portico, had been razed, and in its place stood the new library, 444,000 books and 346,000 videos housed in yet another orange-brick cube. Ruth's Hasty-Tasty Diner (I barely remembered the *really* old days, when it had been Vera's Hasty-Tasty Diner) was now Be Tran's Eggroll. The First National Bank had become "The Fifth Third Bank"—a byzantine series of mergers encoded in its impossible name. Stan Little's Marathon station, where an overinflated bike tire once blew up in my face, was now the "Eastside Service Center." Dietsch's ice cream parlor manifested the ultimate sign of success by expanding. Housed in a new building twice its former size, with a second store out on Tiffin Avenue, Dietsch's now sold wooden figurines of cowboys and horses. One of the original Dietsch brothers, now an elderly man stooped from years of reaching deep into the freezer bin behind the counter, was still there; I wondered if he ever saw the old store with its green booths when he looked up from the vats.

Differential Steel, which had succumbed to the fad of snappy names initiated by Woolco (Woolworth's) and K-Mart (Kresge's), now called itself "DifCo." Morey's Newsstand was still Morey's Newsstand, though the Mentor paperbacks and Penguin Classics that I remembered were long gone, and the books were supplemented with cold medicines and Findlay Senior High Trojans sweatshirts. In deference to post-Watergate journalistic standards, the papers stacked by Morey's window were now called simply *The Courier* rather than *The Republican Courier*. "Republican" was dropped in 1976, the Findlay Publishing Company claims, "to emphasize the newspaper's independence from political bias."

We made a lunchtime pilgrimage to Wilson's Sandwich Shop, supposedly Dave Thomas's inspiration for Wendy's, still there in the "new" building that had replaced the Ghost Town diner and still bearing a name from an era when "hamburger sandwich" was a viable term. The place was packed as always, but the winds of change had not left it untouched. French fries were now on the menu, and the hamburgers were decidedly smaller and drier than we remembered. Dry hamburgers, however, are less problematic in a town that now features a restaurant for every taste, including the Bistro on Main and Japan West. As the Development Foundation proudly affirms, "You don't have to leave Findlay to eat out."

Such incremental changes required only minor adjustments to my mental pictures. Other sites, however, had changed beyond recognition. I kept trying to superimpose onto them the scenes in my mind, like transparencies in an anatomy book, but it was impossible. The marsh along Lye Creek, beneath the Bridge of the First Beer, had been partially drained and reclaimed. Cussins and Fern's Hardware, a wonderland of gleaming tools and fixtures and fittings, was now the Ohio unemployment office. Carter's Music Store had become a tuxedo rental shop, Dyer's neighborhood market was an accounting office, and the Hobby Shop on North Main was a sign store that also offered fax and copying services. The ground floor of LaSalle's department store had become an expansive omelette restaurant called "Breakfast at Marie's." The Fort Findlay Hotel, elegant host to countless proms and wedding receptions, had been replaced by a modernist cube housing a large record and CD store. The Kodak processing plant, where my sister worked during college, was now a professional building filled with doctors' offices. The Dark Horse Tavern, scene of some small triumphs when I was a drummer, was a nondescript abandoned building.

Some places were simply gone, bombed out by time. All that was left of the train station, a reassuring reminder of Findlay's connectedness with the world, was a vacant lot of weeds and gravel. The elegant downtown theaters—the Harris, the Royal, and the State—were gone, replaced by the disorienting empty space of parking lots. The White Castle, a cheaper, late-night alternative to Wilson's, had been supplanted by a radiology lab. Haley's Bar, an ancient dive with an Art Deco facade and the most beautiful door through which drunks have ever been tossed, had been obliterated by a new office block. The studios of WFIN, where my brother spun records while in high school, were being remodeled into a law office. Dave used to bring home stacks of promotional 45s that his boss ordered "out of here" because rock was the "devil's music." The station's politics have loosened a bit, but not much. WFIN, which moved to new facilities out by the airport in 1992, now features an all-talk format for the forty-five-and-over demographic; its syndicated shows include Rush Limbaugh, Dr. Laura Schlessinger, and Paul Harvey. The old studios were clearly a prime attraction of Dave's Findlay. While Sue and I guarded the corridor, he snuck in and rescued a piece of yellowed floor tile, a relic from the start of the fifteen years he spent in broadcasting before moving into computers.

. . .

A short drive south of town confirmed the impossible: Ghost Town had survived and prospered. As if emboldened by the example, Findlay had done the same. The quarry on the south end was now the Lake Cascades Corporate Center, complete with fancy condos. More new housing stretched out toward the reservoir, populating those lonely township roads. Findlay College had become, as an elaborate brick and concrete sign announced, "The University of Findlay." Six Flags had refused to stand still. Indeed, plans are currently being developed for a revitalized downtown that will combine cutting-edge technology with theme-park nostalgia. The old-fashioned trolleys slated to cruise up and down Main will stop, among other places, at Findlay's new "silicon alley."

In places like Findlay, things are always looking up. The high school class of 1997 had a composite score of 22 on the ACT, one point above the national average. As if to reward the kids, Ralphie's Family Sports Eatery, located some 350 steps from the front door of Findlay High, petitioned for a liquor license, despite considerable citizen resistance. The University of Findlay, which has tripled its enrollment to over three thousand students, is now nationally known for its program in "Equestrian Studies." In the old days Findlay College routinely ran a faintly desperate ad in the high school yearbook. One year the ad proclaimed that "The grass isn't necessarily greener on the other side." The following year it showed a picture of the college gate with a sign that read "Hello."

The Findlay Racing Pigeon Club, founded in the mid-1950s, is still going strong. The Butt Hut, which sells "cigarettes, pop, and candy," has its own website, as does "Toyota Bob," owner of LaRiche Toyota. Cooper Tires recently advertised for a tire engineer who "must be team oriented"—nothing, I would guess, is worse than a rogue tire engineer. The *Findlay Courier* was seeking interns who "must have a driver's license and are paid $220 a week." And just outside of town a gutsy dreamer who calls himself "Alpaca Jack" has established a thriving alpaca farm, new meat and wool for the old Midwest. Findlay is also the home of Closet Monster Productions, a full-featured recording studio that charges thirty dollars an hour. One band that recorded there is "Coma," which Closet Monster's website once described as "a young and aggressive three-piece band from Northwest Ohio, but by their writing style they could blend into the Seattle scene." The members of Coma could tell you that a trip to Seattle begins with a single step; on June 21, 1997, they played at the Mount Blanchard Community Festival.

As in the Findlay of memory, booster dreams can embrace real estate developers and grunge rockers alike. Art and commerce are not oil and water in small places where nearly everyone doubles as someone else. In high school I played drums in the pit orchestra for a Fort Findlay Community Playhouse production of *The Music Man*, in which a prominent dentist was cast as Professor Harold Hill. He was pretty good, too, though I can't help thinking that the number of open mouths he saw increased dramatically after that show. Art, as every true Findlayite knows, shouldn't just imitate life; it should materially improve it. Findlay students recently mounted a production of *How to Succeed in Business without Really Trying* at Central Auditorium, where I once beat time to Professor Harold Hill. Then as now, Central Auditorium is a pretty good place to learn that you have to get along to get ahead—or maybe it's the other way around. Either way, we small-town Ohioans, whether musically inclined or not, have always believed in progress. Construction is our way of life. As a website devoted to cataloging the nation's speed traps recently claimed, Ohio's true state flower is not the carnation but "the orange road barrel."

. . .

My sister embraced Six Flags Over Findlay with no regrets, because she had been given ample time to adjust to its changes. My brother and I, by contrast, felt vaguely cheated. We went to Findlay expecting to find ghostly confirmation of the images in our heads. Instead we found a living town in which *we* were the ghosts, two incarnate anachronisms peering uneasily into the storefronts on Main Street. Like all ghosts, Dave and I were rattled by the shock of the new, by irritating signs of modernity that kept breaking into our dreamscape. What was a Taco Bell doing here? Or that Blockbuster Video? Who was debasing our memories with all these Seven-Elevens? Who had bolted *USA Today* boxes to these hallowed sidewalks? It was unsettling to see current Findlayites bursting our nostalgic bubble with their Nike sneakers, Tommy Hilfiger windbreakers, and Ralph Lauren bomber jackets. And what were all these late-model cars doing here? Clearly, the Six Flags entrepreneur had neglected verisimilitude on this one, frustrating our nostalgic hunger for sculpted fins and huge grills. He had apparently skimped on the number of cars, too. Although the day after Thanksgiving is supposed to be the busiest shopping day of the year, we glided up and down Main Street with neither effort nor delay, pale riders in a ghostly van.

The action, we learned, had shifted to the Fort Findlay Village Mall. Originally surrounded by fields, the mall was now engulfed by a subdivision whose trees were sufficiently large to prove that Findlay's urban sprawl had been going on for some time. I found myself uncharitably miffed at the fact that the mall could have been anywhere. With its lot filled with SUVs, its landscaped entrances, and its indulgent spread of low-slung chain stores, it gave off the wrong kind of familiarity, rudely frustrating my quest for first things. I felt like Ben Franklin alive again, grumbling at the elevated highway that now bisects his old neighborhood in Boston. In the days of flesh, a boy could walk from Milk Street to Old North Church without having to thread under a concrete overpass, godless and sterile and rumbling with unearthly noises. My equivalent to the Fitzgerald Expressway was Tiffin Avenue, with its garish string of All-American eateries: Chi-Chi's, Red Lobster, McDonald's, Arby's, Pizza Hut. As if to appease Franklin's ghost, Boston is finally replacing its ugly highway with a tunnel. But I lack Franklin's clout; Tiffin Avenue is probably here to stay.

I would guess that most Findlayites welcome the Tiffin Avenue boom as economic "trickle-down" at its best. Findlay is—and always was—Republican heaven. Bob Dole, who made a campaign stop in Flag City during the 1996 election, voiced goals as appropriate to the town's aspirations as to his own. "I want to be number one," he gruffly declared, "and we're going to make it." Dole knew he was preaching to the choir, and in the choir's language. Hancock County would choose him over Clinton by 17,000 to 9,000 votes. In the same election Mike Oxley won his eighth term to the U.S. House of Representatives, beating his Democratic opponent in the Fourth District by a more than two-to-one margin. In 1994 Oxley ran unopposed, but in 1992 there was a real race: Oxley received 145,000 votes to the Democrat's 91,000. In 1992 Hancock County supported George Bush over Clinton by 17,000 to 8,000 votes, with Ross Perot receiving only about 900 votes fewer than Clinton. In 1988 Bush trounced Michael Dukakis, 20,000 to 7,500. But that was then; what about now? America held its breath as Floridians agonized over chads and dimples, but the citizens of Hancock County suffered no such ambivalence: George W. Bush beat Al Gore by 20,500 votes to 8,500, while Oxley crushed yet another hapless Democrat by 20,900 to 6,500. And this is near equity compared to the days when Eisenhower and Nixon were running—the days of my father's water-cooler defenses of FDR against the attacks of his Marathon Oil coworkers. Among its many changes, Findlay has progressed to a one-and-a-half-party town.

. . .

My brother and I walked the streets of Six Flags furtively and self-consciously, worried that we might be spotted and forced to summarize our lives in ten-minute conversations. These fears were groundless. We kept forgetting that ghosts are invisible; neither of us looked anything like we did when we lived here, and whenever we saw people we thought we knew, their ages were all wrong. As he stared at a man who was walking down Lima Avenue, Dave momentarily wondered how Jim Whitaker, class of '59, had managed to stay so young. What was he doing with a fanny pack? And why had he exchanged his crew cut for one of those Billy

Ray Cyrus mullets? I thought I saw my algebra teacher, unchanged except for an Indians baseball cap and a sweat suit, jogging down West Main Cross. Sue, who was definitely *not* a ghost here, had to remind Dave that his alleged classmate was, if anything, his classmate's son. Ditto for my teacher, who would be in his late seventies now and unlikely to be jogging anywhere.

During lunch at Wilson's, I actually did see someone I knew, a friend from junior high. Now a middle-aged man with jowls and white hair, he was sitting with his family. I considered going over to their booth, but what would I have said? My likely greeting—"Look at what time has done to us!"—would surely have spoiled his meal. At one point the man glanced my way but showed no sign of recognition. He was a real Findlayite with real matters to attend to, like distributing the correctly garnished hamburgers to his wife and two teenagers. Ghosts are not supposed to materialize in the midst of so ordinary a scene. If you're not expecting to see a ghost, you won't recognize one even if it is sitting four booths away—maybe *especially* if it's sitting four booths away.

Knowing where ghosts belong, we guessed where *our* people were, or at least a fair number of them. When we arrived at Maple Grove Cemetery we stopped first at our grandparents' grave. As long as our mother was still able to drive up from Columbus, she had always placed a few Fig Newtons, their favorite treat, by the stone. Regretting that we had forgotten to bring some along, we pulled weeds for a while and then wandered off in different directions to catch up on thirty years of life and death in our three Findlays.

To read the stones was to conjure up faces more vivid than the people I had seen on Main Street. Here lay a friend from high school, a girl who played cymbals in the marching band. Here lay the old man who owned the Hobby Shop; he routinely accepted IOUs when kids didn't have money to pay for something. Here lay our family dentist. One time Sue had excitedly told him "Guess where we're going for Texas!" Without missing a beat he replied, "Christmas?" Here lay a neighbor who served in the Ohio Senate and then the U.S. House as the unbeatable Mike Oxley's predecessor. I also found the graves of my driver's-ed teacher, a boy in my sister's class who had been killed in Vietnam, a second-grade teacher at Whittier School, my eighth-grade social studies teacher, the doctor who removed my tonsils, one of Dad's Marathon Oil friends, and a popular boy one class ahead of me who had died just five years before—from what, I didn't know. On the stone of another friend from the band—a fellow drummer who died in a car crash at college—a tiny drum set was carved in the upper right corner.

Dave and I figured that we had seen enough for one day, and maybe enough for another three decades. After a stop at one of those intrusive Seven-Elevens so Sue could get something to drink, we drove on in silence, lost in our separate reveries of Six Flags Over Findlay and what we had learned there. As the houses thinned out and South Main became Route 68, we decided to stick with the old road rather than "new" Route 15 or I-75. No sense rushing our return to the present.

. . .

Seeing Findlay again shattered any illusion that my past was still anchored in a real place. As a result, the town in my mind became stronger for what it had always been, a dreamy realm where larger truths might endure even as smaller ones faded. There was bittersweet satisfaction in finally claiming the inner Findlay as my own. The actual town would continue to go its own way, stubbornly refusing to be anyone's theme park. Conceding Findlay's wild ungovernability, I understood that my real hometown was as much a Ghost Town as that businessman's dream, a private destination for only one tourist. Such thoughts might seem fittingly philosophical, but they did not come without resentment. It was hard to shake the feeling that I had been suckered, not so much by the Six Flags entrepreneur as by my youthful gullibility. I felt sheepish at having once set so much store on so small a place.

This sort of regret comes sooner these days, if a website called findlaysucks.com is any indication. The site, maintained by a Michigan college student who grew up in Findlay and whose father works at Harris Semiconductor (that is, if he wasn't laid off), is "Dedicated to telling you why Findlay SUCKS, as well as skateboarding, punk rock, and anything else I find interesting." To this kid Findlay is "F-town," a place so suffocating that he lists a hundred numbered reasons for hating it. Reason fourteen sums up most of the others: "Kids don't have anything to do besides drugs, drinking, have sex, or drive the circuit." This description, which actually sounds more like Las Vegas than the town I remember, lends support to the webmaster's plenary denunciation. "All rivers in Michigan flow south," he declares, "because Ohio SUCKS!"

If small-town Ohio sucks, it has never been for lack of human drama. There was always a saving undercurrent of weirdness in Findlay, where eccentrics were tolerated because they were *our* eccentrics. It was simply part of the scheme of things that Sammy Rogers, an accomplished smoker in fifth grade, routinely extorted our nickels and dimes outside of Dyer's market. It was old hat to see Tom Fierstadt strolling down East Sandusky in the dead of winter, shirtless and flipping an axe in the air. We came to expect that Larry from next door, a thirty-five-year-old man with a mental age of eight, would occasionally stare, wide-eyed and bland-faced, into neighborhood windows. Indeed, there was weirdness aplenty. The Carey Tombstone, which marked the graves of a reputed murder-suicide couple, featured spectral faces—I once *saw* them!—that were rumored to come back each time the stone was replaced. Every year one or two high school boys were lured to mysteriously random deaths—who would be next?— while drag-racing on the county roads. Prominent Findlay citizens were constant objects of speculation involving booze, affairs, or boozy affairs. For years Osborn Avenue ended abruptly at the Bridge to Nowhere, a half-completed span that tempted local daredevils to move aside those orange road barrels and test their Findlex Corporation brakes by playing chicken with the Blanchard River. The Royal Theater was periodically plagued by ringworm and rumors of ringworm. A huge steaming mound by the fairground stables was said to contain a century's worth of testicles from castrated horses. Junior high kids routinely "shot" Haley's Bar, bursting through the Main Street door on bikes and racing through to the back alley as patrons barely glanced up from their mugs of Old Dutch beer. Ghosts of slaves were said to cry out at night from a mansion on East Sandusky that had been a link in the Underground Railroad leading to Detroit and Windsor. Those voices, we were told, belonged to the slaves who never made it to Canada.

Small-town normality has always found its underside in flat ignorance. When I was ten and heard that a "Jewish" boy was coming to spend the summer with a neighborhood family, I expected a kid who spoke Hebrew and wore flowing, biblical robes. It turned out, of course, that he came from

Cleveland, spoke perfect English, and was a better baseball player than anyone in the neighborhood. Children of migrant workers harvesting sugar beets appeared briefly at school only to disappear—what had we done wrong?—just as we were getting to know them. I knew of only two black families in town when I was growing up, and not much has changed regarding Findlay's blinding whiteness. According to the 2000 census, African Americans constitute about 1 percent of Hancock County's population, and only 5 percent of county residents identify themselves as minorities of any kind. When our Michigan student complains that the town has "no diversity," he is, for once, understating the case.

The webmaster's lament that there's nothing to do in our old hometown gains credence from the Findlay message board sponsored by "USA-Talk." When I examined its archive a while back, there were only two messages. On March 11, 1998, at 11:07 P.M., "Q-Ball 187" posted the following communiqué: "hi girls." "Duckman," who posted the second message on May 6 at 10:22 P.M., simply typed "Helloooooooooooooooo"— a loopier version of that Findlay College ad in my old yearbook. When I recently checked the message board again, a man from out of state had posted a question about a coworker from Findlay—he gave her full name —who was telling everyone in the office that she had been Miss Ohio of 1968–69. Was this true? Some local kill-joy had posted the answer, which was of course no. I don't begrudge the woman her rich fantasy life. As "Joe Bob" put it in yet another post, "Findlay needs somthing [sic] that the Teens can hang out around in the evenings other than the Library Parking lot." Another message posed a temporary fix, one which Joe Bob probably rejected: don't miss the First Assembly of God crafts fair.

Members of the Christian Parents' Educational Fellowship, whose national headquarters are in Findlay, would probably agree with the crafts fair organizers that an idle mind is the devil's playground. The devil aside, they would surely be right in asserting that boredom can be lethal. The local mania for drag-racing, for instance, has not gone away. Twenty-one people died on the county roads in 1988, the worst record in recent memory; sixteen died in 1996. But in Findlay, even county-road carnage can provide a forum for community progress: in 1997 the deaths reached a record low, at seven. This is clearly a problem on which the town fathers have been working. A billboard next to the Sandusky Street bridge, the

Bridge of the First Beer, featured a picture of three police cars and the message "Drink & Drive . . . We'll Provide the Chaser." The problem, however, is far from solved; this past Memorial Day weekend, Hancock County saw twenty-two arrests for drunk driving.

For those who survive teenage restlessness, Findlay continues to offer tamer walks on the wild side. A few winters back, local cops and state liquor agents raided the Moose Lodge, the AMVETS, the Eagles Lodge, the Elks Lodge, the Olde Town Tavern in nearby McComb, the DAV, the American Legion Post, and the Flag City Post of the VFW. It was a red-letter day for law enforcement but a bad day for Findlayites with little to do. Twenty-four gambling machines were confiscated, along with a truckload of betting slips and nearly forty thousand dollars in cash. Twenty-six liquor citations were issued, and the Moose Lodge alone sustained twenty-five gambling-related charges. Two months later a dozen members of these clubs picketed the courthouse to protest Ohio's anti-gambling laws, and by late spring the Moose were petitioning the Findlay police to return their seized property.

At the corner of Main and Front we saw a young man on a bike waiting for the light to change. His face was painted red with cat-whisker white stripes, and when the light turned green he let out a resounding whoop before pedaling off. This, I thought, was typical Findlay. Even in crazy Indian makeup, the kid dutifully waited out a red light. Still, you have to start somewhere, as the members of Coma might tell you between sets at the Mount Blanchard Community Festival. A Findlay man wanted for questioning in a series of local bank robberies recently made the "Top Ten Most Wanted" list of northwest Ohio. How many wanted guys could there *be* in northwest Ohio? Maybe some of those fugitives lost their heads and voted Democratic. Other miscues are recorded in the Findlay police blotter. A man recently filed a harassment complaint against his estranged wife for allegedly calling him 101 times on the telephone; what was it about that 101st call that made him file charges? A twenty-nine-year-old Findlay man wanted since 1993 on rape and sexual misconduct charges was finally captured in Detroit, where he was trying to hide his six-foot-four, 250-pound frame in the back seat of a taxicab. One woman kicked another on the dance floor of Wooly Bully's on Tiffin Avenue. A man was arrested for passing a bad check at Pioneer Quick Lube, and the Butt Hut reported forty-four stolen cartons of cigarettes. Somebody scratched a profanity on the door of a parked van, several cars in the police impound lot were vandalized, and a newspaper deliverer was assaulted at five in the morning by a man with "a deep low voice." Judging from the website of the Crime Stoppers of Findlay/Hancock County, every crime in town has been committed by a single culprit: a white male in his twenties. Maybe Joe Bob isn't spending *all* his time in that library parking lot.

There were always two Findlays: the tranquil Republican town and the cauldron of minor-league antsiness just beneath the surface. Each is indispensable to the other, of course, because nothing will seem abnormal unless you harbor a gut-level affinity for normality. Fostering such affinity is what places like Findlay do best. If you grow up in such a town, you might join the findlaysucks webmaster in complaining that not much happens there, but you will also absorb this unaccountable feeling that something unusual is about to break through the bland surface of things, and maybe soon. This expectation will keep you moving brightly through tedium for the rest of your days. You will not be easily bored—or more accurately, you will develop a begrudging affection for boredom, a habit of teasing it into significance. A Findlay man, a former Mandrake student who bills himself as a "gospel clown," recently made a bid for the Guinness Book of Records as "the world's fastest magician" by performing over three hundred "magic effects" in a minute and a half. The feat is vintage Findlay, not unlike the amazing Montaville Flowers and his one-man *Ben Hur.* Consider the red-faced bicyclist with streaks of white, his war cry shattering the midafternoon calm. Or consider our young webmaster, who has already turned his uneventful past into an ongoing source of amusement. While I don't share his harsh take on things, I sympathize with his motives. I also suspect that someday he will make his own peace with the place. Give him a few decades out in the world, and he'll come to appreciate the empty, dream-filled days he once spent on the banks of the Old Mill Stream.

The webmaster clearly grew up waiting for something to happen. So did Joe Bob as he hung around the library parking lot. And so did I. This habit of mind, the chief legacy of places like Findlay, is not without its uses. This past summer a runaway freight train pulled out of a railyard near Toledo and careened sixty miles through the countryside. Reaching speeds of over forty miles per hour, the riderless train passed through Findlay as it headed south. Another train loaded with state officials promoting rail-crossing safety had to be sidelined while crossings were blocked and schemes were hatched. The freight was finally stopped near Kenton when a veteran railroader jumped aboard, climbed into the cab, and applied the brakes. Naturally, the hero was a Findlay resident—a man uniquely prepared for something to happen whenever it did. Hancock County's chief deputy sheriff, as quoted in the *Courier*, summed up the local response: "You see a thousand trains in your life, but when you see one go by without anyone in it, it's kind of ghostly." Representative Oxley, who immediately fired off a letter to the Federal Railroad Administration, insisted that "We must be absolutely sure that there are safeguards in place to prevent potentially calamitous incidents like this from happening." These two reactions pretty much sum up the Findlay mindset: a persistent habit of seeing ghosts, coupled with a Republican's faith that if we just shape up, they'll leave us alone.

· · ·

As I trudge on toward Arlington, I am reminded of how clarifying a flat landscape can be. It dawns on me that my boyhood contentment is itself a product of nostalgia, the final illusion that Six Flags over Findlay has both intensified and dispelled. Aren't these the same sort of broody thoughts I once had when I rode my bike down these straight country roads, intent on figuring something out? Chief among those old thoughts was the certain knowledge that I would someday leave town. Although my friends and I knew that our lives would play themselves out somewhere else, we rarely spoke about it. We had no interest in diminishing the tangible days and nights we were living by worrying about some vague, placeless future that would break upon us soon enough.

There's nothing like midwestern flatness to make a person seek out the corners and edges of things, crisp borders to oppose and contain the fields that stretch out inconclusively—as far, so the saying goes, as the eye can see. Northwest Ohio has the kind of landscape that opens you up. It teaches you, without your realizing it, to want things that you cannot yet see. There is no mystery to this; if there's not much to look at in a place, you end up gazing harder at what's there and trying harder to imagine what's not. That flat horizon begs to be filled up with *something*.

You can hear forever on these roads, too. I am dimly aware of the whine of an engine far behind me, and as I turn around and jerk up my thumb, a pickup truck comes into view. When the truck slows down, I see Dave in the passenger's seat waving for me to climb in. The driver is a big, friendly kid who looks to be around twenty, dressed in a denim jacket with a white fleece collar.

As we drive on toward Arlington and the special grace that comes from finding an open gas station in the middle of nowhere, we learn that our rescuer grew up on a nearby dairy farm and is majoring in computer science at Ohio Northern University in Ada. Home for Thanksgiving, he has escaped his family's postholiday torpor for a solitary cruise down the old roads. His ambitions are bigger than working in Findlay's planned silicon alley. With an old Tom Petty song blaring on the radio, he tells us of his plan to move to the Bay Area after graduation and make his mark in systems analysis or network design. My brother the software designer has roused himself from his own Six Flags reverie and is chatting with the kid about Unix and Java and C-Plus-Whatever as the fields and farmhouses and silos fly by. The kid keeps brushing his lank hair out of his eyes and bobbing his head up and down. He has an infectious, goofy laugh, and his accent sounds familiar. I like him immensely.

Ohio States

When I was little, one of my favorite toys was an Ohio road map that my father picked up at a gas station. It was huge when spread out on the living room floor, large enough to nap on—though I would never do that for fear of ripping it—and covered with an inexhaustible fund of words and colors and shapes. At first the map was simply a dazzling thing to look at, but once I understood what it was, it became magical. Here was an entire world cast into child-size, foldable form, gorgeous with red lines, yellow lines, hatched lines, double lines, bright hues clashing at the state borders, and the deep blue of mapped water. One starred city was our "capital," with other cities spreading out into irregular yellow shapes. There were hundreds of mysterious names and numbers and, here and there, tiny green pine trees and tents that meant, in one of my first experiences of legibility, "You can camp here."

I spent hours sprawled on my belly, tracing and retracing Ohio journeys with my finger. Once I learned that our house faced north (for a map-child, there was a profound rightness to that), I aligned the red, white, and blue Sohio ellipse at the top with our front door and imagined leisurely trips from this place to that and back again, always by a different route. These journeys usually started from our hometown, and always from a sense of well-anchored security that came from my opening ritual: Findlay, Ohio, is *here*. I am *right here*. When I was learning to read I practiced on the map names, eager to learn where I had been and where I would go next. Should I take the short, straight line up to Toledo, where the zoo was? Should I venture into the unknown, maybe south to wander a meandering black line leading to, say, Chillicothe? Or should I follow one of the many routes converging on the sprawling yellow of Cleveland? Cleveland had a cluster of names so tightly packed I could hardly distinguish them, and I instinctively moved my finger more slowly in order to take them all in.

If you spend time playing with an Ohio map, you will become a whiz kid of Buckeye geography without even trying. I knew what lay northwest of what, where the rivers ran, how to get from point A to point B without ever having to cross a bridge. These were not insignificant journeys; the map reinforced a child's sense of living in a manageable, self-contained world—in my case, a world of wall-to-wall Buckeyes. I thought we were lucky. We inhabited a state whose shape was particularly satisfying. No characterless rectangle like Colorado, no vast expanse like Texas, no pinched-in seeming afterthought like Connecticut or Rhode Island—Ohio seemed the perfect balance of nature and people, its boundaries a mix of lake and river and surveyors' lines. There was something for everybody, and as far as I was concerned, everybody lived within its confines.

I knew, of course, that people lived in places called Indiana, Michigan, Kentucky, Pennsylvania, and West Virginia, but those places dropped mysteriously off the edges of my map, its red and black lines extending into a child's terra incognita. I still get a muted thrill when I think of those first pointers to the unknown—"To Erie," "To Detroit," "To Fort Wayne"—my versions, I suppose, of those ominous marginalia on medieval maps: *Here Be Monsters*. Not that I thought of Pennsylvanians or Michiganders as monsters, exactly, but I *did* assume that they were somehow different from us. Ohio's borders seemed to contain all that was knowable—and there was comfort in that. I didn't worry about these other places, because they were for later. I couldn't know it at the time, but this was a typical assumption for an Ohioan to make.

The Sohio map instilled a habit of feeling situated in a landscape larger than what I could perceive. Years later, when I rode my bike out to the reservoir, climbed the embankment, and looked north, I thought I could almost *see* the skyline of Toledo, forty-five miles away, so strong was my conviction that it was there. The world—or more accurately, Ohio—felt like a palpable, understandable thing. Just beyond those trees to the southeast lay Carey, and beyond Carey lay Upper Sandusky, and beyond Upper Sandusky lay Marion and Delaware and Columbus, the city with the star.

The map prompted considerable curiosity about my state, along with the natural assumption that this curiosity could be satisfied, that Ohio could be mastered. How could it not? After all, I lived there—or rather *here,* in this small town located on the thin black line of Route 68 between Bowling Green and Arlington. As it turned out, however, Ohio was not as easy to read as those pine trees and tents. Individual facts (entered the Union in 1803; home of the Great Serpent Mound and the Olentangy Caves; birth state of General Grant, Thomas Edison, the Wright Brothers) were straightforward enough, but not what those facts added up to. This became a problem, one that was especially disturbing to a child devoted to the legibility of things. The more I learned about other states, the harder it became to pin down the essence of mine. I remember feeling jealous of how *identifiable* other places seemed. Texas had beef and oil wells. Wyoming had cowboys. California had the movies. There was Iowa's corn, Wisconsin's cheese, West Virginia's coal mines, Michigan's car factories, New York's crime—and so on. But what did Ohio signify? What did *we* stand for? The nickname "Buckeye State" offered little help; what did that brown, shiny nut say about *us*? North Dakota, South Dakota, and Kansas seemed to offer similar blanks, but I didn't live in those boringly squared-off places. I lived *here:* the meaning of Ohio was *my* problem.

· · ·

As I got older my growing knowledge of Hoosiers and Golden Staters and Georgia Peaches, however slight, caused me to redouble my efforts to get a handle on us relative to them, and my search for the sum and essence of Ohio sent me back to the map. Maybe the town names would provide a clue. Like most children, I sensed the importance of names (just get a child's name wrong and watch the response: "I'm not John! I'm *Jonathan!*"). And if it's a big deal to have your own name or to name a pet, what if you had to name a town? This, I figured, was my key to Buckeye clarity. The people who had named our towns were pioneers, grownups who knew what they were doing. Surely they understood what Ohio meant.

My initial forays into Ohio's names boded well. My hometown, for instance, had been named for Colonel Findlay, a local hero of vague military significance. Heroes' names also graced Steubenville and Zanesville. Columbus honored an even earlier hero, though hardly a local one. It made sense, given my budding midwestern faith in progress and achievement, to name a place after a discoverer, a soldier, or a rich man who had coaxed a railroad or a canal to come *here* instead of there. These people had worked hard and played it smart and gotten ahead, all worthy activities. To name towns after such enterprising souls was a good deed, like respecting your elders.

This, then, was Ohio. Tennessee was the Volunteer State, and Florida was the Sunshine State, but I lived in the Respect-Your-Elders State. It was easy to picture a parade of distinguished elders named Tiffin, McComb, Worthington, and Kettering. In my mind these Buckeye luminaries all resembled President Grover Cleveland, the inspiration, I wrongly presumed, for our biggest city. Mansfield gave me some trouble. Had a field once been owned by a man named Man? Had there once been a nearby town named Womansfield—the result, perhaps, of a nasty frontier divorce, Debbie Reynolds and Eddie Fisher in buckskins?

I also discovered that you could name a town after what you found— or hoped to—once you got there. Defiance and Independence were stirring examples of this, but what the settlers found was usually more down to earth. There was no great mystery to Rocky River or Springfield and its etymological near-twin Bellefontaine, once I looked it up. I could guess what lay beneath the hills of Ironton. Upper Sandusky made sense, too: it lay "above" Sandusky—that is, on higher ground than Sandusky, which was on Lake Erie and named, I assumed, for a distinguished elder called Mr. Sandusky. Middletown must have been halfway between two other places (absent, of course, a distinguished elder named Mr. Middle). Then there was Akron, which always had a harsh, un-Ohio sound to it. Once I learned that the name was Greek for "high place," the mystery vanished. Wasn't Akron the seat of Summit County?

So *this* was Ohio: the State of Respecting Your Elders in a New Place. But not all Ohio names started from scratch. People frequently named new towns after the ones they had left behind, though it seemed strange that anyone who had bothered to leave a place would want to use its name all over again. New Concord, New Boston, and New Philadelphia were obvious examples. I learned that there was a Dover in England, as well as an Arlington and a Kent. Once I saw in the dictionary that "Wooster" was how you pronounced the first two-thirds of Worcestershire— as in the steak sauce and the English county—another mystery was solved. Ohio also had a Cambridge, an Oxford, and a London, all of which must have been founded by Brits with big plans. East Liverpool made sense, too, until I remembered that it actually lay *west* of the Beatles' Liverpool. Maybe its founders had come to Ohio by way of China.

So far so good. Ohio was the State of Respecting Your Elders in a New Place but Without Forgetting Where You Came From. I soon realized, however, that Ohio's namers of things had embraced a far larger world than I had suspected. Toledo and Lima (pronounced *LY-muh*) were named for dreamy places where people wore colorful shawls, ate spicy food, and spoke Spanish. Milan (pronounced *MY-lun*) suggested elegant buildings and the Mafia. So did Parma, one of those squeezed-in names near Cleveland, and Ravenna, six inches southeast of Cleveland's sprawling yellow. Ohio also had a Lisbon, a Cadiz, and a Medina. And when I looked up Gallipolis, down on the Ohio River, I discovered that it meant "City of Frenchmen." This did nothing to further my progress toward Buckeye clarity. How did a city of Frenchmen, berets at a tilt and wineglasses on their gingham-covered tables, square with my hometown of slim farmers and beefy, narrow-tie Republicans? What American Dream was reflected in towns named after Spanish sword centers, Inca capitals, and Muslim holy cities? Arcadia, ten miles northeast of Findlay, looked nothing like that peaceful shepherd place described in our encyclopedia.

Clearly, the state of Respecting Your Elders in a New Place but Without Forgetting Where You Came From, or Didn't, was getting out of hand. Where was the "Ohioness" in all this? And what to make of all the Indian names, with their beautiful sounds and spooky reverberations? Although I had once believed that there had been a Chief Gallipolis, I soon learned that Ohio had plenty of legitimate Indian names to go around. Even *Ohio* was an Indian word, meaning "beautiful river." *Ohio River*, as our seventh-grade geography teacher pointed out, was a redundancy: the Beautiful River River. This was no help at all.

Echoes of the pristine, forested place that preceded *this* place—Ashtabula, Ottawa, Maumee, Miami, Wapakoneta, Coshocton, Cuyahoga Falls, Sandusky (there was no Mr. Sandusky, as it turned out), and Delaware—added to the incomprehensible mix of long-gone Buckeyes, a motley crew of Indians, easterners, Englishmen, Germans, Dutchmen, and Frenchmen forming a swirl of Ohio ghosts, a midwestern Babel whose capital city was named after an Italian who didn't get where he was going and never really knew where he had been. I understood that the Indians had died off or headed out a long time ago. Their first stop westward must have been Indiana, where they managed to name another state before being shoved farther into the *real* West—the one that those clearly defined Californians showed us in the movies. Still, these names invoked tribal presences who spoke as loudly as the others, and not just in the Cleveland Indians' Chief Wahoo or in the warrior pictured on the label of the grape pop bottled in Wapakoneta, later famous as the birthplace of the first man on the moon.

Indian ghosts might be peering sullenly out from the trees, but there were ancient Greek and Roman ghosts, too. This new knowledge demanded adjustments. When I read the story of Cincinnatus, Chief Cincinnati joined Chief Gallipolis in the happy hunting ground of nonexistence. For a while I even thought that the real Ohio was Roman at heart. To be called from your plow to defend your people and then to return to your fields afterward sounded like a quintessentially "Ohio" thing to do, something that Grover Cleveland might have done. Never having been to Cincinnati, I imagined it as a gleaming cluster of temples and amphitheaters nestled on the banks of the Beautiful River River. The Romans, I learned, traced their ancestry back to the Trojans—and didn't Troy lie a little north of Cincinnati? Troy, Ohio, certainly had a ring to it, but was this the town that launched a thousand ships? When our family drove through on a visit to the great Smoky Mountains (a rare venture into terra incognita), I half expected to see spear marks in the storefronts. Instead, Troy looked a lot like Findlay.

Maybe, I thought, Ohio could be summed up more tersely than I had imagined: the State of Aiming High but Falling Short. Not far from Troy lay Urbana—"City Town." But despite its founders' hopes, Urbana was hardly a city. There were lots of other remnants of lofty classical dreams:

Attica, Delphos, Euclid, Utica, Bucyrus, Sparta, Macedonia, Minerva, Xenia, Antioch, Fostoria—Ohio's own "city of light," from the Greek—and, more grandly, Athens, Rome, and New Rome. I figured that Twinsburg must have been named for those wolf-suckled Roman boys, Romulus and Remus. But the towns I had seen gave off little of the glory that was Greece or the grandeur that was Rome. I was beginning to think that Ohio was less a place of new dreams than of old daydreams. I could still imagine Cincinnati looking like a set from *Spartacus,* because I hadn't been there. I had been to Fostoria, though, and seen its narrow streets and abandoned glass factories. Clearly, something had gone wrong in our City of Light.

Where was I now? I was a citizen of Ohio—the Aim High Like an Indian or a Roman Even Though You Will Fall Short, and Respect Your Elders in a New Place and So Forth state. But forty miles southeast of the Greek high place where they made the tires lay the biblical high place of Salem. Ohio's rich supply of biblical names added yet another layer to the mix. Having learned something about the Bible from my grandmother, I guessed that those Salem settlers had aimed high with a vengeance. If you name your town after the Holy City, you probably aren't anticipating empty warehouses or juvenile delinquents. Ditto for the founders of Zion. But how, exactly, did biblical holiness connect with my Ohio? Was there a balm in Mount Gilead? Was the Hebron east of Columbus a city of refuge, like its namesake? And what about Lebanon, Zoar, Goshen, Galatea, Damascus, Berea, Gilboa, Palestine, and East Palestine? Did the flinty-eyed ur-Buckeyes who settled these places hope to imitate the sanctity of those Bible lands? Did it make any difference that they would be substituting oats and winter wheat for date palms and olive groves?

I tentatively added Be Holy to Aim High Like an Indian or a Roman Even Though You Will Fall Short and So On and So Forth. After all, Ohio contained St. Marys (both a town and a lake), Marysville, Marietta, and Marion, the latter the home of Warren G. Harding, whose unpresidential behavior surely disgraced the Town of the Virgin. Curiously, I never ran across a Jesus, Ohio. I supposed that such a name would create too much pressure; if a town named Jesus ever had a corrupt mayor or lost its only supermarket, despair would surely be loosed upon the land. There was no God, Ohio, either—the closest was Lordstown, with its huge GM plant—but that was probably a good thing. If there ever were a God,

Ohio, it would surely become the adopted hometown of every politician in the state. "Friends, I stand before you as a man of God." Warren G. Harding would have moved there just to save face, though it probably wouldn't have done any good.

Given all these biblical names, maybe Ohio was simply God's Country. That certainly sounded like a fine thing, and perhaps capable of encompassing all the conflicting strands. But some Ohio towns seemed to reflect a flat-out opposition to God. Rome and Athens and Antioch might have been honorable classical places, but you couldn't be pagan and Christian at the same time, could you? Once I learned that these cities were also in the Bible and that Paul had tried to rescue them from false gods, I figured that a few old-time Buckeyes had intended to plant their crops and worship Mars. What about Gahanna, on the outskirts of Columbus? The fact that it sounded suspiciously like Gehenna, Jerusalem's valley of Hell, did not bode well. And if Ohio was really the Devil's Country, what to make of all these Methodists and Baptists? Was there anything about my home state that wouldn't shimmer or break up, that wasn't canceled out by something else?

I began to suspect that no meaning was possible for a state that had been cobbled together from shards of this and that, a hopeless mix of conflicting dreams. Even individual dreams, on closer inspection, had a way of shrinking to insignificance. It was disturbing to learn that a number of proto-Buckeyes had established brassy, self-promoting towns. Moses Cleaveland—not President Cleveland—had founded our biggest city, in an act, I now thought, of monumental arrogance. A Connecticut lawyer, Cleaveland chose the site and immediately headed back east; a newspaper later dropped the "a" from his name to save space. The respectable President Cleveland, it turned out, wasn't even *from* Ohio. I darkly guessed that Colonel Findlay had probably pressured people to name my town after him. So much, I sadly concluded, for respecting your elders. So much for aiming high and being noble like an Indian or a Roman and being honored for it. So much for the meaning of Ohio.

. . .

I couldn't know that I had bitten off more than any kid could chew. Ohio really *is* an enigma, and not without reason. It has always been a place in which the past and the future count for more than the present. If the present is diminished, people will consider the very ground on which they stand to be temporary. They will see themselves in a holding pattern, potentially just passing though. This is a natural legacy of Ohio's long-standing status as a way station. Once the original "West," Connecticut's Western Reserve to be exact, Ohio soon became the first Gateway to the West, a role that never ceased even as the frontier grew increasingly distant. Ohio was coming into its own just as those westward places were coming into *their* own, and the old thoroughfares—Zane's Trail, the National Road, the tight nexus of railroads—soon became funnels to get you *through* Ohio to somewhere else. The Erie Canal, which linked the East with the Great Lakes and created the ports of Ashtabula, Cleveland, and Toledo, soon became like that. Lake Erie led to Lake Huron, which led to Lake Michigan, which led to that big-shouldered Hog Butcher for the World and rail lines leading still farther west, where the real action was. The old railroads—the Chesapeake & Ohio and the Baltimore & Ohio— quickly outgrew their Buckeye dreams, too. Within a few years of its founding, the C & O fossilized the *O* in its name by making Chicago its western terminus; the B & O did the same by extending to Chicago and St. Louis. Long before those Buckeye brothers Wilbur and Orville came along, Ohio was already becoming, in a phrase I've been hearing more and more lately, "flyover country."

Ohio's traditional role as the Not-Quite-West has always fostered among its citizens an acute awareness of impermanence. Even sixth and seventh-generation Buckeyes, whose ancestors shod horses and pumped gas for more adventuresome souls as they passed through, retain a feeling of just marking time, waiting for their own chance to move on. Born observers of a passing parade, most Ohioans grow up assuming, rightly or not, that they will someday join it. It's hard to resist such thoughts if you live in a place that remains nobody's destination. Even today the Ohio Turnpike serves as an extended bypass traversing a Lake Erie plain that exists merely as ground to be covered by the steady flow of East Coast–Chicago traffic. Travelers a little farther south on Interstate 70, which supplanted the old National Road and U.S. 40, pass through Columbus with Indianapolis beckoning as Oz and St. Louis as a greater Oz. Interstate 75 similarly connects Detroit with points south, good weather, and Florida beaches ahead—though not soon enough ahead. Ohio is a perennial midpoint between desired ends, an entire state as Middletown.

The University of Akron has an uplifting but oddly poignant slogan that could stand for the state as a whole: "You can get there from here." The slumping midwestern economy has aggravated the old Buckeye itch to get there from here, or wish that one *had*. A charter member of the Rust Belt and a place of small farms unable to compete with modern agribusiness, Ohio has fallen hard during the past fifty years. Any middle-aged Ohioan will confess to nostalgia for better times. In 1950 Cleveland was the seventh-largest city in the country, with nearly a million kielbasa-eating souls. Cleveland has since shrunk to half a million and now ranks twenty-sixth, though its metropolitan area still ranks a respectable fourteenth. Houston, in 1950 an upstart at around half a million, is now pushing two million—the equivalent of two 1950 Clevelands. When I was growing up, Ohio's factories, buoyed by frenzied postwar production, were stamping out steel, auto parts, and heavy equipment in record quantities. All that money brought other, less tangible gifts. Ohio State was number one in basketball, and the Browns and Indians were champions in football and baseball. Jerry Lucas, Lou "The Toe" Groza, and Bob Feller were fabled warriors of the Buckeye Golden Age, but like all golden ages, ours didn't last.

Pushed by economic necessity, more and more of us have acted on the old impulse to join the caravan. Half the people you meet in Sun Belt cities seem to come from Ohio, though Michigan might run a close second. An astonishing number of Texans, Floridians, Arizonans, and Californians have Ohio roots, though they never describe themselves in such terms. Why proclaim yourself a former Buckeye, only to watch your face lose its features? When a Texan moves to Cleveland, he's a Texan in Cleveland. But when a Clevelander moves to Houston he's a Texan, then and forever. There's no mystery to this: if you have no identity, finding one will feel intoxicating. That's why you won't see anyone in the bars of Dallas, Phoenix, or Los Angeles hoisting a Coors to the ol' Buckeye State. You will hear no flushed, teary renditions of "Beautiful Ohio," even though its draggy waltz offers an ideal rhythm for drunks trying to sing. There will be no slurred toasts to Toledo or Dayton (the launching pads, respectively, of Gloria Steinem and Martin Sheen), no prayers for the deliverance of Steubenville (ditto for Dean Martin), Cadiz (Clark Gable), or

Fredericktown (Luke Perry). I'm beginning to suspect that Barberton (City of Barbers?) is called "Magic City" because half its citizens have vanished into thin air—which is to say, into the suburbs of Houston and Atlanta. If *Ohio* has become a word that an increasing number of Americans use as a synonym for the past, it's important to remember that we Buckeyes were born to this long before the factories closed and the small farmers went bankrupt. When I was a child and assumed that those states off the edges of my map were for *later*, I had already absorbed every Ohioan's innate sense of the transient.

. . .

When I moved to Washington, D.C., at the age of twenty-seven, I learned that my suspicions regarding Ohio's placenessness were true. In the past two decades I have heard people repeatedly confuse my state with Iowa or Idaho or Oklahoma. As a college teacher I frequently hear colleagues— smart folks and holders of Ph.D.'s—conflate Ohio State and Ohio University into an apocryphal "University of Ohio," a thing to set Buckeye teeth on edge. For easterners, that old *New Yorker* cover in which the Hudson serves as a River Lethe to soft-focus oblivion was not far off the mark. Ask a New Yorker and a Philadelphian, if you can get them to stop badgering each other, and they'll agree that Buffalo and Pittsburgh are the ends of the line, twin gateways not to the West but to Palookaville. As for Ohio (East Coast people routinely infantilize the place by over-pronouncing it: *Oh-HI-oh* rather than the native *Uh-HI-yuh*), "Fuhget-taboudit!" Cleveland is a blob somewhere between Here and Chicago. Columbus and Cincinnati, hovering in the uncharted ether between Here and St. Louis, are two more blobs in the vast blur of a continent that refuses to click into focus until L.A. smog and San Francisco fog render the world visible again.

Ohioans in exile are painfully aware of our nondescript origins. Whenever two of us meet on non-Buckeye soil, there is often a mutual cluck or a shrug, the subtle acknowledgment of people who once got minimally acquainted during a shared inconvenience like a delayed flight or a stuck elevator. Sometimes there is a hint of admiration for another soul who found a way out. About the old sod itself, though, we have little to say. "I'm from Ohio, too." "Oh? Whereabouts?" "Zanesville." "Ah."

We Buckeyes have always known that ours is one of those placeless places, the ones that aren't labeled on national weather maps because people don't go there unless they have to. Watch an Ohio flight boarding, and the first thing you'll notice is that nobody is cutting in line. Pasty-faced businessmen lugging samples cases wait patiently behind sunburnt Buckeye families whose vacations have just ended. Here and there, college-age Buckeye sons and daughters lug their backpacks through the gate with expressionless placidity. There are no reduced fares because as the airlines know, an Ohio flight is a captive market, like the post office on April 15. If your sales territory includes Cleveland and Cincinnati, you will be flying to Cleveland and Cincinnati. That week at Epcot was great, but if you live in Akron, you'll be returning to Akron. When grandma dies in Toledo, you'll be heading for a funeral in Toledo. This is the stuff of which Ohio journeys are made. Despite the recent hoopla surrounding the Rock 'n' Roll Hall of Fame and the Indians' Jacobs Field, when was the last time you saw an ad for a vacation package to Cleveland?

By the 1990s, tourism was bringing over eight billion dollars to the state—about the same as Michigan, with all its lakes and forests. But these numbers are inflated by the Buckeye law of just passing through. Most Ohio tourists are merely in transit, stocking up on Stuckey's pralines and Bob Evans sausage and Marathon gas on their way to—or back from—faster times and bigger things. In an attempt to sell more pralines, sausage, and gas, the state's tourism board recently adopted this slogan: "Ohio: The Heart of It All." That's pretty catchy, but doesn't a heart pump blood *elsewhere?* And if you're the "Heart," then isn't the "All" somewhere else?

• • •

It would be easy for a Buckeye to feel bitter, to sulk invisibly in a tent that nobody sees. On those occasions when the burden of formlessness seems too heavy, I could almost say that I'm mad as heck (to use Buckeye-speak) and I'm not gonna take it anymore. Maybe all those Ohio jokes have taken their toll. The worst thing about them—the never-ending litany about Cleveland ("The Mistake on the Lake"), Woody Hayes, farmer savants, shoat-to-boar 4-H projects, the "Mother of Presidents," middle-class "normalcy" (Warren G. Harding's word)—is their fill-in-the-blanks quality. They have less to do with a specific place than with a general impression of incompetence and smallness. The fact that Ohio jokes actually say nothing *about* Ohio has renewed my old quest to redefine something that was never defined in the first place, to find the *quidditas* of Ohio and the core of my unsheddable identity as a Buckeye, through and through.

Lately I've been thinking that I had it right the first time, when I was lying on my belly and poring over that colorful, cryptic map and thinking of it as my whole world—or at least, my whole country. Maybe Ohio, in its stubborn indefinability, really *is* the whole country. This would offer a reasonable and honorable excuse for remaining imageless. A state could do worse than to play America in microcosm, to offer a hodgepodge so thoroughly and weirdly jumbled that its very "thereness" lies beyond recovery. Granted, we Ohioans seem bland. But can we truly *be* bland if we're the products not of nothing but of damned near everything, an entire spectrum blending into white light? And besides, who says that blandness cannot be redemptive? I've wondered all my life whether a definable "Ohio" exists or does not exist, but I'm beginning to suspect that the question, so framed, poses a false dilemma. Why can't both options be true? If Ohio's being seems to edge perilously close to nothingness, maybe its being resides *in* nothingness.

This revelation excites me. If Buckeyes are to achieve identities as crisp as those that descend upon Montanans, New Yorkers, and Californians as a birthright, we're going to have to embrace the distinguishing possibilities of indistinction, to accept shapelessness as our defining shape. The beauty part, especially for a middle-aged ex-Ohioan (and the "ex-" feels tellingly natural), is that this assertion of everything-through-nothing runs true to who we really are. Ohioans are nothing if not pragmatic ("Paint your feet blue? Why would you want to do that?"), and any solution that verifies what we already know will seem right as rain, as maddeningly down-to-earth as *we* are, our faces startlingly plain in reflections from Manhattan storefronts or the waters of San Francisco Bay.

Ohio's natureless nature makes us Buckeyes think of ourselves—when we think of ourselves at all—as unwritten pages, blank slates ready for anything and eternally poised to *become* something. We are, God bless us, an open people. If you grow up knowing that the City of Barbers is a suburb of the City of the High Mound of Tires, or that a drive eastward on Route 224 will take you, in fairly quick succession, through Tiffin, Attica, Willard, New Haven, Nova, Sullivan, Homerville, and Lodi, any juxtapositions that the world throws at you will not be unduly startling. You will find, in fact, that you have an innate taste for odd juxtapositions, that you are uniquely equipped to *see* them as juxtapositions in the first place. In practical terms, this means that you will possess a keen appreciation of the weird, even though—or more accurately, precisely because—the weird is utterly alien to you. Whenever people paint their feet blue, they are surely hoping that an Ohioan will be watching them with mild surprise. They are rarely disappointed.

This, I've come to believe, is an Ohioan's mission: to serve as a counterweight to whatever seems unusual, as a foil to whatever's happening once something actually starts happening. Wherever we go, we Buckeyes form a roving cultural ballast whose heraldic emblem might well be Beige Field with Nothing, *couchant.* An Ohioan is a walking zero at the intersection of America's x and y axes, a point from which everything else gains distinctiveness by veering away. Upholding this imagined, shifting center is what we were born to do.

This might seem a thankless job, but it is not without rewards. Among an Ohioan's blessings is the possibility, nowadays so rare, of being left blissfully alone. All those corny jokes about us—"Second prize, *two* weeks in Cincinnati!"—are too vague to cut very deep. Wouldn't it be worse to come from Tennessee and endure more pointed comments about moonshine, Elvis, and the Grand Old Opry? How often do uprooted Californians hear wisecracks about earthquakes, tofu, and Third Eye crystal fondlers? And what about the poor New Yorker who moves through life as everybody's Tough Guy, doomed to watch people constantly flinching in anticipation of the next rim-shot insult? This business of being *known* by total strangers, even through half-truths, strikes me as terrifying in its vulnerability—so public, in Dickinson's phrase, like a frog. I certainly would not like to be a frog. I'd much rather be a Buckeye, gloriously swathed in anonymity.

Emerson once remarked that to be great is to be misunderstood. A Buckeye, who defiantly offers nothing to understand, surely embodies this greatness. Ohioans are pure mystery, human ciphers capable of sinking into whatever American place we enter. Take some well-known

Clevelanders—Bob Hope, Arsenio Hall, Drew Carey, Teri Garr, Hal Holbrook, Tracy Chapman, David Birney, Tim Conway, Debra Winger, Jack Weston, Paul Newman, the Eagles' Joe Walsh—and ponder their collective affect, their steady projection of generic Americanness. Cleveland and Cincinnati together produced Phil Donahue, a kind of hyper-Ohioan, a Buckeye squared. Unassisted, Cincinnati gave us Roy Rogers, Steven Spielberg, and Doris Day (I wonder whether her forebears founded Dayton, until I remember that her real name was von Kappelhoff). Canton gave us Jack Paar; Columbus, James Thurber, Beverly D'Angelo, and Tom Poston; Toledo, Teresa Brewer and Jamie Farr. Lima, where I was born, produced Phyllis Diller. I'd like to claim Hugh Downs as my spiritual kinsman because he grew up there, but he was born in Akron.

These are my people, their inscrutable but comfortable blankness shining through even in celebrity. Even Joe Walsh, long enshrouded in a mystique of rock 'n' roll hipness, looks like a hundred guys I used to see schlepping along Cleveland's Euclid Avenue. And speaking of hipness, what about Chrissie Hynde of the Pretenders and the robotic lads of Devo, Akronites all? What about Marilyn Manson, that skinny Canton boy who got tired of being Brian Warner, went Goth, and made a mint? These folks are exceptions that prove the Buckeye rule. If they ever checked out the Akron-Canton airport during their formative years (as they surely did when their sunburnt families returned from those Florida vacations), they learned precisely how *not* to look—how *not* to be—if you want to make it big. If you're seeking the Yin to which every self-respecting rebel must be a Yang, the Akron-Canton airport is not a bad place to start looking. And because Yin and Yang are locked in eternal embrace, Ohioans remain predictable even in dissent, the flip side of the standard-issue Buckeye. I get homesick whenever I see a picture of Chrissie Hynde. Not only was her Industrial Bad-Girl look already around when I was an Ohio teenager, but when I visit my parents for the holidays I see dozens of her younger sisters—pasty faces, low bangs, and owl eyes—scurrying through the malls buying presents for their little brothers.

The chief lesson that Marilyn Manson and I learned at the University of Ohio is that people who are nobody can be whoever they want. We Buckeyes have that freedom, and in full measure, because we are baggageless, devoid of particular expectation. Our job, after all, has always been to watch the other people passing through. A watched person might need a special outfit—a Stetson and boots, perhaps, or maybe one of those Gloucester fisherman's caps, or a floral print shirt that renders its wearer visible as a citizen of Miami (though probably born in Columbus). But if you're one of the watchers, it matters little whether you wear Armani or Sears off the rack. Occasionally, a Buckeye will don a contrived getup—a fright wig and a husband named "Fang"? Gothic makeup? a British backup band?—and take the stage. However uncharacteristic this turning of the tables may be, a Buckeye will know exactly how to do it. All those years of watching are not lost on us.

· · ·

When I was a kid, the *Toledo Blade* ran Earl Wilson's syndicated column, with its chatty gossip about New York showbiz and nightlife. Its running title was "An Ohioan on Broadway," a phrase that brought a rush of pride whenever I saw it. One of *us*—whoever *we* were—had somehow gotten himself to the center of it all and was now soaking up the energy and feeding it back to the home folks. Whenever the smart set gathered for after-theater drinks and repartee at Toots Shor's, Earl Wilson was our stand-in, a homegrown Edward R. Murrow reporting on the action from a far hipper front than Cleveland or Cincinnati. As I grew older, though, the notion of "An Ohioan on Broadway" began to stink of self-diminishment, of an intentional dumbing-down of who we were, whoever we were. Why should any of *us* play the star-struck yokel just to satisfy an easterner's notion of what an "Ohioan" was? How many New Yorkers were coming to Toledo to gaze at *us*?

Earl Wilson even looked the part: his picture revealed a nondescript man with a bovine face and a bland smile, like an Ohio insurance salesman. But now that I've turned fifty and look like an Ohio insurance salesman too, I've come to see Earl Wilson as a kind of pioneer, a model Buckeye. Could there possibly be light without shadow? Broadway wouldn't even exist unless somebody had a heartfelt acquaintance with slower, duller places. Places like Broadway *need* a steady supply of cultural and geographical centrists—solid, generic Ohioans—to crane our necks and take it all in. If life is to retain its spice, somebody has to be capable of viewing it from an undifferentiated, spiceless center. Somebody has to observe—to swell a scene or two—as a necessary foil for the observed.

It is this, finally, that makes Ohioans not only visible but indispensable. It is this that defines our niche in America's cultural geography. When a Texan leaves home, he becomes Somebody: a Texan in another place, encouraging or enduring all those faux drawls, cowboy jokes, and quips about the lucrative "erl bidness." When Ohioans leave home, we become Everybody: dependable, middle-of-the-road Americans bearing bread for other people's jam. It is an identity, however shapeless, that the nation cannot do without—and I am resolved to embrace it with honor and even a measure of relief. It's nice, at long last, to be somebody.

My Sohio map, of course, was telling me this all along. I should have heeded the clue embedded in those prominent words at the top: "Standard of Ohio." But I was young and green and had no way of knowing that the *real* Ohio lay in terra incognita, beyond the map's edges in those other places ("To Pittsburgh," "To Lexington," "To Indianapolis") where so many of us would live out our lives. With our special capacity for appreciating wherever we happen to end up, wherever we are *now,* we Ohioans make *your* place seem a little more interesting. Human antidotes to ennui, we expect little and are therefore pleased at most everything we find. If the first man to walk on the moon had not been Neil Armstrong of Wapakoneta, where my favorite grape pop was bottled, the first words uttered on lunar soil might well have been "Houston, there's nothing here." A farther-flung Earl Wilson, Neil Armstrong was only doing what comes naturally to every Buckeye. The instant his boot sank into the powdery surface and he found himself not bored, he had attained an Ohio state of mind. Ohioans, I now realize, become Ohioans only in diaspora. It is only after we have joined our fellow Buckeyes in the realm of elsewhere, a ghostly band of eager onlookers moving unobtrusively though an achingly palpable, non-Buckeye world, that we become our truest and noblest selves. After all, we got here from there.

Ohio States

was designed and composed by Christine Brooks

in 10/14 Palatino

on a Macintosh G4 using PageMaker 6.5;

printed on 60# Supple Opaque stock

by Thomson-Shore, Inc. of Dexter, Michigan;

and published by

THE KENT STATE UNIVERSITY PRESS

Kent, Ohio 44242